J R. Seeley

Introduction to Political Science

Two Series of Lectures

J R. Seeley

Introduction to Political Science
Two Series of Lectures

ISBN/EAN: 9783337076283

Printed in Europe, USA, Canada, Australia, Japan

Cover: Foto ©Suzi / pixelio.de

More available books at **www.hansebooks.com**

INTRODUCTION

TO

POLITICAL SCIENCE

TWO SERIES OF LECTURES

BY

SIR J. R. SEELEY, K.C.M.G., LITT.D.

REGIUS PROFESSOR OF MODERN HISTORY IN THE UNIVERSITY OF CAMBRIDGE
FELLOW OF GONVILLE AND CAIUS COLLEGE ; FELLOW OF THE ROYAL
HISTORICAL SOCIETY, AND HONORARY MEMBER OF THE
HISTORICAL SOCIETY OF MASSACHUSETTS

London

MACMILLAN AND CO., LIMITED

NEW YORK: THE MACMILLAN COMPANY

1896

EDITOR'S PREFACE

ELEMENTARY instruction in Political Science — regarded not merely as a subject cognate to history, for which the study of history is a preparation, but as a method of studying history itself—formed for many years an important part of the teaching given by the late Sir John Seeley as Professor of History in Cambridge. Usually, however, this instruction was given not in formal expository lectures, but in a weekly conversational class. His manner of conducting this class has been clearly described by one who attended it — Mr. J. R. Tanner — in the *English Historical Review* for July 1895 (p. 512). I quote a portion of his description :—

His old pupils carry with them grateful recollections of his "Conversation Class." The subject was political science studied by way of discussion, and discussion under the reverential conditions that prevailed resolved itself into question and answer—Socrates exposing the folly of the Athenians. It was mainly an exercise in the definition and scientific use of terms. What is liberty? Various definitions of the term would be elicited from the class and subjected to analysis. The authors of them

would be lured by a subtle cross-examination into themselves exposing their inconsistencies. Then the professor
would take up his parable. He would first discuss the
different senses in which the term had already been used
in literature. . . . From an examination of inconsistent
accounts the professor would proceed to the business of
building up by a gradual process, and with the help of
the class itself, a definition of his own. . . . It was not
told us on authority as something to remember, but we
assisted ourselves at the creation of it. Thus it became a
possession to be enjoyed with a title analogous to the title
of authorship. It took an hour to define liberty, but the
leisurely process had the highest educational value.

The discussions thus described were repeated
weekly, year after year, with new sets of students;
while Seeley's expository lectures—which were also
delivered usually once a week during term-time—
were for the most part on special historical subjects,
and thus bore no close relation to the matters treated
in the conversation class. Twice, however, he thought
it useful to deviate from his ordinary plan, and treat
political science in a course of expository lectures:
first, in two series of lectures, occupying respectively
the Michaelmas and Lent terms of the academic year
1885-86; and again in a course of half the length,
delivered in the Michaelmas term of 1891.[1]

When Lady Seeley consulted me as to the desir-

---

[1] This second course was repeated, without much change, in the
year 1893, illness having compelled him to make an exception to
his principle of composing a new set of lectures every year.

ability of giving to the world some part of the
numerous sets of lectures which her husband had left
behind completely written, it seemed clear to me
that our first choice ought to fall on one of the two
courses on Political Science ; as representing a funda-
mentally important part of his work as a teacher,
and expressing, more fully and systematically than
any of his writings hitherto published, his general
view of the true aims and method of historical
study.   The difficulty was to choose between the
two courses above mentioned.   Had they been of
equal length, I should, as a matter of course, have
chosen the later.   But, after carefully comparing the
two courses, I found, on the one hand, that the
general views expressed in both were in the main the
same ; while, on the other hand, the compression of
the subject into a single term's lectures had neces-
sitated the omission, or a comparatively meagre treatment, in the later course, of many topics of interest
which were fully discussed in the earlier course.   On
the whole, therefore, it seemed to me best to publish the earlier and longer course ; but, at the same
time, to incorporate in it as far as possible such
portions of the later lectures as appeared to indicate
any change of view either as to the matters discussed
or as to the manner in which they should be treated.
This incorporation has been effected in two different
ways : some passages from the later course have been

added in the form of notes or appendices; in other
cases I thought it best to substitute the later passages
for the earlier, in order to avoid wearisome repetitions. The method of substitution is used almost
solely in Lectures VI. and VII. of the first series in
this volume; the latter of which, as here printed,
is in fact mainly composed of Lecture VI. in the
1891 course. This extensive transfer appeared to
me necessary, in order to represent the later views
of the author; since I found that — in spite of
the severe limitations of space under which he
worked in composing the later course — he had
treated the topics discussed in the lecture in question much more fully than in the longer course of
1885-86. I therefore inferred that in 1891 he would
à fortiori have regarded the earlier treatment as too
scanty for the longer course.

A further change was rendered necessary by this
substitution; for there remained a fragment of the
older Lecture VII., which had to be retained, because
it commenced a discussion continued in Lecture VIII.
As this fragment could not well stand alone, I thought
it best to combine it with the original Lecture VIII.
This combination led to the excision of certain passages,—chiefly repetitions which had been caused by
the division of the subject between two lectures;
and it also rendered it necessary for me to compose
a couple of opening sentences for the new Lecture

VIII., as the connection of thought had been broken by the large transfer of matter from the 1891 course in Lecture VII. Further, I have not hesitated to make one or two minor consequential changes of phrase which appeared to be rendered necessary by the insertions that I have just described, in order to prevent slight inconsistencies between the earlier and later expressions of the writer's views. I have also here and there omitted repetitions more suitable to an oral lecture than to a book, and once or twice altered the position of sentences; and, generally speaking, have made such corrections as I thought it probable that the author would have made before publishing the lectures. In the books prepared by himself for publication, Seeley was, as I know, unsparing of pains in rewriting such portions as did not come up to his ideal. I have felt, therefore, that it would be unjust to his memory to let this posthumous book go forth without such correction of inadvertencies as I was able to make. No reader can feel more strongly than I do how inadequate a substitute this is for his own revision.

In reading these lectures it is important to bear in mind that, being written for oral delivery, they were composed on a plan materially different from that which would be appropriate in a manual of political science designed to be read. Their aim was not to impart a complete system, but to communicate

a method, and to excite the hearers to an independent
exercise of thought in applying it. It is from this
point of view that the lecturer's incisive and unsparing criticism of current notions and accepted
generalisations should be judged: since even those
who may think it occasionally somewhat one-sided
can hardly refuse to admit the stimulating quality
of this criticism. I do not mean to suggest that
Seeley ever artificially forced his ideas into a paradoxical form; such a procedure would have been
incompatible with his habitual sincerity and his ideal
of academic duty. But the conversations, always
deeply interesting, which I from time to time had
with him on different subjects at which he was working, led me to think that truth was apt to come to
him in the garb of paradox—using the word in its
strict sense; that the new ideas which his original
and penetrating intellect developed had a natural
tendency to assume, quite spontaneously, a form
strongly opposed to the popular drift of thought on
the subject; and that it required a subsequent deliberate effort to qualify and reduce this opposition.

As regards the general view that these lectures
enforce and illustrate—the two-sided doctrine (1) that
the right method of studying political science is an
essentially historical method, and (2) that the right
method of studying political history is to study it as
material for political science—I think it may be said

that this was one of his deepest and most permanent convictions. He announced it in the inaugural lecture which he delivered on his accession to the Chair of History in Cambridge; and it grew stronger and clearer as years went on, and assiduous study enlarged his knowledge and deepened his insight into the development of historic polity. Indeed, he once said to me that he valued the wide popularity of his *Expansion of England*, not only for the effects that might be hoped from it in furthering practical aims that he had at heart, but also not less because the book seemed to have proved itself a persuasive example of his method : because it had brought home to Englishmen throughout the Empire, that, in order to know what England ought to be and do now, they must study what she has been and done in the past.

In conclusion, I must express my gratitude for the help ungrudgingly afforded me in preparing this book for the press by Mr. B. E. Hammond, Fellow of Trinity College, and Mr. J. R. Tanner, Fellow of St. John's College, whom I have consulted throughout on all points of importance, and whose advice and suggestions have been of much value to me. I have also to thank Lady Seeley for the kindness with which she has rendered my task as easy as it was possible to render it, and for her aid in revising the proofs.

H. SIDGWICK.

CAMBRIDGE, *January* 1896.

FIRST SERIES

(Michaelmas Term 1885)

LECTURE I

IT has been my practice ever since I was appointed to this chair—now sixteen years ago—to give instruction in two subjects which are commonly held to be altogether distinct,—in history proper and in that which hitherto in the scheme of our Tripos has been called Political Philosophy, and which it is now proposed to call Political Science. But I have not usually adopted the same method of teaching in the two subjects. History proper I have expounded in formal, public lectures; Political Philosophy I have taught by means of a Conversation Class.

This plan of conversation I was led to adopt in consequence of the want of a satisfactory text-book to which I could refer students. I hold, indeed, that the conversational method is always useful in teaching a subject which requires exact thinking and a precise use of terms. But it is not only useful: it seems to

B

me indispensable where the subject is of this kind, and yet has never been mapped out, arranged, and put before the student in a methodical text-book. Political science, as I conceived it, was in this predicament. Such books as Aristotle's *Politics* did not seem to me adapted to the needs of the present generation of students, while the manuals that have recently appeared either did not seem to me satisfactory or were for one reason or another not accessible to the Cambridge student.

But the conversational method is only appropriate to a small class, and there are some reasons why it is desirable occasionally to expound the subject also in formal lectures. I have done so in former years, though not very recently. I propose to do so again in this year. But this time I shall try the experiment of treating the same subject at the same time, both by the conversational method in a conversation class, and formally in this lecture-room, so that during this year my conversation class will bear the same relation to this class as the individual teaching by examination papers and conversation bears to their public lectures in the work of my colleagues.

Perhaps on this announcement a thought may occur to some of you which, if you put it into words, would take this form. "What! you are a Professor of History; and yet you tell us that during this year you are not going to lecture on history at all, but on

a different subject, — Political Science or Political
Philosophy ! " Now, if I heard this objection from
you I should not admit it to be well-founded. I should
answer, Certainly I am going to lecture on Political
Science, but when did I say that I was not going
to lecture on history? True it is that I do not
intend this year to select a period and investigate
or narrate the occurrences which took place within it.
That no doubt would be lecturing on history, but
there is another way of doing so. And in my
opinion, to lecture on political science is to lecture
on history.

Here is the paradox—I use the word in its
original sense of a proposition which is really true,
though it sounds false—which I have tried for many
years to commend to the consideration of students
commencing the study of history in this University.
Even when my subject did not allow me to dwell
long upon it, I have taken pains to state it fully
at least once in an opening lecture. But in this
course, which is devoted to political science, I shall
not content myself with a mere statement. It is my
point of departure ; it is the first aphorism in the
system of political science which I am about to
expound to you, that this science is not a thing ,
distinct from history but inseparable from it. To call
it a part of history might do some violence to the
usage of language, but I may venture to say that

history without political science is a study incomplete, truncated, as on the other hand political science without history is hollow and baseless—or in one word :

    History without political science has no fruit;
    Political science without history has no root.

To establish the truth of this aphorism will be the object of the present lecture. I need not make any long introduction to show that if true it is important. History has usually been taken to be concerned simply with facts. Evidently it would be entirely transformed if we came to consider the facts established by history as mere raw material out of which a science was to be constructed. Such a view would on the one side impart a new interest of a very vivid kind to historical research; on the other hand, perhaps you may think it would deprive history in a great degree of the peculiar charm which it has hitherto possessed. Hitherto there has hung about historical study a delightful atmosphere of leisure and enjoyment; it has had a dainty flavour of romance, curiosity, poesy, which we may regret to see replaced by the potent, pungent, acrid taste of science. Whether the loss would be more than counterbalanced by the gain is a further question; in any case, the revolution which would take place in the study could not but be momentous, and for you who are on the threshold of the study it is all important to decide in what spirit you will apply yourselves to it.

Now you have always, I am sure, heard history spoken of as a serious study. "How delightful it is," may be a reflection more frequently made because it is not quite so obvious; that a knowledge of the great events which have happened in the world must needs be in the highest degree useful and instructive is perhaps seldom expressly stated because it is scarcely ever denied or doubted. It appears, then, that we do not quite literally investigate historical facts for their own sake : a knowledge of them, we hold, is useful ; that is, it is a means to an end. But in what way is it useful? "In a hundred ways," we shall be told ; but when we press for a more precise answer we shall find that the conviction that history must be useful is based more or less immediately upon the principle that what has occurred may occur again. There is regularity in human affairs; the same causes will in the main produce always the same effects ; evidently, therefore, he who wishes to be wise, since wisdom consists in understanding the relation of causes and effects, cannot do better than inquire into the past experience of mankind, or, in other words, cannot do better than study history.

Now this argument is obvious enough, but what I wish you to observe is that the application of it is not in any way confined to what we now call specially history. It is the fundamental argument which applies equally to all knowledge, which makes knowledge a useful and indispensable thing, and justifies the ancient saying of the wise man, " Wisdom is the principal thing; therefore get wisdom: and with all thy getting get understanding." We live in a universe which proceeds according to regular laws; the same causes produce the same effects; therefore if we would guide ourselves aright we must register what we observe, then we must compare our observations and generalise upon them; so we shall obtain general laws, and thus the knowledge of the past will lead us to a knowledge of the future.

I need not here enter into the old controversies about innate ideas, truths of the reason, truths given in consciousness and the like. It is enough that the vast mass of our knowledge is inductive or founded on the observation of facts. If, then, we take history to mean the record of what has happened, we may say that the vast mass of our knowledge is founded upon history. It does not matter what inductive science you select, its conclusions will be found to be based upon history. Our astronomic knowledge is based upon facts which at a given time and place were observed by this or that astronomer to take place in the heavens; our knowledge of the laws of life, though it may now take a general form, rests ultimately upon facts in the history of this or that plant or animal which were registered by some naturalist, that is, some historian of nature.

The practice has gradually been formed of appropriating the word history to the record of a particular sort of facts. But it is worth while to remember that the word need not be, and originally was not, thus appropriated, and that in the main facts of all kinds are recorded in the same way and for the same purpose. Plato says Natural History where we should say Natural Science; Pliny's great collection of wonderful and curious natural facts is called "Historia Naturalis," and till quite recently it was usual to call zoology by the name of Natural History. It has now become the custom to exclude from books called historical a vast number of facts, in themselves memorable and curious, on the ground that they are more fitly recorded in books of science. We do not look in a history of England for a record of the interesting meteorological or biological phenomena that may have occurred in England. We have come to think that facts of this kind do not belong to history. And yet if history registers events in order to discover laws, and so to guide the life of man, it ought certainly to register these, for precisely such observations have led to the great discoveries in natural science. And in the infancy of history such facts filled a large space. In the earlier books of Livy, where he draws from the most ancient sources accessible to

him, there frequently occur paragraphs in which he
sums up the curious natural occurrences that had been
noted in a particular year, how at Privernum a bull
had been heard to speak, how at Corioli blood had
fallen for rain. Now assuredly we have not become
less, but infinitely more curious in the observation
of nature than those primitive chroniclers; we may
smile at their credulity, but we respect them most
sincerely for registering what natural occurrences
they fancied themselves to have witnessed. Why,
then, do modern historians omit to register occurrences
of this kind?

The answer is obvious. Such occurrences are now
sifted and registered with a care which in those remote
periods was unknown, but they are not registered by
historians. The phenomena that occur in the world
have been divided into classes, and to each class a
special body of investigators and narrators is assigned.
Of occurrences such as I just now instanced, one
would fall to the meteorologist, another to the physiologist. And there follows upon this change of practice a peculiar alteration in the case of the words
"history" and "historical." These occurrences, which
originally were regarded as historical or belonging to
history, do not, properly speaking, in any way cease
to be so because they are recorded under a particular
heading by a particular class of specialists. And yet
we cease to speak of them as historical. We give

them henceforth the name of the science which deals
with them. They are supposed to be taken away
from history and appropriated by science. We speak
of them now as meteorological or biological facts, not
as historical facts belonging to meteorology or biology.

History, then, as the word is now used, is the name
of a *residuum* which has been left when one group of
facts after another has been taken possession of by
some science. We are accustomed to think that history records the facts which concern human beings,
and this is roughly true, but it is only true because
what we call natural science was earlier successful
and established itself earlier on an inductive basis
than the sciences that concern man. Even now there
are a vast number of facts concerning man which we
do not consider to fall within the province of the
historian,—physiological and pathological facts for instance. We do not expect from the historian information about cases of disease, however important they
may be, except where an epidemic has appeared on
so large a scale as to produce social and political
effects. This is because the sciences of physiology
and pathology have successfully taken possession of
some classes of facts relating to man. Other sciences
are already grappling with other human phenomena.
Now suppose these sciences to be successful, in the
end, I ask you, what will become of history?—that is
of general history, history proper, or history pure and

simple.[1] When each new human science has carved
out a province for itself, will not the *residuum* at last
entirely disappear? Political economy is dealing with
the facts of industry, the science of jurisprudence is
dealing with the facts of law. Already the historian
feels that on economical questions, for example, he
can afford to be sketchy and summary, because he
may refer the reader for fuller information to
economical authorities. Now it is only reasonable to
suppose that all these sciences will make rapid progress. Will not the day then soon come when on
almost every subject the historian will be able to
refer to some scientific authority who has spared him
the trouble of minute exposition, who, in fact, has told
his story better than he could tell it himself? And
will not this day be the eve of another day when the
historian will feel himself to be superfluous altogether,
when we shall cease to speak of human history as we
have already almost ceased to speak of natural history?
Dann wird einst ausgesungen Das alte ewige Lied. The

[1] "A distinction must be drawn between two different kinds of
history, of which the one may be called special and the other
general. There is scarcely any department of human activity
which may not be made the subject of history in the special sense.
We have histories of art, of science, of invention and discovery.
We might well have a history of history. To this special kind of
history there is no end, nor can any one say that it is not legitimate, or that it may not produce most important results. Yet no
one calls this sort of history by the simple name of history. History proper is understood to be general history; you know very
well that I could not in my character as Professor announce a
course of lectures on the history of the Tuscan schools of painting."
—(From the First Lecture of the 1891 Course.)

old, endless tale will then be told, and history will be swallowed up in science.

When I picture this sort of disappearance of history, you will understand that I only mean history considered as a grave serious pursuit, a study for ∿ grown men. Some writers have lately protested— one of them, Mr. Birrell, did me the honour to select me personally as the object of his attack—that history has no relation whatever to any kind of science, and cannot therefore be affected by any conceivable advance of science, that Clio is a Muse, that in other words men have a natural joy in great actions and great events, and that history is only the natural literary expression of this joy. According to this view, the historian is only an eloquent, sympathetic narrator, and will always have his function so long as men feel and enjoy ; history, like poetry, will exist as long as human beings exist.

I do not care to question this, and far be it from me to undervalue literature and poetry. As a matter of course men will always enjoy lively narratives of famous events, but considered as a mere branch of literature I do not think that history can even rank high. The great ancient historians have been admired partly no doubt for their eloquence, but mainly for their truth and depth. That is, they have been on one side, as it were, literary men, and on the other side men of science. The development I have described would deprive them of the latter character and leave them only the former. If all the more serious part of their work—investigation and generalisation—were taken out of their hands by specialists and no function left to them but that of eloquent narration, their importance would sink very much. Their works would contain no solid information that could not be found more fully and precisely given in the works of the specialists, and as mere literary artists they would be at a great disadvantage compared to the poets and romancers. For they would not be allowed to invent or embellish; they would be in strict bondage to fact; and that is not a predicament in which artistic genius can display itself. They would be mere popularisers, and their narratives would be in request chiefly among young people. Certainly history, so understood, could have no place in a university. However, I fully concede to Mr. Birrell that history of the old kind will probably always subsist as a somewhat insignificant branch of literature.

It is history, the great teacher of wisdom, the great instructress of statesmen, that I am thinking of, and it does seem to me that the *residuum* which now exists must go the way of the rest, and that the time is not very distant when a science will take possession of the facts which are still the undisputed property of the historian. But I also think that the change

will not be so great as might be supposed, for this
reason, that the group of facts still remaining will
not dwindle gradually or be distributed among a
number of sciences, but will become altogether the
property of a single science. What science ? Political
Science.

You see, then, what I meant when I said that to
lecture on Political Science is to lecture on History.

In my view a science has for a very long time
past been insensibly growing up by the side of
history, and every one has perceived that it has
some connection with history, and must draw a
great part of materials from history ; this is political
science. On the other side, within the department of
history itself, it has been more and more felt that
the accumulation of facts suggested the possibility
of a science; what was to be done with them if no
generalisations were possible which might reduce
them to order? But all this time it has been overlooked that the science which lay so near to history
was itself the very science which historians were
calling out for.

And now I must tell you more distinctly what I
mean by political science.

We start of course from the fact that man is a
social or gregarious animal, but we deal, not with
the sociability of man simply, but with one peculiar
phenomenon connected with it. For the sociability of

man has many aspects, and brings into existence
several sciences; for example, the science of language
and economic science. The phenomenon in question
is this. As a matter of course human beings, like
other animals, are united together in families, and we
might be prepared to find the family tie stronger and
the family organisation somewhat more developed
in them than in inferior animals. But we observe
something more, something which, when we think
philosophically,—that is, when we contemplate it as
if we had not been familiar with it all our lives,—is
very surprising and unexpected. We find that men
have another bond of union beyond that of the
family, and another higher organisation.

In nature there is seldom breach of continuity,
and so this higher organisation is seldom quite distinct from the family, and sometimes might be
explained away as if it were not distinct at all.
Usually, however, it is tolerably distinct. Almost
in any place, in any circumstances where a human
being might be found, if you questioned him you
would find that he considered himself to belong to
some large corporation which imposed duties and
conferred rights upon him. Each man has a name
which belongs to himself alone, and another name
which he has in common with all other members of
his family; but if you would describe him and class
him sufficiently you must learn a further fact about

him, you must know to what state he belongs. |
State? But what is state?

When I say "I am an Englishman," what do I
mean? Does it refer to my parentage or family?
Well! I cannot absolutely say that it does not. I
regard myself as being in some sort of kin to other
Englishmen, as though we were all alike descended
from some primitive Anglus. I feel this very strongly
in the presence of foreigners, for I find that they speak
a different language and seem both mentally and bodily
of a somewhat different type. But whether it really
is so is after all of no practical importance. I am an
Englishman, and should be so just as much if my ancestors were Frenchmen. And yet that I am an Englishman and not a Frenchman is all-important to me.

Mankind fall into classes in different ways according to the observer's point of view. The anthropologist divides the species according to some bodily
difference; e.g. Blumenbach according to colour,
Retzius according to the shape of the skull, recent
anthropologists according to the character of the hair.
The ethnologist introduces new distinctions founded
upon language, and these are distinctions unknown
to the anthropologist. He talks of Indo-Germanic
and Semitic races; but the anthropologist protests
that he knows of no such distinction, and that to
him all the races called Indo-Germanic and all the
races called Semitic appear to belong to one variety.

Now in political science the groups are different again. Language, bodily conformation, decide nothing here. We and the Channel Islanders speak different languages, we and the Anglo-Americans speak the same; but in political science we and the Channel Islanders are in the same class, we and the Anglo-Americans in different classes, because here men are grouped according to states.

The division of mankind into states is of vast importance, first, because of its universality; secondly, because of its intensity and the momentous consequences it has had. When I speak of its universality I admit that I stretch considerably the meaning commonly given to the word state. In the Greek or Roman, or in the European sense of the word, the state has been and is by no means universal; on the contrary, it is somewhat rare among mankind. But we want some one word to denote the large corporation, larger than the family yet usually connected with the family, whatever form it may assume, and the word state is the only word which can be made to serve this purpose. Sometimes it would be better called a tribe or clan, sometimes a church or religion, but whatever we call it the phenomenon is very universal. Almost everywhere men conceive themselves as belonging to some large corporation.

They conceive themselves too as belonging to it for life and death; they conceive that in case of need

this corporation may make unlimited demands upon
them ; they conceive that they are bound, if called
upon, to die for it.

Hence most interesting and memorable results
follow from the existence of these great corporations.
In the first place, the growth and development of
the corporations themselves, the various forms they
assume, the various phases they pass through ; then
the interaction of these corporations upon each
other, the wars they wage, the treaties they conclude, all the phenomena of conquest and federation ;
then again the infinite effects produced upon the
individual by belonging to such a corporation, those
infinite effects which we sum up in the single expres-
sive word civilisation ; here, you see, is a field of
speculation almost boundless, for it includes almost
all that is memorable in the history of mankind, and
yet it is all directly produced by the fact that human
beings almost everywhere belong to states.

This peculiar human phenomenon then, the state in
the largest acceptation of the word, distinct from the
family though not unconnected with it, distinct also
from the nation though sometimes roughly coincid-
ing with it, is the subject of political science. Or
since the distinctive characteristic of the state,
wherever it appears, is that it makes use of the
arrangement or contrivance called government, we
may say that this science deals with government as

C

political economy deals with wealth, as biology deals with life, as algebra deals with numbers, as geometry deals with space and magnitude.

Such is the subject of the science. The problems it presents will evidently arrange themselves under two heads. First will come those presented by the internal structure and development of the state itself, the manner in which government enters into it, and the machinery through which government works; then will follow the problems of the interaction of one state upon another, or the external action of the state.

And now what shall be our method in dealing with these problems? You know how much depends on method in scientific investigation. Especially you know what a peculiar difficulty rises when we investigate human phenomena. For here we are under an almost irresistible temptation to mix up what ought to be with what is. As we know it to be all-important that we should go right in political action, we are tempted to think that political science, if it is to be worth anything, must show us what is right, and under this strong prepossession we are apt to enter on the inquiry with no other category in our minds but the category of right and wrong. If we set out in this way we shall make it our object to find the perfect or ideal state. Our first step will be to ask for what purpose a state exists, and having determined this to our satisfaction, we shall proceed to inquire what institutions, laws, and practices are best adapted for the attainment of this object. This is the ancient method of treating political science of which Plato and Aristotle have left us examples.

We may adopt quite a different method and treat states just as if they were natural growths, just as if they were trees or animals. We may look at them, as it were, from outside and register impartially what we see as if we had no personal concern in it. The naturalist does not proceed at all in the method I just now described. He does not, in considering plants, begin by asking what is the object for which a plant exists, and proceed to deduce what must be the characteristics of the perfect plant. He hardly professes to know whether plants have an object at all; certainly he does not profess to decide that one plant is better than another. He has nothing to do with the category of right and wrong, but contents himself with (1) classifying the plants he observes; (2) with analysing the structure of the plant, and distinguishing the functions of the several organs; (3) with tracing its growth and development, and noting the morbid affections to which it may be liable; (4) with speculating on the origin of the different species and on the nature of vegetable life in general.

Now I think you will see at once that it is possible to study states in just the same way. These, too, can be classified, the different organs of the state can be described and their functions noted; phases of development and morbid conditions present themselves in states, and the theory of evolution can be applied to states.

But, you will say, to proceed thus is very strange and unnatural. After all, a state is not a mere natural production, but the result of human will, invention, and ingenuity. After all, states do fall under the category of right and wrong; some institutions, some laws are good and others bad; if it were not so, how vain would be all the trouble we take, all the excitement we undergo, about politics; and if it is so, the all-important thing is to distinguish the right from the wrong, and in comparison with this all classification and analysis are irrelevant and unimportant.

Now it is quite true that states are to a certain extent products of conscious contrivance, or, in one word, machines. But it is equally true that they are not mere machines. It has become a political axiom that states are not made but grow. They have their roots in the instinctive unconscious part of human nature, and for this reason, though they ought not to be treated solely as natural productions, yet they ought to be treated as such.

Moreover, experience has taught us in almost every department of thought the danger of too much haste,

of attacking too directly and too eagerly the problems
which it is practically urgent to solve. Thus the first
theorists in medicine wanted a universal panacea, the
first chemists wanted to turn everything into gold.
When we look back upon the first modern essays in
political science, the theories of an original contract,
and the patriarchal theory, we see illustrations quite as
striking of the same mistake. However this may be,
it is sufficient for my immediate purpose that states *can*
be treated in the same way as plants or as animals.

Let us now inquire what aspect our science would
wear if it pursued this method. Inductively pursued, political science would live and move among
historical facts. It would begin by collecting these
facts with great industry and verifying them with
most scrupulous care, for it would be keenly alive to
the danger of confounding mere rumour or legend or
party-statement with such facts as science can recognise. Next, it would not attempt to bolster up with
the facts so obtained some preconceived theory; all
such theories it would put on one side, and honestly
wait to see what theories arose naturally out of the
facts. For this purpose it would begin by grouping
and classifying the facts, placing together, for example,
such facts as bear on the internal growth of states,
and in another group such as relate to their external
action or to the interaction of states upon each other.
It would not be wonderful, considering the intricacy

of the subject, if this work of classification proved to
be very difficult and ponderous, as in some other
sciences, especially botany and zoology.

But further, we know that the inductive sciences
obtain their facts in two different ways. In some
cases it is by experiment, that is, the observer
creates artificially the facts he wishes to observe.
But in other cases, owing to the peculiar nature of
those facts, this is impossible. For example, in
chemistry experiment is possible; if we want to
know what affinity there is between two kinds of
matter we bring them together and observe the result.
But in astronomy experiment is impossible; the sun
and the moon are not at our beck and call; we must
wait on them, they will not wait on us. Now in this
latter class of sciences observation, being the only
resource, requires to be pursued with the utmost
industry and care. Everything here depends upon
a large supply of—what shall I say? I was going
to say "historical"—facts carefully observed and
exactly registered.

Having established, then, that our political science
is to be inductive, we proceed to inquire whether it
can work by experiment or is reduced to depend on
observation. And it will be evident at once that in
this respect it resembles astronomy rather than
chemistry. If we want to discover, for example,
what would be the effect of suddenly introducing

democratic institutions into a country, we cannot take ⸴a state, pass the necessary Reform Bill in it, and then stand by watching the result. No, all we can do is to study the states that are before us, or those that have left record of themselves from past times. Thus only can we obtain the facts which are essential for our science. Political science, like astronomy, will need an immense supply of trustworthy registered observations. ⋈

But a state is not, like the sun or moon, a mere physical, but rather a moral, entity. It is not visible to the eye or through a telescope. What is done by it is only done constructively; literally, it is done not by the state but by some individual. Much again is done secretly, and sometimes false accounts of what is done are intentionally laid before the public. Hence the authentication of the facts with which political science deals is far more laborious than in other sciences. Many other causes concur to produce this result. Especially this, that we have before us a vast mass of observations, recorded by various observers at very various periods, which are only partially trustworthy, sometimes because the observers were not scientific, or because they were prejudiced, or because they made their observations rather for amusement than with any serious object, or because they lived when the art of writing was either unknown or little used. We cannot afford to put all this mass of observations aside, and yet we cannot use it without subjecting it to tests which in other sciences are not needed, and which have to be invented for the occasion.

You will see that this mass of observations of which I speak is neither more nor less than what we call history. All that perplexity about the object of their labours which besets historians, all that perplexity about their method which hampers those who would form a political science, disappear together if we regard history as the mass of facts, brought together by observers who were but half conscious of what they were doing, out of which an inductive science of states is to be constructed.

I say these observers have been but half conscious; altogether unconscious they have not been. If you examine history as it is and as it has long been, you will see both by what it records and by what it omits that it is instinctively aware that it is concerned with the state. I have spoken of those large classes of facts which it once recorded but now deliberately omits. There are classes of facts which not deliberately but, as it were, instinctively it either omits or passes over slightly. These are sometimes facts of immense importance. The historian of James I.'s reign scarcely mentions Shakspeare's plays; he says a great deal about the rise and fall of Robert Carr; the historian of William III. says little about

Newton's discoveries, but a great deal about Fenwick's plot. Which was more important, Shakspeare
or Carr, Newton or Fenwick? But the influence of
Carr affected, and the plot of Fenwick endangered,
the state; whereas Shakspeare and Newton worked
in another region. Historians are instinctively
aware that it is not *their* region. They pass over
phenomena of this kind or relegate them to a sup-
plementary chapter, though sometimes they understand their own correct instinct so little as to express regret that they are obliged to speak of the
pomp of kings or the crimes of ambitious warriors,
while they pass over greatness more genuine and
peaceful triumphs more glorious. There is really
nothing to regret in this. The question is not of
glory or greatness, but of accurately knowing the
laws which govern the organism called the state.
Now, government and legislation, and wars and
alliances, concern the state, but scientific discoveries
or artistic masterpieces do not.

When, twenty years ago, Mr. Buckle succeeded in
flashing upon the English mind the notion of a science
of history, he threatened us with a revolution in
historical writing. We were to read henceforth
comparatively little about governments and parliaments and wars; history was to resolve itself into a
discussion of the physical environment of a people,
the climate, the geography, the food. The view I

present, you see, is different, and it is not at all revolutionary. I do not dispute the importance of those physical inquiries, and the results of them must be used by the historian; but his own province, according to me, is distinct. He is not an anthropologist or an ethnologist, but if I may coin a word, he is a politicist. The political group or organism —the state—is his study. On this principle it will appear that historians hitherto, instead of being wrong in the main, have been right in the main. Their researches into legislation and the growth of institutions have laid a firm basis for the first part of political science, which is concerned with the classification and analysis of states. Their investigation of wars, conquests, alliances, federations, have laid a basis for the second part, that which is concerned with the action of states upon each other.

All that is needed is that they should pursue with clearer purpose the path they already tread. They have been right in the main, but hesitating, and therefore somewhat desultory. They have been haunted with the notion that they were bound to record everything of importance that had happened in a given country; in short, that their subject was the country, whereas in truth their subject was the state. They have been haunted with the notion that they were literary men, not men of science, that their function was similar to that of the poet,

who works upon the feelings by narrating heroic
deeds. It is not wrong that great deeds should be
related in noble style. But the notion that this
function is inseparably associated with that of the
investigator of states, so that the handler of docu-
ments, the weigher of evidence, the expert in political phenomena, the discerner of historical sequence
and causation, should be bound to be in his own
person also the eloquent narrator, the epic poet or
ballad-writer in prose, this notion forgets that we do
not live in the days of Herodotus, or Thucydides, or
Livy, but in a time of specialised study. There was
in those ancient historians a popular element and a
scientific element; these have since been separated
and differentiated. We have now the eloquent
narrator who at times, as in Carlyle's *French Revolution*, may almost rise to the dignity of the epic poet.
We have also, but seldom in the same person, the
historical scientist. He is a student of the state, but
he studies it inductively, that is, by the aid of
history.

This is what I endeavour to do, and would lead
you to do. If we would succeed we must carry on
two processes at once. We must think, reason,
generalise, define, and distinguish. We must also
collect, authenticate, and investigate facts. If we
neglect the first process, we shall accumulate facts to
little purpose, because we shall have no test by

which to distinguish facts which are important from those which are unimportant; and of course if we neglect the second process, our reasonings will be baseless, and we shall but weave scholastic cobwebs.

But in this course of lectures I lead you through the first process. I speak of the state in general, not of any particular state. And I think you understand by this time why I consider that it belongs to my function, as a Professor of History, to do this.

[The following passage, which forms the conclusion of the first lecture of the 1891 Course, may be fitly placed here as an Appendix to the present lecture.—ED.]

When on former occasions I have laid this general view of history before my pupils, the objection has sometimes occurred to my own mind that if it were really possible, as I suggest, to make the facts of history an inductive material out of which to construct a political science, this would have been accomplished long since. There were political speculators in the eighteenth century, such as Montesquieu; and in the seventeenth there were Locke and Hobbes. While other sciences were established on a solid foundation, why was this one, so important, still kept waiting? But an answer to this objection also occurred to me. It was this. The inductive basis was wanting. A Montesquieu or a Locke did not and could not know the history of the world. I mean this more literally than you may suppose. It is surprising how

little sound knowledge of mere historical fact was possessed
a hundred or a hundred and fifty years ago. This may
be partly estimated from the occasional historical illustrations which the writers I have mentioned produce. They
are commonly worthless, and betray clearly the infancy
of historical criticism, the uncertainty in the handling
of authorities, and the newness and rawness of the whole
subject. In fact, almost all that we now call history has
grown up since that time.

If this be so, if history itself be a growth so modern,
it is not surprising that the elaboration of a science out
of history should be still in a great degree reserved for
the future. What was called history in the middle of
the eighteenth century was too unsound to form a basis
for anything. The case is different now. The present
generation has a vast treasure of historical knowledge
which is trustworthy and available for the purposes of
science.

LECTURE II

I MADE sufficiently clear in my last lecture what is the phenomenon which is to be investigated. Human beings, as we see them around us, are found to be enrolled or regimented in certain large groups which are organised in a peculiar way, held together by the contrivance known as government, and called states. So it is now in the nineteenth century and here in Europe. But when we consult the mass of observations we find that it was so not less many centuries since. Nay, when we bring before us by means of the dead languages the life which was led by human beings two thousand years ago, though we observe many differences, yet in this respect we find that men were the same then that they are now. Ancient men, too, lived in states and submitted to government. And if we go to countries remote from Europe, to China, which has always been unaffected by western civilisation, or to India, which has usually been so, we still find governments and states. It is true that these ancient or remote states differ very much from those with which we are familiar.

They differ, indeed, more than we readily understand. Observers and students, instead of being
surprised at the resemblances, have been too much
disposed to assume them and exaggerate them.
They have taken for granted that men, wherever
found, must have kings and nobles and governments
like those of Europe. And perhaps some error has
crept into history from this cause; as, for instance,
it has recently been maintained that the Spanish
accounts of ancient Mexican institutions are too
much coloured by Spanish prepossessions. But when
all due allowance has been made for this cause of
error, we do find states, even if states of a different
kind, just as we find languages everywhere, though
the unlikeness of the Bantu or the Chinese language
to Greek or German may be greater than we could
at first have conceived possible. In large regions of
the globe, however, especially where the soil is exceptionally unfruitful, as in the deserts of Arabia or
Central Asia, and in certain mountain districts, we
find less of this kind of organisation than elsewhere.
Here it is customary to say that states are not found,
for it would seem improper to apply that title to
the Arabian tribes or to the clans of the Scottish
Highlands.

It is important on the threshold of the subject to
decide whether in our investigation we ought to conform to this custom. Ought we to say, "Political

science concerns itself of course only with civilised states; it cannot be expected to take notice of the wild and confused associations in which savage, or at least barbarous, men may be pleased to live ?" This, indeed, has usually been the position taken in books of political science. All the classification with which we are so familiar, all that is said about monarchies and republics, aristocracies and democracies, does not apply to primitive tribes, or barbarous communities with strange fanatical ways of life. Nay, if you examine the book which has furnished the model to most political speculators, Aristotle's *Politics*, you will see that he almost excludes from his investigation all states but that very peculiar kind of state which flourished in his own country. Not only is he almost silent about barbarous communities, but even about all states that are not also cities; and perhaps, indeed, we ought to think that he attached a more restricted meaning than we do to the word Politics, so that it ought not to be translated Science of States, but Science of Cities.

But it seems to me that this exclusive way of handling the subject, this intolerant way of pushing on one side the institutions which we disapprove or which excite our disgust, does not suit the inductive method which we have elected to adopt. It is natural and appropriate to those who are inquiring for the perfect state, since it is evident that the most

civilised states fall short of what such investigators
want, and that therefore to cast even a look at uncivilised states must be a mere waste of time. But we have
resolved, for the present at least, to give up the quest
of the perfect state. Nor do we even propose at this
early stage to pass judgment at all upon the states
we study. We content ourselves with distinguishing
and arranging the various kinds in the same purely
observant spirit which a Linnæus brought to plants
or a Cuvier to animals. Having once elected to
take this course, we can no longer think of excluding
any state because we do not like it, any more than a
naturalist would have a right to exclude plants under
the contemptuous name of weeds, or animals under
the name of vermin. Accordingly we must throw
open our classification to political organisms the most
unlike our own and the most unlike those which we
approve. The analogy of plants and animals will
suggest to us that there are lower as well as higher
organisms. Look at the classification of the animal
kingdom. When we use the word " animal " we have
commonly in mind one of the higher animals--a dog,
or a horse, or a lion—though we may be vaguely aware
that there are lower organisms which also in strict-
ness are animal. But when the classification is made
on the true comprehensive principle we find all the
animals with which we are familiar, all which seem
fully to deserve the name of animals, confined to

one out of the four sub-kingdoms. Actually three
parts out of four are assigned to strange outlying
organisms in which the vital principle is either but
slightly developed or developed in such a manner
that the organism bears little external resemblance
to what is popularly called an animal,—strange in-
sects or flower-like molluscs and sponges. Let us
imagine political organisms handled in the same
manner;—it would not be surprising if all the states
described by Aristotle, and all the states of modern
Europe into the bargain, should yield but a small
proportion of the whole number of varieties, while
those states less familiar to us, and which our
manuals are apt to pass over in silence as barbarous,
yielded a far larger number.

But this inductive method, though less intolerant,
ought to be just as rigorous as the other. It will
not reject a specimen as bad or as contemptible, but
it will reject the most plausible specimen which does
not really belong to the class of phenomena under
investigation. The zoologist admits all animals, but
he excludes that which is not properly animal. On
this principle the most barbarous tribe or sept in the
most primitive population will have an equal right
with ancient Rome or modern England to our attention provided only that it is really of the same kind.
But perhaps we may for a moment doubt whether
those rude aggregations of men have really anything

in common with the civilised state. Nobody thinks of applying the word "state" to them; perhaps the simple reason of this is that they are not in any sense states, and have nothing in common with the state. Let us consider this question for a moment.

The fundamental fact to which I pointed in my last lecture, which seems so surprising and so profoundly deserving of study, is that men should conceive themselves as belonging, and belonging in such an intimate and momentous union, to a corporation which is not simply their family. Look at the modern Englishman. He may chance to have no drop of English blood in his veins, and yet we hold that there is actually no sacrifice which England might not, in case of need, demand of him. At the same time, though the tie is not simply, and in a particular case may not be at all, that of kindred, yet it is not wholly distinct from kindred, and in general Englishmen do regard themselves as of kin to each other. The English state may be held together in some degree by a common interest, still it is not a mere company composed of voluntary shareholders, but a union which has its root in the family, and which has grown, and not merely been arranged, to be what it is. Now, it is surely impossible not to admit that this phenomenon, vast and highly developed as it now appears, is in its large features similar to the most primitive and barbarous tribe.

That, too, is a great association, to which its members are attached for life and death. For that, too, its members fight; about its interests they debate. In the tribe, too, we can often discover that individuals may have no attachment by kindred to the whole; they may have come in as slaves and received emancipation, or as foreigners by adoption. And yet in the main and on the whole the tribe is an extension of the family, a family on the large scale.

In short, compare the most advanced state with the most primitive tribe, and you will see the same features, though the proportions are different. In the state there is more of mind, in the tribe more of nature. Free-will and intelligent contrivance have more play in the former; blood and kinship rule in the latter. Still the state has not ceased to a tribe; kinship still counts for much in it, as the nationality-movement of the present century has strikingly proved. On the other hand, the tribe, wherever we can get information about it, is found to be also in some degree a state. The rigid family organisation always shows itself insufficient, needing to be supplemented by more artificial institutions. Thus, apart from kinship, there is a common characteristic which brings together the most primitive and the most advanced of these associations—I mean the principle of government. Here, again, the proportion may be different—this is what gives rise to varieties—

but the common characteristic is there on which
depends unity of kind. The apparatus of command
and obedience has become by familiarity so trivial
in our eyes that we may omit to give it the attention it deserves. Yet upon this simple arrangement, by which the will of an individual determines
the actions, not of himself only, but of a multitude,
depends almost everything important in human
history : and, as I said before, political science may be
called the science which investigates the phenomenon,
government.

Here, then, is the first peculiarity of a system of
political science which is frankly inductive. It
begins by putting aside as irrelevant the distinction
of barbarous and civilised, and by admitting to an
impartial consideration all political aggregates, all
societies held together by the principle of government.
This is seldom done consistently and uniformly by
historical speculators who take the widest view. Most
of them abandon only partially the old dogmatic
method. They may be less exclusive than the
eighteenth-century school, may be prepared to see the
good side of medievalism, to appreciate or even over-
appreciate some forms of political life which used to
be treated with contempt. But the system I put
before you goes much further, for it does not ask at
all that the phenomena it studies shall be good or
noble. It simply wishes to find out as much as

possible by observation and induction about the
nature of states and the laws of their development.
For this purpose all facts are welcome, and if corrupt
or morbid phenomena appear these will have, not
indeed the same interest as the phenomena of health,
but another interest peculiar to themselves. The only
facts which will be unimportant are those which
present nothing new, but only confirm in a superfluous
manner what was well known already.

When we have once got rid of the notion that the
tribes and clans of barbarism are contemptible and
unworthy of attention, we obtain a somewhat different
view of the state. Before we naturally regarded
states, since they were peculiar to civilised people, as
being more or less of the nature of inventions, like
the art of writing; but now we see that they are more
like language itself, that is, that though they may
differ infinitely in the intelligence they display, yet
they are found uniformly and universally, or nearly
so, wherever human beings are found. Everywhere
the human being belongs to something which may be
called a polity, and is subject to something which may
be called a government. How then shall we deal
with this universal phenomenon, how shall we set
about investigating it? Shall we begin by laying
down some grand proposition with respect to the
object for which the state exists? This was long
usual. The state exists to put down violence and

protect the weak against the strong. It exists to do justice between man and man and to compose differences. It exists to defend the country against foreign invasion. It exists, in fact, to attain any end which we anywhere find the state aiming at. One school urged particularly that a high and noble view should be taken of its functions. It should consider itself to exist for the sake of virtue or of man's highest wellbeing in whatever way that may be conceived. Another school took a more modest view : holding that the state ought to rest content with keeping order and protecting property, and that the promotion of virtue ought to be left to other agencies.

This is an example among many how the discussion of high and important subjects falls into a groove in which it moves on interminably, blending with party politics and imparting to these a dignity they sadly want, but settling nothing because it proposes no definite question. Do we want to know what the state *should* aim at or what it *does* aim at ? The first question is quite legitimate, and it is all-important, but it is wholly distinct from the other, and we may add that a general answer to such a question, an answer deduced directly from the abstract idea of the state, is scarcely to be expected. What the state should aim at now is likely to be quite different from what it either did or could aim at in ancient Rome, or Sparta, or Persia, or India.

I suggest that we should abandon for the present
the enterprise of deciding what the state ought to be
and to aim at, and consider by way of pure observation what it has actually been. When we do this,
and especially when we take note of the more primitive forms of the state, we may surely doubt whether
we ought to speak so glibly of the object of the
state. We do not speak of the object of a tree or an
animal. Now certainly the state is not so purely a
natural product as a tree or an animal; still it is in
part a natural product, and to the extent that it is a
natural product it must be said to be in the strict
sense without an object. Nay, further, long after its
development has begun to be influenced by human
will, conscious intelligence continues to be wanting;
the will that acts in it is mere instinct. So that only
states that are far advanced and that are composed of
modern men can be treated in the abstract method,
can be referred to and judged by a theoretic standard.
But if this method is not satisfactory, what other
method shall we adopt? In what way shall we bring
the mass of facts which history and observation
present to us into some system ?

In those subjects which we are able to contemplate
calmly, because they do not immediately affect our
interests or excite our feelings, the first step which
science takes is to arrange the phenomena in classes.
Some little classification has to be done at the com-

mencement of every science. Euclid begins by arranging the simple phenomena with which he has to deal, lines, plain figures three-sided and four-sided, etc., curved figures. The astronomer distinguishes the small number of classes of heavenly bodies, fixed stars and planets, satellites, comets, etc. Now it is evident that political science also will have a task of classification to undertake. Some of the technical terms of political classification are very famous. The names monarchy, aristocracy, democracy, etc., constitute almost all the political science most of us know.

But there are some sciences in which the preliminary work of classification is not so easily dispatched as in astronomy or geometry. In dealing with plants and animals, it has been found so difficult and so large a work as almost to require a separate science to itself. Thus by the side of vegetable physiology, which analyses the plant and deals with the laws of life in its vegetable form, we have botany, a science wholly occupied with the description and classification of plants ; and it was found in the eighteenth century, when the Linnæan system grew up, had its day of acceptance, and then gave way to the natural system introduced by Jussieu and others, that in mere classification difficulties may arise, mistakes may be made, and the higher faculties of the mind may be called into play, scarcely less than in the discovery

of laws.   Zoology stands in a relation precisely
similar to animal physiology.   But this has taken
place only in certain sciences.   The question therefore suggests itself whether in a science of states we
may expect that classification will be soon and easily
dispatched, or are to prepare ourselves to overcome
serious difficulties.

Look at those two sciences of classification; you
will see at once that they deal with phenomena of the
same sort, viz. with living organisms.   This suggests
to us that it must be specially difficult to classify
living organisms.   And as soon as the suggestion is
made we see that it is true.   For wherever life is at
work it displays itself in vast numbers of organisms
which show striking resemblances, but at the same
time infinite, almost indescribable differences. "No two
men are alike," we say.   True, but on the other hand
no two men are very different.   And what is true of
men is true of other animals and also of plants.   This
infinite blending of resemblances with differences is
peculiar to living organisms.   Nothing similar presents
itself in the substances dealt with by inorganic
chemistry, still less in the abstractions dealt with by
mathematics.   And therefore those sciences have no
equally difficult problem of classification.   For it is
precisely where an infinite number of complex
individuals exhibit a small number of types and
innumerable differences that classification becomes

difficult. We may expect, then, that a science which
has to do with living organisms will present a serious
problem of classification. Now, are not states living
organisms?

Let us consider what is meant by organism. It is
derived from a Greek word meaning a tool, and may
be said to mean etymologically much the same thing
as a machine, that is, a composite tool. But in
English both organ and organism are usually applied,
not to mechanical but to living tools. Thus a pair of
pincers is a tool or machine for holding ; the hand,
which performs the same function but is alive, may be
called an organ for holding. Now it is a characteristic
of life which has been made very prominent in recent
science, that substances informed by it receive what
is called organisation, that is, the different parts
acquire different capacities and adapt themselves to
perform different functions. Each part becomes more
or less a living tool or organ.

Take something inorganic, e.g. a stone. One part
of it is like another, or if accidentally it differs in
shape does not differ in its capacities. But an organic
substance, e.g. an animal, is a complex, not merely of
parts, but of organs, that is, of tools specially adapted
to do work necessary or conducive to the well-being
of the whole,—eyes for seeing, feet for walking, and
so on.

But this is precisely what characterises a state

A state is a number of human beings not merely crowded or massed together but organised. This is so strikingly true that all the technical terms applied to physical and political organisation are interchangeable, and the word organisation itself is applied in both departments alike without metaphor. We say a man is a member of a state. What does the word member mean? It means "limb." We say the eye or the ear performs a function. What does function mean? It is a political term meaning the discharge of a public office. These examples show how early and how instinctively the analogy between that differentiation which in the physical body creates organs, and that selection which in the state assigns special functions to special men or to special classes, was perceived. The same thing is illustrated by the ancient fable of the Belly and the Members, which you may read either in Livy or in Shakespeare, and by passages well known to all of you in Plato's *Republic* and in St. Paul's Epistles. There should be no schism in the body, says St. Paul, and Plato says, as we do not say, "A finger has pain," but, "A man has a pain in his finger," so in the state we ought not to say, "Some one suffers," but "The state suffers in some one."

The analogy of course must not be overstrained. There are points of difference as well as points of resemblance between physical and political organisation. Nevertheless, it is no mere fanciful or rhetorical, but a really important analogy. In any case the resemblance is sufficiently close to justify us in anticipating the same difficulty of classification in political that we find in physiological science. The states that we see scattered over the globe at present, or over the wide field of past history, are just as bewildering in their differences and correspondences as the plants and animals which exercised the classifying talent of Linnæus and of Cuvier. Here as there certain great types strike the eye, but at the same time each state is so complex, the organs are so many and afford room for such infinite small differences, that we find ourselves compelled to make subdivision after subdivision, and often uncertain under what heading some individual ought to be placed.

I must confess that I cannot find that very obvious classification which comes down to us from Aristotle, and which is still assumed and accepted almost on all hands, at all satisfactory. Let us consider it. States differ, it tells us, according to the number of persons which compose the government. This may consist either of one person, or of a few, or of many. Hence we get three classes, now commonly called Monarchy, Aristocracy, and Democracy. Aristotle, you know, introduced a further distinction, and after admitting these three classes as legitimate under the names

of Monarchy, Aristocracy, Polity, placed by the side
of each a perverted variety of it. The perverted
Monarchy he calls Tyranny, the perverted Aristocracy
Oligarchy, the perverted Polity he calls Democracy.
It seems to me strange that though everything in
politics has altered since Aristotle's time, though the
states we deal with are marvellously unlike the city
communities he had in view, we should still think
such a classification as this sufficient. And yet
it seems to me that in all our political discussion
we still use, and even confine ourselves to, these
simple categories. Parties still dispute on Monarchy
and Non-Monarchy, which they call Republic, on
Aristocracy and Democracy: adhering to Aristotle,
except in this that whereas he, almost as a matter of
course, held Aristocracy to be the best form and
classed Democracy among perversions, we have come
to speak of Democracy as a sort of ultimate ideal,
while the word Aristocracy, in the Aristotelian sense,
has gone out of fashion.

This classification presented itself almost inevitably to Aristotle, who saw on one side Persia and
Macedonia exhibiting in a commanding form the
Monarchy which he also read of in Homer, while in
Greece itself he had before him the sharp contrast
between contemporary democracy and contemporary
oligarchy. In modern Europe the types are much
less simple and distinct. When we take a modern

state and inquire whether it is governed by one, or by few, or by many, we find it usually impossible to obtain a satisfactory or plain answer. For what are we to think if we find that the functions of government are divided between a king and one or several assemblies? Aristotle does not seem to contemplate such a case. In Persia the great king, in Macedonia Philip or Alexander, did not seriously share their power with any assembly; in Athens no individual and no small assembly could enter into competition with the vast democratic *Ecclesia.* The contrary is the case almost everywhere in the modern world, as indeed it used to be a boast of English constitutionalists that the English constitution was a beautiful compound of the three forms of government, and had the advantages, with none of the drawbacks, at once of Monarchy, Aristocracy, and Democracy. Since popular institutions were introduced during the present century into almost every continental country, France and Germany and Italy and Spain may, if they choose, make the same boast. Everywhere, and even in the United States, we find government divided between the one, the few, and the many. England is called a Monarchy, but beside the Monarch it has a House of Lords and a House of Commons. So has Italy, so Prussia, so Belgium, Holland, Spain and Portugal. France and America profess to be democratic Republics, but both beside a popular

assembly have a smaller Senate and also a supreme
President. The American Senate has decidedly
greater power than our House of Lords, and the
American President decidedly greater power than
our Monarch.

Under which heading then are we to class these
states? It is usual to say England is a Monarchy,
America is a democratic Republic. This ought to
mean at the very least that in England the One, if
not ruling alone, yet has greater power than the Few
or the Many, and also greater power than any One in
the American Republic. The contrary is the case.
The One here has far less power than the Many, and
decidedly less power than the One, the President, in
America. The accepted classification then tells us, I
do not say nothing, but the contrary of the truth.[1]

The truth is, that though we continue to use the
ancient words we do not use them in the ancient
sense, but in a sort of metaphorical manner which is
not admissible in any discussion which professes to
be exact. It is no doubt possible to lay it down that
in a given state, whatever the formal institutions may
be, the predominant influence is in the hands perhaps

---

[1] In the corresponding lecture of the 1891 course, after pointing
out the predominance of the assembly, representing the many, in
the so-called English "Monarchy," the author adds—with reference
to the principle of Aristotle's double classification—"If we are required to say whether this assembly governs honestly for the good
of the whole or pervertedly for its own good, I do not know what
answer we could make but the unsatisfactory one,—partly for the
one, partly for the other."

of the people, or of a class, or of some influential individual. We may express this popularly and shortly by calling such a state democratic, or aristocratic, or monarchic, but we must not dream that by using the words in this metaphorical way we are adhering to the old classification. That classification was intended to be taken literally, and it referred to the recognised institutions of the state, not to some hidden influences which we may be able to detect by looking below the surface. If we go in search of such influences and choose to treat them as determining the character of the state, we adopt a wholly new and very strange principle of classification, even though we may abide by the old technical terms.

But if we take those terms, as we ought to do, always in their literal sense, then I think we shall seldom find the old classification serviceable. The case of Rome, for instance, appears almost as complex as England. The *comitia tributa*, a democratic assembly, sometimes seems quite supreme, but more usually the senate, which is aristocratic. The senate, however, at no time possesses undivided power, for the many, represented by the comitia, and the one, represented by the consuls, have always large competence. And when we travel beyond the ancient city states, and go to the medieval or modern states, an instance of government in the hands either of one, or of a few, or of many, is seldom to be found. In one or two

E

cases all power has been thrown by exceptional causes into the hands of an individual, and in some small and poor communities, lost to view among barren mountains, what little government is needed has been done by the many. Otherwise government has been a complex thing, and has been distributed among a number of individuals and assemblies. Some functions are almost everywhere assigned to the one, others almost everywhere to the many; almost everywhere, too, there has been found occasion for select councils representing valuable qualifications possessed only by the few.

But even if this old classification were valuable, who can for a moment regard it as sufficient? Do states differ only or chiefly in the number of their rulers? In the old histories of Greece or Rome the writers seem so much preoccupied by thoughts of republican liberty that they quite overlook a peculiarity of those ancient states which might seem even more interesting and obvious. They seem scarcely to notice that those states are cities and not countries. What an enormous, what a pregnant difference! Ought not this to enter into our classification? Ought we not to say, There are not only aristocracies and democracies; there are also city-states and country-states. To the former class belong the famous states of antiquity, the states which Aristotle studied; to the latter almost all the states of modern Europe.

This is now one of the great fundamental distinctions of political science, but it was almost overlooked in the speculations of the eighteenth century, except where it was exaggerated by Rousseau.

Again, take a government like that temporal state of the Pope which was taken from him in 1870. A serviceable classification would seize the dominant peculiarity of this and bring it into the same list with other governments which are really of the same kind. But how can a classification which only inquires after the number of rulers do this? It can only discover that the government in question is a monarchy, and therefore to be classed along with the government of Louis XIV. or that of Queen Victoria. Surely this arrangement will not help us much.

It is evident that the peculiarity of this government is that it is priestly. Do we find elsewhere in history governments of the same kind? Yes, the government of the Jews after their return from captivity, when the High Priest assumed the position of a prince, was similar. Somewhat similar was the authority of the earliest Mohammedan caliphs, an Omar and an Ali. And everywhere history testifies that priestly authority has a tendency to convert itself into political authority, and will do so when circumstances favour it. But if so, ought not this kind of government to have a place in our classi- fication? The truth is that in the records of history theocracy is a phenomenon almost as prominent as aristocracy or democracy. Yet it is almost over-looked by Aristotle, and has been but slightly referred to by most modern writers on political science.

The result, then, is that in political science classi-fication may be expected to be most important and difficult, and also that the accepted classification suggested originally by the very partial and peculiar experience of the Greek philosophers is scarcely applicable to the states with which we have chiefly to deal, and is also insufficient. /

IN my last lecture I brought together the civilised
state and the rude primitive community to which
we usually deny the name of state, and I asserted
that they belonged together as much as the insect
or mollusc belongs together with the bird and beast.
I asserted that political science ought to find a place
for the rude communities and not to pass them by on
the ground that they are uncivilised, while it confines
its investigations to states which it dignifies with the
name of civilised. Still civilisation is a great thing,
and a thing, if we may trust its etymology, particularly important in political science, for it seems
to be a way of living or thinking peculiarly adapted
to the *civitas* or state. When I maintain that the
rude community should not be overlooked, I do not
maintain that it should be put in the same class with
the civilised state, any more than in zoology the
mollusc is put in the same class with the vertebrate.
And as we propose to busy ourselves with the classification of states, and must therefore go in quest of
large differences, we can scarcely find a larger or

more striking difference than this to begin with.
The question why it is that some communities are so
different from others that we are inclined altogether
to refuse them the name of states, will probably, if
we can find an answer to it, yield us the most fundamental and the broadest of the distinctions we want.

I indicated slightly in the last lecture the most
prominent point of difference between the primitive
and the civilised state. The primitive *man* may, no
doubt, differ from the civilised *man* in a hundred
different ways, but the primitive *state*—that is, the
political organisation of the primitive man when compared with that of the civilised—always, I think, differs
from it in the same way, viz. that it is far more closely
connected with the family. Take any highly civilised
state, whether from ancient or from modern history,
you scarcely perceive any relation or affinity between
its organisation and that of the families composing it.
In modern England or France, in the Greece or Rome
of Demosthenes and Cicero, the family has ceased to
have any political importance. So much is this the case
that those who, in the seventeenth century, speculated
upon the origin of states often show themselves
unaware even that in their origin and first beginning
states were connected with families. The very
tradition of the connection has been lost. It is
supposed that a condition of lawless violence, in
which the weak were at the mercy of the strong,

originally prevailed, and that this was brought to an
end by the invention of government, that is, by an
agreement to surrender to a single strong man a part
of the liberty which each man originally possessed, in
return for protection. This theory seems to conceive
the primitive community as a mere unorganised
crowd of individuals.[1] But the beginning of political
organisation is given by nature in the family relation.
The authority of the paterfamilias may, or may not,
be primeval and universal; but certainly in those
cases where we are able to trace the history of states
furthest back, the starting-point seems not to be a
condition of universal confusion, but a powerful and
rigid family organisation. The weak were not at the
mercy of the strong, because each weak man was a
member of the family, and the family protected him
with an energy of which modern society can form
no conception. In these cases, too, we are able to
trace that the state was not suddenly introduced as a
kind of heroic remedy for an intolerable confusion,
but that the germ of organisation given by nature
was developed artificially; that the family grew into
something more than a mere family ; that it developed
itself gradually so much, and acquired so much
additional organisation, as to disengage itself from
the literal family, which now reappeared in an inde-

---

[1] The MS. has here a pencil note : " This is more true of Hobbes
than Locke."

pendent form within it; and that at last the conventional or fictitious family acquired a character of its
own, until it first forgot and then at last denied and
repudiated its connection with the natural family.

Observe, I do not mean to assert that the state has
in all cases grown up in this way; only that in the
most conspicuous instances, where its growth can be
traced most certainly, it has gone through these
stages.

For an example I will take one of the states best
known to you—ancient Rome; I might equally well
take ancient Athens.

In the time of Cicero the state had a character as advanced and independent as it has in
England or France; and those who speculated upon
its origin often forgot as completely to connect it
with the family as in modern times did Hobbes and
Locke. They said that Romulus had opened an
asylum to which robbers had flocked, and that this
robber community had afterwards stolen wives and
transformed itself into a state. But certain institutions still existed in Rome, which were of immemorial
antiquity, and which to Cicero and his contemporaries
had become quite unintelligible, but which, atten-
tively considered and compared with the traditionary
history by modern scholars, have betrayed the secret
of the development of the Roman state out of the
family. Particularly, there was the institution of the

gens. The second name of every Roman, ending always
in *ius*, Fabius, Julius, Tullius, showed to what *gens* he
belonged, and yet Cicero almost confesses that the
nature and meaning of the *gens* are quite obscure to
him. But Athens had just the same institution, and
the analogy of other primitive communities shows us
that we have here the clan, that is, the conventional
family—a family enlarged and strengthened by means
of various legal fictions. What puzzles Cicero is that
in the condition of the *gens* in which he saw it the
fictions were too transparent, so that he cannot think
of it seriously as a family. But we know that there
is an earlier stage in the development of law when
legal fictions are taken quite seriously. We can
therefore easily conceive that five hundred years
before Cicero these institutions, the *gentes*, may have
been thoroughly intelligible and full of vitality. And
now, when we take up the early books of Livy and
read the account of that strange primitive party-
struggle between the patricians and plebeians, we
are able to discern the primitive nucleus of the
Roman community in the original clans, the patrician *gentes*. For we find references to an ancient
maxim that no plebeian belongs to a *gens ;* now as in
later times this had ceased to be true, we see that
the struggle had been not merely for office but also
for status, social as well as political ; in short, that it
was the effort of expansion by which the old family

mould was broken and the state proper disengaged itself from the clan.

Again, the history of the city of Rome shows us that the nucleus of it was composed of a number of primitive clans living each in its separate settlement, but side by side, for the oldest districts of the city have the names of the ancient patrician *gentes*. In short a number of indications concur to show that Rome—though in the time of Cicero the fact had been quite forgotten—first took shape as a league of cognate but distinct clans, each clan being a conventional family into which admission could only be procured through the fiction of adoption.

The same fact is almost as evident in the history of Athens. And in almost every state the development of which has been at all recorded it is possible to recognise that the family is infinitely more prominent in the earlier stages than in the later, so that the further you ascend the stream the more you see the state taking the form of a tribe or clan, or league of tribes and clans.

So far, then, we have arrived at a grand distinction which roughly corresponds to the distinction between civilised and uncivilised states. For the most part we find that the uncivilised state is only a tribe that is a more or less conventional family.

But is this all? No; when I compare in my mind the so-called civilised with the more primitive states

I am struck with another difference equally pregnant.
I am struck with the immense political importance
of religion in the primitive state. I use the word
religion here in its most literal popular sense, the
worship and apparatus of worship of special deities
in literal temples. In the higher sense I should
maintain that religion rather gains than loses by the
advance of civilisation in a state, and I do not myself
believe that the state can disengage itself from
religion taken in this higher sense. But as the state
gradually disengages itself from the family, so it is
a historic law that the state as it develops tends
to disengage itself from the particular form of
religion with which in its primitive period it had
been connected, and in its earlier stage the state is
very frequently found thus intimately connected
with some such special form of religion.

This has been somewhat concealed from the
readers of history, owing to the fact that many of
the most famous histories have been written in a
time of scepticism with respect to the religious
system with which they have to deal. Thucydides,
Polybius, Livy, Tacitus, are not believers in the
ancient national religions of Greece and Rome
respectively. The same is true also of Aristotle.
Accordingly all these historians and speculators
rationalise somewhat, and in their accounts of early
history the religious colour is in a great degree

washed out. Still, in the early books of Livy it is
clearly recognisable that a strong religious feeling
entered into the struggle of patricians and plebeians,
and that the former regarded themselves as defending
the ancient religious institutions, the "sanctities of
old." And in general we may perceive that both in
Greece and Rome the later generations when they
looked back perceived that religion had formerly been
much more prominent in public life than it was in
their own time, as we ourselves feel when we compare
modern politics with the politics of Charles I.'s time.
"Majores nostri, religiosissimi mortales," says Cato,
and Sophocles tells of Athens that it boasted itself
to be "most religious" ($\theta\epsilon o\sigma\epsilon\beta\acute{\epsilon}\sigma\tau\alpha\tau\alpha\iota$), as indeed it
appears in the ideal picture of it given both by that
poet and by Aeschylus. The legends of Numa
Pompilius and of Epimenides; the ancient priesthoods, more ancient commonly than purely secular
institutions; many survivals, such as the Amphictyonic
Confederation and the Comitia Curiata,—all these
indications in Greek and Roman history, and others
quite similar in the histories of other states, lead us
to conclude that of states it may be said, as the poet
has said of individuals, "Heaven lies about them in
their infancy." These examples have been drawn
from heathen religions, but the history of the last
two centuries has shown that in Christian states, too,
a time comes when the State tries to disengage itself

from the particular institution of Christian religion with which in earlier times it has been connected. Down to about the time of Queen Anne the English state was also in some sense the English Church, but since that time it has been in a manner secularised, and so visibly that the very complexion of its history has been altered. About the same time the same change passed over the leading Catholic states, so that an ever-growing hostility to the spiritual power is throughout a characteristic of continental history in the eighteenth century.

Looking upon states in general from our own point of view, which is that of a somewhat secularised state, we perceive a great difference between states like our own and others in which politics are closely connected with religion. Like our own are the states of modern Europe, and also the classical states of antiquity in their later periods; to the other class belong the medieval states, most of the Oriental communities, and most communities anywhere that are in a primitive stage. This particular influence of religion, its influence upon politics, tends to become exhausted after a certain time, just as the influence of the family does, because after a time the state becomes independent, and able, as it were, to stand without props. Hence we see that political theory forgets the influence of religion as it forgets that of the family, because political theory commonly

belongs to an advanced period of the state when it
has become independent. Aristotle in the *Politics*
is almost entirely silent on the subject of religion.
Not only does he not recognise that one most
important and common form of government, the
theocracy, is absolutely founded on religion, but he
does not seem to recognise that even in primitive
periods religion is a leading cause of the development of states out of tribes. We shall find it quite
impossible to follow him in this respect when we
found a political science upon induction and history.
Historically, religion is a ruling influence in most
states during their period of growth; in some
conspicuous cases it seems almost to create the state;
and many centuries commonly elapse before it
becomes possible to distinguish the two ideas of
state and church, much more to think of dividing the
two institutions. Accordingly we have here another
leading difference between the states called civilised
and those which are more primitive; in the primitive
state not only the family but also religion is far more
prominent, and has a substantial political importance.

How does this influence work? As to the family,
we saw how, by a gradual extension and sophistica-
tion of the simple idea of the family, the state may
gradually come into existence. But historically we
see states at times springing into existence in quite
another way, through religion. Look at the great

states of Islam. A religious doctrine was preached in the seventh century among the Arab tribes, and forthwith those populations, till then feeble and disunited, took the form of a mighty state, and in the course of a century had founded cities, overthrown empires, and established a great federation of states, covering a considerable section of the globe, and united among themselves by the bond of a common religion. This is the largest phenomenon of the kind; but we have all read in our Bibles how two thousand years earlier another prophet had given a law in the same neighbourhood, which law had in like manner created a state. These are extreme and striking examples of the state-building power of religion, because they seem to show us religion creating states, as it were, out of nothing. But as a concurrent factor religion is seen wherever the formation of a state can be traced. In the Semitic or Hamitic East, wherever a barbarous tribe has raised itself at all above the level of barbarism and taken any development, it has done so usually through conversion to Islam. In Europe it was by alliance with the Church that the Germanic nationality first achieved durable political creations; thus did Clovis create and Pepin restore the Frankish Empire. In England, too, it was religion that first brought the tribes together and laid the foundation of an English state.

The reason why the family is capable of developing into the state is that it creates a strong link between individuals. The son belongs in the most intimate sense to the father; the members of a family belong together. Once given such a solid bond, human contrivance and invention may by degrees add suitable organisation; but the bond is indispensable. Now perhaps the only other influence which creates such a bond is religion. It forms churches which, so long as the religious influence continues genuine, unite their members for life and for death as the family does. These unions may be barbarous; the deity worshipped, the rites practised, may appear to the outside world repulsive, as in other cases they may appear noble and admirable; but whether good or bad, the bond created by religion is of that strong, natural, elementary, instinctive kind, that it lasts for centuries, and allows infinite modifications and developments in the body which it holds together to take place without dissolution of the body.

We see then two ways in which the state may come into existence. It may have its root in the family, it may have its root in the Church. But are these roots really distinct? Do churches spring up quite independently of clans or tribes? We do not intend here to speculate; we wish to follow the indications of fact and of history. Whatever may be possible in the abstract, in historic experience they are generally found together. The family influence and the religious influence operate side by side. Mohammed did not bring together individuals that had been isolated, but tribes that had been distinct, and, moreover, in spite of their distinctness, cognate. Moses made a church or rather a church-nation, but he made it out of tribes, and behind the Mosaic we see the patriarchal, Abrahamic community. Take other examples. The early history of Rome shows us a religious legislator, Numa Pompilius, endowing the community, while it was yet in political infancy, with an elaborate organisation of worship. We cannot lay any stress upon the personality of Numa, but it is clear that early Rome passed through a phase of intense religious feeling, for all evidence shows that the religious institutions in Rome were more ancient than the political, that Rome had many priesthoods, many temples, at a time when she had scarcely any magistrates. The nucleus of the world-state was a group of sacred shrines, the Ara Maxima by the Tiber, the shrine of Faunus on the Palatine, and then the great temple of Jupiter on the Capitoline. Shall we say then that Rome developed itself out of a primitive church? I think we may say so. But it is equally clear, as I said before, that Rome grew out of a league of tribes or clans. The tribal character is just as manifest as the theocratic character in that primitive community, not less so than in the earliest

F

phase of the Hebrew community. It appears, then, that the ecclesiastical form is not diverse from the tribal form, but may be superimposed upon it—nay, possibly springs out of it by normal development. ✓

However this may be, it is certain that in some communities the theocratic stamp is most marked, in others the tribal; while again both these classes of state appear to us primitive and old-fashioned, because we are accustomed to a third class in which both the influence of religion and that of the family have ceased greatly to influence the state, which now assumes to be independent of either.

This is a large generalisation, but it is not at all recondite. It merely collects together some facts which, if they are often overlooked, are overlooked only on account of their largeness and obviousness. The word *state* and the conception *state* seem wanting in some communities, which in other respects also appear to be imperfectly developed. Accordingly such communities have been passed over by political speculators who were in search of states, since they do not even profess to be states. But as my object is to bring together all the political phenomena which are really of the same kind, and as these communities appear to be of the same kind as the recognised state, though they do not adopt the same name, I desire to include them. I find two large varieties of them. That which strikes me first because it is most barbarous, most unlike the civilised state, is the *tribe*, which I find chiefly in the great desert regions of the world, in North Africa, Arabia, and Central Asia. But I find another variety which cannot be called the tribe, for it has quite other characteristics. The Turkish Empire is the great example of it. It is often of great extent, and often has much organisation. It reminds us of what we ourselves, the nations of Europe, were in the Middle Ages, and we think of it rather as medieval than as barbarous. The prominent feature of it is not the family but religion. In the Turkish Empire no question is raised of a man's nationality, but only of his religion. True believers are all equal, and men differ only as they are true believers or infidels.

We have then three great varieties of state. There is the state proper, there is the tribe, and there is this ecclesiastical community, which I have just described,—we may call it perhaps the theocracy.

They are all states in this sense, that they are all alike corporations to which men belong for life and death, but corporations distinct from, and larger than, the mere natural family.

In what do they differ? In the motive which attaches men to them; in the conception which the members have of the corporation to which they are thus closely attached. Ask a tribesman what binds him to his tribe, what he means when he says he belongs to it: he will answer that "blood is thicker than water," that he belongs by kinship to his tribe, that he is a Macgregor or a Gordon, and must go with the Macgregors or the Gordons; ask the same question of a Jew or a Mussulman—they will speak of the God in whom they believe and of their circumcision; ask an Englishman or a Frenchman—they will give again a different answer, one not so easy to express in a few words, to the effect that it is of infinite advantage to them to belong to a great England or a great France. Thus one speaks of community of race, another of community of religion, another of community of interest. But all alike are agreed that the tie, whatever it is, is infinitely strong; and that if the corporation to which they are attached should be endangered they would be morally bound to make all sacrifices in its behalf.

States, then, may be classified according to the motive which holds them together, and this is perhaps the most comprehensive principle — that is, the principle which is independent of all differences in form of government, and which includes the least developed organisms that can pretend to be political. It is useful in the same way as all principles of classification that are founded upon real and important differences—that is, it brings together and makes available for use a large number of scattered facts. But at this stage we know only that the political

community appears in these three shapes; we must
not for a moment assume that we have here three
different species, as the word species is understood in
physiology—that is, varieties so rigidly separated that
they can either not at all, or only in very long periods
of time, pass into each other. On the contrary, all
appearances show that we have here only three
different stages in the development of the same state.
For it is important to remark that the three motives
are not generally found operating separately. One
of the three is commonly predominant, but the other
two are generally observable either in germ or in
decay. This cannot be better illustrated than by
considering our own state and the way in which we
ourselves regard it. Among us the state has gained
independence; we are in an advanced stage of
development. We belong to it mainly because we
hold it useful, beneficial; the bond that holds us all
together is community of interest. But does this
mean that the other older motives have quite ceased
to act, that the older ties have quite fallen away?
Not at all; we are still Englishmen. When we speak
of the colonies and rejoice to think that they will not
lightly separate themselves from us, we still use the
old phrase and say that blood is thicker than water.
Nor has the religious tie by any means ceased to
hold not only individuals but also the state together.
In the presence of Mohammedans or idolaters we

feel in the most vivid manner that we are Christians,
and when we travel in Italy or Spain we mostly feel
in the same manner that we are Protestants.

Thus in the advanced communities all the three
motives act at once. They are states proper, held
together by interest; this is their predominant
character. But they have by no means entirely
ceased to have the nature of theocracies, held together
by religion, nor have they ceased to have the nature
of tribes held together by kinship.

I have already remarked in like manner that in
the theocratic state, though the theocratic motive
predominates, the tribal motive is commonly also
operative; the theocracy is a tribe or league of tribes
at the same time. Conversely, it is not to be supposed
that the tribal motive has in it no germ of theocracy.
What I have called shortly the sense of kinship is
in those primitive minds in which it is most influential
by no means the simple rational thing it is in ourselves. There it is closely blended with religion; it
is a worship of ancestors, and as the ancestors are
regarded as gods, so the gods are regarded as ancestors,
so that no line can be traced where family feeling
ends and religion begins.

Once more, both in the tribe and the theocracy
there are observable very distinct germs of the state
proper. The notion of a common interest has not
indeed detached itself, and we can observe that when

it begins to do so those who have been accustomed
to the older motives receive a shock, cry out on
utilitarianism, and predict the downfall of the nation.
But implicitly the notion must always have been at
work, and however little avowed must have worked
powerfully. For such primitive communities are
under an intense pressure from danger and from
suffering. The enemy is often at their gates, the
men are exposed to massacre, the women and children
to slavery. In such circumstances the community
of interest is much more palpable, more undeniable,
than in the vast nation-states and empires of a more
civilised time; and if it is not so much mentioned
this is only because the older notions are still vigorous
enough by themselves to hold the society together
and satisfy the minds of the citizens.

Thus, when we make the experiment of bringing
together the rude and civilised communities, we discover that the difference is not so much one of kind
as of degree of development, and this is what the
common expression, progress of civilisation, would
lead us to expect. In the main it appears that the
barbarous states, or those we call Oriental, of the
present day, are not essentially different from our
own, but only less developed—that they are now
what we were once.

I have distinguished three different state-motives
and three different forms of state corresponding to

them. But can we find no fourth motive and no fourth kind of state?

I daresay your first impression will be that it is easy to find states which do not fall under any of these three heads. You will cite for instance the Roman Empire, which was composed of various races and various religions. And you will ask, What common interest held together the conquering Romans and the provincials who were plundered by Roman proconsuls and proprætors? And similar to the Roman Empire are all states founded on conquest, where a ruling race lives in the midst of dependent races; such states occur in history as frequently as those which we have hitherto contemplated. Evidently, then, there is a fourth state-motive, simpler and no less effective than the three we have examined, viz. force. Sheer superiority of force on the part of the ruling class, inspiring first terror, and after a certain time inert passive resignation,—this is the explanation of, perhaps, half the states in the world.

This brings us to another distinction which is very fundamental. We began by laying it down that the state is an organism, and that the processes by which it is developed are analogous to those by which animal or vegetable organisms receive their peculiar form and organisation. But these are natural processes, the result of the power which life has of adapting itself to its environment. We see something analogous to this when a group of men, held together by some living bond and pressed by some difficulty or danger from without, takes a shape and puts forth organs that may enable it to withstand the pressure. We see here the natural genesis of the state. But among the mass of states which history presents we find a whole class which have not arisen in this way at all. They ought, no doubt, to form a fourth class by the side of the three which we have distinguished, if it did not seem more just to refuse them the name of state altogether. For these so-called states are not natural organisms. They are inorganic.

The natural states exist side by side, and are often crowded together in a narrow room. Hence wars arise between them, and for the most part not such wars as we see now among European states, which are closed by a treaty and an indemnity, but wars in which either state aims at the destruction of the other. This destruction is often accomplished. Government is swept away, organisation is dissolved, the victorious state enters the territory and has the conquered population, now reduced to a mere crowd, at its mercy. What does it do? Sometimes it annexes the territory to its own. In this case it will set up a new government, which will be in the hands of alien officials. From this time there will be nominally one large state where before there had been two smaller states. Now, as most actual states have often engaged in war, this process has occurred very frequently indeed, and most states now include some territory and some population which was originally incorporated in this way.

But for our purpose it is essential to draw a sharp distinction between the natural organic union out of which the living state grows and this sort of violent incorporation. Not because we may disapprove of such violence, for, as I have said, our moral approval or disapproval is wholly irrelevant to the question of classification ; but because the difference between the society held together by force and the natural society is so great that they ought not to be described by the same word. At least, if we must in conformity with usage call the former "state," let us add the epithet "inorganic."

Properly speaking, such a society is a double thing. The conquering class or horde, taken by itself, is a real state, a vigorous organism. Thus I quoted the Turkish Empire as a typical example of the theocracy. It is so if we think of the ruling Mussulman population, but outside this in the same territory there are the subject Christian populations, who form properly no state at all, either by themselves or in conjunction with their rulers, but an inorganic crowd.

Nevertheless the inorganic quasi-state imitates the organic state, and has one characteristic of the true state in a high degree. For we said that the state is characterised by government, which means command enforced by punishment; this, then, the inorganic quasi-state has, and indeed depends exclusively upon it.

It is time to sum up the results of this lecture. History and observation show us that human populations are often united by an organic process analogous to that which combines natural substances into a living organism. The family, in withstanding external pressure, extends and modifies itself by means of legal fictions till it becomes the clan, and several clans unite themselves by means of a federal league. Again, the worshippers of a deity engage in religious war against the worshippers of some other deity, and the pressure of war gives rise to organisation. Hence we have two types of organic governed society; but these two types are commonly found blended together. After a certain time the society thus founded on kindred or common religion or both, becomes aware that its union is a thing valuable for its own sake, that government and organisation and co-operative life are useful in themselves to the individuals who possess them. Hence there springs up the conception of a common good, a common weal, which is independent of such considerations as kindred or religion; by degrees the society disengages itself from these props, and begins to rest by preference upon utility, the word being understood not necessarily in any sordid sense.

Hence the organic state appears in three different forms: clannish, or theocratic, or properly political; but these forms are, to all appearance, only different stages of a single normal development.

By the side of these organic forms history shows us another sort of political society which, if the state is an organism, can only be called a quasi-state. It is not organic—that is, it is not developed from within. It is the result of conquest, but has a similar appearance to the organic state, because it adopts and imitates the organisation of it. In history, however, since conquest has been very frequent, this quasi-state occurs at least as often as the organic state. If we speak seldom of it in these lectures the reason will be, not that it does not deserve study, but that it ought to be carefully distinguished and studied separately, and that our present undertaking concerns rather the organic state.

LECTURE IV

THE practical use of the classification I laid before
you in the last lecture is that it helps us in understanding the history of primitive and uncivilised
states, and enables us to conceive that, however
different in appearance, they are substantially phenomena of the same kind as the modern civilised state.
For these purposes it is, in my opinion, of very great
use. Everywhere in history the ordinary student
suffers lamentably from the want of general ideas.
Some compass we must have in the sea of facts. In
modern and recent times we are not quite without
this compass, for we understand in general that
constitutional freedom is the object aimed at, and
despotism the evil struggled with. But in primitive
times all is different. Here we want other categories,
other generalisations, yet we are scarcely aware of
this, and hence we try to make the familiar categories
serve again. But it is not really true to say that the
struggle of the plebeians against the patricians was a
struggle for liberty, and it is of little use to apply
modern principles to that long stretch of primitive

history which is so familiar to us in the Old Testament. In all these parts of history we should dismiss the notions of liberty, constitutionalism, checks on royal power, writs of *habeas corpus* and petitions of right. Wholly different notions are required here, and the clue is given when you understand that the clan is struggling with the theocracy, and the theocracy with the state proper. Some Numa or Mohammed or Moses breaks the hard tribal organisation by some grand religious proclamation. Augustine breaks in upon the rude heptarchy, Clovis holds out a hand to Catholicism. The community assumes a theocratic form. Then at a later period the theocracy too is put upon the defensive. Political ideas are now gaining head; a royal house establishes itself; the theocracy, as represented by the prophet Samuel, is indignant that the people should ask for a king; or the royal house itself has been allied with the theocracy, or it may be an aristocratic government has endowed itself with priesthoods; in this case the rising movement will attack aristocracy or monarchy, the precinct of religious privilege will be invaded, and the plebeians will break into the priesthoods and pontificates.

Such are the party struggles of the primitive age, but the primitive age is nearer to us than we are apt to suppose. The rationalistic mode of writing history effaces, as I said, the religious colour of

national life. We have a trick of dividing ecclesiastical history from civil and relegating it into special
treatises; but it is in this ecclesiastical history that
the primitive ideas under which the state was first
formed are preserved. Thus, in our struggle with
the Stuarts there is evidently a very large ecclesiastical element, but we do not allow to it all the weight
we ought, because of the prejudice which leads us to
think that this does not belong to history proper, but
only to ecclesiastical history. If we allowed ourselves
to contemplate that struggle as a whole, we should
see that it was not a mere struggle with monarchy
for freedom, that it was at the same time the effort
by which the state made itself independent and
passed out of its theocratic stage.

We may pass now to another of the large distinctions by which states are divided into classes. I
take intentionally such as are most obvious, because
I want to take note of the largest differences first.

Those who in our modern period study the history
of Greece and Rome are not perhaps at first struck
by the fundamental difference between the classical
states and those of modern Europe. Compared with
the primitive state, or even with the medieval state,
Greece and Rome have quite a modern appearance.
The school of Voltaire used to couple the age of
Louis XIV. with the great age of Greece and Rome
as being of the same kind, and to treat all that came

between as deserving only to be forgotten. Since Voltaire's time the modern state has grown still more like the classical one, for it has acquired liberties and popular assemblies. And yet what a difference! A difference that must take by surprise those who think that states differ almost exclusively in the number of their rulers!

It flashes on us after a time that by a state the ancients mean a city, and that we mean a country!

When I say the ancients I mean of course the Greeks and Romans. Outside the classical world we see traces of a similar arrangement in antiquity, for Carthage seems to be a sovereign city like Rome or Athens. But antiquity, too, has large country states, the Macedonian Monarchy, the Persian Empire, the primeval Egyptian state. Substantially we have to deal with the fact that in two countries, Greece and Italy, the political vital principle seized small groups of population and turned them into highly developed organisms, whereas in modern Europe (and now also in America) and in Asia, the political organism is very large and tends also to become larger.

In modern times the substance of the organism is commonly a population speaking the same language. Sometimes, however, it is a population with two or three languages, but one of them generally preponderating. So Switzerland has three languages, but German greatly preponderates; Austria has several languages, and much difficulty is caused by the fact that no one now preponderates quite decidedly.

In ancient Greece and Italy language had no political effect. The polity embraced only a small number of those who spoke the same language. So it was in Greece, where the language was spread over no great space, and yet within that space there were dozens of independent states. So, too, in Italy, where languages closely cognate were spread over a large section of the country, and yet we find Rome and Veii and the cities of the Latin league contending together in much the same way as Athens, Megara, and Corinth.

In the modern world something similar has been seen again in Italy, and also in Switzerland. In both countries in the fourteenth century, owing to the failure of the power of the Emperor, cities became for practical purposes again sovereign, and in the cases of Florence and Venice highly developed. In Germany, too, from the same cause, a number of free cities, such as Nürnberg and Frankfurt, became practically almost independent republics. These have been momentary glimpses, in the case of Italy something more than a glimpse, of the ancient classical world, but in the end the modern tendency has set more and more decidedly against the small state,

G

and seems likely now to replace its large states by states larger still, states of 20,000,000 by states of 80,000,000.

If you will reflect you will see that a difference so great as this must necessarily involve innumerable other differences of organisation. The government of a town council cannot possibly follow the same rules as the government of a great country. This simple fact shows us how hollow must have been the political theories of the last century, which aimed at the imitation of the classical states, and yet for the most part forgot such a fundamental difference.

I mention it here for the sake of founding upon it a classification, but, as a matter of fact, a great part of history is occupied not so much with the proceedings of states of these two kinds as with the struggles and confused endeavours of human society to form states of these two kinds. In particular, the gradual growth of the large nation-state in the bosom of the dissolving Roman Empire occupies many centuries full of history on the largest scale. Though I have not space to treat of this, I may find room here for a suggestion as to the causes which may have led the political vital principle to embody itself in different countries in these two different ways.

We might perhaps imagine that that rational way of setting up a state which charms philosophers so much may really have given birth to the old city-

states, though not to the modern country - state.
The city-state was so compact and developed itself
so fast that it looks not quite unlike the invention
of an ingenious thinker. And yet the gradual
growth of the city-state out of the family and the
religious community is as well attested as that of the
country-state. Primitive Athens and Rome are not
a whit more philosophical, they are quite as mythical
and religious as primitive Germany and England.
We must look therefore for some other explanation.

You will observe that the thing we call kindred
has no natural limit or end. Every man's relation-
ships are infinite, but he only keeps in memory a
certain number of them. A tribe is bound together
by kindred, but kindred does not end with the
tribe. All that ends there is the consciousness of
kindred. Now when we study primitive society we
are usually able to distinguish very clearly two sorts
of kindred, one within the other, one narrow and
conscious, the other wide and unconscious. Those
original tribes of Athens and Rome had conscious
kindred, each within itself, but they dwelt in the
midst of other tribes whom they regarded also as
cognate. This latter relationship did not influence
them; they were not even consciously aware of it,
but they were certainly not ignorant of it. For every
Athenian believed himself to be a Hellen, and could
not but know that his language was intelligible to the

visitor from Thebes or from Corinth, but not to the visitor from Tyre or from Babylon. The common kindred of all Greeks was in a manner always assumed and yet never considered ; no consequence was drawn from it ; it had no effect on the formation of states.

Thucydides remarks that Homer has no collective name for the Greeks. There is indeed such vagueness in Homer's conception of the nation as a whole that the reader is never made to understand whether the Trojans are of different nationality from the Greeks or of the same. Now it is curious to observe that the German tribes too labour under just the same vagueness of conception as to their nation. They too have no collective name. There are German tribes, who blindly feel themselves to be related to each other, and there is a German language. Roman observers can see their unity, but they overlook it themselves, and it was actually not till the eleventh century, or a thousand years after Tacitus, that a collective name *theotisc, deutsch*, grew into use among them. I might make a similar remark about the Arabs before Mohammed. It seems, then, that in the ordinary circumstances of early society the large family, the tribe, has vitality, but the larger family still, the nation, has scarcely any vitality. Now it may chance that in the whole course of development the tribe and the nation may preserve this relation to each other.

So it happened in Greece and Italy. Within each country the cognate tribes pressed close upon each other and made war against each other, knowing each other mainly as enemies, until each separately, or small leagues of them, under this mutual pressure developed through the stages I enumerated last week, became first from the clan the theocracy, then from the theocracy the state proper. Meanwhile the nation as a whole remained undeveloped, and when a great danger from Macedonia called for a general rally the nation had no organisation ready by means of which it could answer the call. Each town was armed against its neighbours, but the nation was not armed against a foreign enemy. It was thus in ancient Greece, it was thus again by a remarkable correspondence in medieval Italy, when the cities fell in like manner before Charles V. In ancient Italy the development was the same, but the result was different; there one town swallowed up all the others, and when the Carthaginians, Gauls, and Germans threatened Italy the great union of federated towns served the same purpose as a country-state.

But it is possible to imagine another course of circumstances in which after the early stage the tribe might not gain but rather lose vitality, so that it may not grow into a state, and on the other hand the faint glimmer of consciousness which the nation had at the outset might be strengthened until it eclipsed the consciousness of the tribe. The result of this may be that the city-state may be arrested in its development, and in the place of many city-states one great nation-state may come into existence.

We notice that Greece, Italy, and Switzerland are mainly mountain-countries. Here invaders are kept aloof, and in the perpetual petty struggle of the cognate tribes strong natural fortresses present themselves. The federated tribes gather round some double crag, where a citadel and a temple rise side by side; in the plain below is the forum. Here begins the development of the city-state. But north of the Alps we have in the main large plains. Over these plains tribes wander without much mutual pressure; they do not much build towns. It was said of the Germans that they hated towns. Here, therefore, the tribal stage continues without much development for a long time. Suppose now this undeveloped nation assailed from without by a great invasion. At first it will be more helpless than the region of city-states, for it will have no strongholds. Thus before the onset of the Huns and the gradual advance of the Slavs the Germanic tribes did not defend their territory, but abandoned it and swarmed across the frontier of the Empire. Thus in England the tribes yield at first with little resistance to the Danes. But such a nation holds in reserve a resource which the nation of city-states has parted with. What

the Greeks could not do because all their political
energy was drawn off by the city-states, they can
still do. They can form a nation-state. This is
what in many cases we observe to take place. The
English nation-state first formed itself under Alfred
in the great nation-rally against the Danes. In like
manner the Germans, who in the fifth century had
given way before the Huns, in the tenth century
rallied successfully under Henry and Otto against
the Magyars. Henry is called the town-builder of
Germany because he first made the country defensible,
and it is from this period of the greatness of the
Saxon dynasty that we seem able to date the national
consciousness of Germany ; soon after this was heard
the collective name—*Deutsch.*

These seem to have been the causes at work. The
fact in any case is most remarkable and fundamental,
viz. that the political principle in its more advanced
stage, when it has left tribal and theocratic life somewhat behind and is calling into existence the state
proper, creates this in two wholly different forms,
the one small and intense, the other indefinitely large
and therefore for a long time languid. This is one of
those facts which observation reveals easily, for it
lies on the surface of history, yet probably we should
never have arrived at it by any amount of abstract
reasoning on the nature of the state. Since there are
two such forms there may well be more than two ;

perhaps other such forms may already lie before us in history but may have passed undistinguished; perhaps the future may reserve others for us. But this distinction of the city-state and nation-state is made specially memorable by corresponding to the two periods of cultivated intelligence which history has known. Hellenism (and, we may add, the Italian Renaissance also) is the triumph of the city-state; the European brotherhood of nation-states has produced the vast growth of every kind of power and science which distinguishes modern civilisation.

But our object is classification. Let us look, therefore, a little closer at this difference in order that we may see how much it involves. For it may seem at first sight that between ancient Athens and modern England there is only a difference of extent of territory. Athens possessed but a narrow portion of land surrounding the city, but there is a very large territory round London. Now evidently this is not all. On the one side Athens is the organism, not Attica; on the other side England, not London. There the people were called from the town, Athenians; here they are called from the country, Englishmen.

When we compare this fact with the speculations of Aristotle we see that it has had the greatest influence upon them. The technical name which he gives to the ripened political community is not, like "state," a term originally indefinite, but actually the word

"city." We may see, too, that the great country-
states, such as Macedonia or Persia, which were
known to him did not strike him as belonging to the
same class of phenomena, for when he settles the
characteristics of the perfect state he tells us it must
not be so large that the whole people may be unable
to attend the same assembly.

The simplest rudimentary conception of political
action is this, that one man imposes a command
upon another. But, under primitive conditions, this
means that the two men meet. Suppose now that
the state, instead of including a town and a few fields
round it, covers a circle with a radius of two or three
hundred miles. The simple action of government
becomes at once impossible. The world has been
occupied through something like half its history in
struggling with this elementary difficulty.

Of course it would be easy to divide the territory
into manageable districts and plant a ruler in each.
But if this is done without reserve the result is, not
one large state, but as many small states as there
are districts with separate rulers. Evidently, then,
some special contrivance is needed. It is a very
simple contrivance, and it is in reality everywhere
the same, however many names or disguises may be
given to it.

A distinction is drawn between two kinds of
government. It is recognised that some affairs are

the common concern of the whole population, but
that other affairs concern only a particular neighbourhood or locality. These last, which it is most difficult,
are also those which it is least necessary to deal with
from headquarters. It is possible therefore to set up
a ruler in each district, who in respect of certain
affairs shall give independent orders, but in respect
of all greater and more general affairs shall receive
instructions from a ruler of rulers who shall be
stationed at the centre.

I say *a ruler* in each district for simplicity. There
may be in each district several rulers, or there may be
a complicated organisation of officials and assemblies.
So, too, in the centre there may be a despot, or a
council, or a parliament, or a combination of all three.
I disregard all these differences and call your attention
to the one characteristic which is and must be possessed
by all governments in large territory. This is that a
distinction must be recognised between local and
central government, between affairs that can be settled
on the spot by a local ruler and affairs that must be
carried to headquarters. This distinction cannot be
dispensed with, though it may be reduced to the
lowest point by certain contrivances. The contrivance
called centralisation, so long used in France, has the
effect of paralysing as much as possible local government. It cannot destroy the local official nor even
his independence, but it can reduce this within very

narrow limits, and bring him very near to an automaton. On the other hand, in large empires we frequently see *central* government paralysed in an equal degree. In the old Persian and the old Mogul empires the satrap and the Nizam were almost independent sovereigns, the intervention of Susa or of Delhi had become almost formal, and in the other extreme of the political world we come upon the same phenomenon when we note how nearly the authority of Downing Street has disappeared in the government of our greater colonies.

But in these extreme cases the two kinds of government are visible side by side; if either kind seems on the point of perishing, this means not that a large state can do without it, but that some great change is at hand. In the city-state, on the other hand, if we suppose it small enough and still at a primitive stage, we can imagine a state of affairs in which no such different kinds of government are known; when all controversies are brought to the same king who sits in the gate; when one man, or it may be many men, or even every man by turn, bears rule and the others obey, but yet all government is of the same kind, and the state is thought of always as one inseparable whole, which always in great matters and in small acts together; when there are not yet, as in the world we live in, two states, the great one which resides in the capital and has its kings and parliaments, and the little one in our own neighbourhood, with its mayor and town council or its sheriff and quarter-sessions.

Some local government, no doubt, may be found even in the city-state. There were "demes" in Attica by the side of the great Demos;—Aristophanes in his play of the Acharnians enables us to understand the relation between them. Still the one Athens, the one imperious, noisy, all-deciding, all-governing Ecclesia, gave its character to everything, so that we can enter into the view of Aristotle that there can be no real "Polis" where the whole people does not meet together.

We may say then that the great difference between the city-state and the country-state is not a mere difference of size, but consists in this, that whereas in the city-state government is one great simple thing, in the country-state it is double. Here we have the great government and the little government, the mother-country and the mother-locality; for in these country-states the locality is often a former state that has been deprived of its independence; such for instance are some of the shires of England, such were the provinces of France before the Revolution.

A kind of middle-state may be imagined, and the Roman Empire furnished an illustrious example of it. This was an aggregation, no less than England or

France, but an aggregation largely of city-states to a
city-state. As an English shire may be a heptarchic
kingdom humbled, so the cities of Italy and the
Greek world in the Roman Empire were city-states,
reduced to the rank of localities. And though it
covered so vast an extent of country the Roman
Empire never completely assumed the character of a
country-state.

But having marked the fundamental distinction
between the city-state and the nation-state we may
take note of a number of less striking differences of
the same kind. In the city-state local government is
practically *nil*, in the country-state it has a substantial
existence. This gives us two classes. But the latter
class, which has local government, splits up into a
number of sub-classes. For local government may
have strikingly different degrees of importance. It
may be there, but in a state of comparative insignificance, or it may hold its own fairly against the
encroachments of central government. Again, it may
have excessive importance, and this also in two
degrees. Central government may hold its own
against it, but with difficulty. Again, central government may fail to hold its own, and may be reduced
to insignificance.

It is here that I introduce the familiar distinction
between the unitary state and the federation. Against
the common way of conceiving this distinction I

have the same sort of objection that I have to the
distinctions of monarchy, oligarchy, and democracy ;
it is too purely formal and verbal. We say that in
some cases states unite themselves in bundles or
clusters, and that these bundles of states are called
federations, and sometimes federal states. Hence we
get two classes of states—the one simple, the other
composite. But in what way are these states united
together? Surely not by literal ropes! As soon as
we give to ourselves an account of the metaphor, we
see, I think, that the latter class of states is not a
whit more composite than the former. For we have
seen that every country-state is composite to this
extent—that it consists of a number of districts, each
of which has its own government in a certain degree
independent, but which are united together by a
common central government. This shows us in what
way governments are said to be united. When in
several districts, in other respects self-governing,
certain affairs are reserved for the decision of a
central government, those districts are politically
united. Now, just in this way and in no other way
are states united together to form a federation.
Compare the union of the states in the United States
with the union of the boroughs and counties in the
English State or of the departments in the French
State. There is great difference in the degree, but
no fundamental difference in the kind of union. The

states in America are said to be united because in each
certain affairs strictly defined by the Constitution cannot be settled by the state government, but must be
settled at Washington.   In no other way are the
counties and boroughs united to form the English
State ; only the affairs which in England must be sent
up to London or settled by persons coming from
London are much greater and more numerous than
those which in America require the intervention of
Washington.

I deny, then, that between the unitary state and the
federation or federal state there is any fundamental
difference in kind; I deny that the one is composite in
any sense in which the other is simple.   But I adopt
the terms as marking conveniently a great difference
which may exist between states in respect of the importance of local government.   In every country-
state there must be a certain proportion in weight
between the locality and the whole.   But country-
states fall into two large classes, those in which the
locality and those in which the whole has the advantage.   In the former the notion of multiplicity,
in the latter that of unity, will necessarily prevail,
and therefore we may very naturally call the former
federal and the latter unitary.

But when we regard the matter from this point of
view we find that country-states fall into four rather
than into two classes.   For unitary states have two

well-marked kinds differing from each other in precisely the same point, viz. the importance of local government, and in like manner it is well known that there are two kinds of federation, the one strong and the other weak.

In some countries there are so-called local liberties, in others these liberties are wanting. The expression is a very misleading one, as I shall show when we come to consider the subject of liberty. But it expresses a real difference, which is observable in states in which central government is decidedly more prominent than local. In one class of such states the locality has a modest but at the same time a real and valuable independence. It is freely and fully permitted to have its own way and govern itself without external interference in affairs of some considerable importance. In another class this is not so. The independence of the locality is regarded as a necessary evil which should be reduced to the lowest possible point. Pains are taken to attach the local ruler by every possible tie to the central department, and to detach him by every contrivance of separation from the locality. We often call this system despotism and the opposite liberty, but th······ms ought to be appropriated to a quite di   ᴸ The proper name for it is centralisation,   ········   posite ought to be called only decentrali· ti· . ɜoth terms are properly applied only to states i·   ·iich the central government is decidedly more important than the local, that is, to states called unitary. Thus we commonly take England as an example of decentralisation and France of centralisation. But when local government assumes the magnitude which it has had in the United States we do not consider the word decentralisation appropriate to it.

Thus there are two kinds of unitary state, the decentralised and the centralised. In like manner there are two kinds of federation.

The two kinds of federation have been very elaborately distinguished. You may study the subject in the Federalist, or in De Tocqueville, or in Mr. Freeman. I am concerned here only with the results which have been arrived at, and with these only so far as they help us in our classification. To English writers, then, the two kinds are known by the names *Federal State* and *System of Confederate States*, by which it is meant to convey that the first, though it allows very great independence to the component members, still deserves the name of a state, but that the second goes too far and cannot properly be called a state at all. The same point is marked by the happier term⸱ ⸱ ⸱⸱ Germany. There the one is called Bun ⸱⸱ ⸱⸱ the other only Staatenbund; which impli⸱ ⸱⸱⸱⸱⸱ ⸱⸱ ne is a state, though only a bundle-state, ⸱⸱ ⸱⸱⸱ ther is no state but only a bundle of states.

You may say that if the latter form does not deserve the name of state it ought not to find a place in
our classification. And, indeed, the precise organisation which has received the name of Staatenbund
has had attention drawn to it through its great
historical importance as a very common blunder in
state-building, which has frequently led to disastrous
consequences, rather than as a healthy distinct kind.
It belongs rather to the pathology than to the descriptive physiology of states. But though it marks a
degree of weakness in the central power somewhat
below the amount of strength necessary for the dura-
bility of the federation, it indicates that a kind of
federation might exist, somewhat better organised
than itself, which would be wholly different from
that vigorous, strongly and sufficiently organised kind
which is represented by the United States. We may
say then that there are at least two kinds or classes
of federation.

I would observe here, what applies to the whole of
our classification, that it is a real and not a verbal or
nominal classification. We arrange states according
to real differences which they present, not according
to the descriptions they may choose officially to give
of themselves. The United States calls itself a
federation; the Holy Roman Empire which disappeared in 1806 did not call itself so; but in our use
of the word the latter was none the less, and the

former none the more, a federation on that account. Every political union which has not sufficient central power to deserve the name of a unitary state must in our system be called federal. For example, almost all very large empires are really, though they are not called, federations, because in them the central power cannot act vigorously at such a great distance. In like manner the feudal monarchy, wherever it was fully developed, was a federation, and a federation of the weaker kind, since feudalism had the effect of almost destroying the central power.

And this observation suggests another, by which I may conclude this lecture, viz. that the classification which we have laid down has no connection whatever with those favourite categories of ours, popular institutions, liberty and democracy. We may not remark this at once, because when I mention the city-states of antiquity we think at once of republican institutions, and we have the same association with federalism since the United States have given the most successful example of federation. But the old city-states were not invariably republican—nay, they all began as monarchical. In like manner there is no necessary connection between republican institutions and federalism as I define it. The great specimen of federation which for many centuries was familiar to Europe, viz. the Holy Roman Empire, presented the property of federalism in a form so exaggerated that

the result was a helpless confusion; and yet in most
parts of Germany the subject was living under
monarchical rule, which in some parts, *e.g.* in Prussia,
became a rigid despotism. So too, as I have just said,
great military empires are almost always in reality
federations, and yet it is in these that government is
most usually despotic. It was federalism in Persia
that the satrap, or in Turkey that the pasha, was
like an independent prince, but to his subjects the
satrap or the pasha played the part of an Oriental
Sultan.

The result, then, is that we have two great classes,
and under one of these a fourfold division, according
to the importance of local government.

I.—The city-state—L. G. none.
II.—The country-state.
   (a) Centralised unitary—L. G. small.
   (b) Decentralised unitary—L. G. considerable.
   (c) Federal state—L. G. predominant.
   (d) System of confederate states—L. G. all-
          powerful.

Liberty

LECTURE V

THE student of politics is apt to be impatient till
he hears of liberty, especially if he has been trained
in the English school. I do not think that it is
possible to overrate the value of liberty, and yet
when I read many of our constitutional writers I feel
that the science of government assumes a very strange
shape in their hands, owing to the prominence which
they give to this conception. We have laid it down
that the phenomenon which our science investigates
is government—that is, the principle by which the
individual will is in certain cases crushed, sacrificed to
the public good. Now what is liberty? It is the
spirit by, and the principles according to, which
government is resisted! Now these constitutional
writers are so mainly concerned in studying this
spirit and these principles of liberty, and seem to regard this study as so identical and coextensive with
the study of political science, that the reader is
tempted to ask, Is, then, government an evil to which
states are liable, and is it the object of political
science to check and keep under this evil? Does a

state become a state by having a government, or by
avoiding as much as possible to fall under the yoke
of a government?

This curious distortion of the subject is only what
might be expected. In my first lecture I pointed out
what mistakes arise in science when those who
arrange the method of science are intently and
eagerly pursuing some practical object. Those constitutionalists looked at the matter from a practical,
not from a scientific point of view. In practical
politics it so happened that government had come
before them chiefly as an enemy. Government is
a very great power, and we need not be surprised to
find that when once it is set in motion in a state it
works more efficiently, more overwhelmingly, than is
expedient. At an earlier time perhaps the question
had been how to make it efficient, but at the time of
these writers that question had long ago been settled,
and another question had become much more urgent,
the question how to prevent it from being over-
efficient. Towards this end a number of maxims and
observations had been collected during several generations, and these writers treasure them up.

But if we resolve, laying aside immediate practical
objects, to arrange the whole subject in a truly systematic manner, we shall see that the whole subject of
liberty, which in these writers comes first and middle
and last, ought indeed to have a place, and an important

place, to itself, but not a place very near the beginning, nor yet the most important place in the science. Government comes before liberty; we must first analyse it and classify the different forms under which it appears; not till all this has been done, and till in this way we have become tolerably familiar with the nature of government, shall we be ready to consider the danger that may arise from an excess of it, and the necessity of putting limits to it.

But the example set by these writers has in my opinion introduced great confusion, not merely by making liberty too prominent, but still more by accustoming us to the greatest recklessness in using the word. As they represent liberty as "the one thing needful," so they teach us to call by the name of liberty whatever in politics we want. And this habit falls in so well with the style of popular oratory —for if a political speech did not frequently mention liberty, who would know what to make of it or where to applaud ?—that it becomes inveterate, and the subject is marred by a great, formless, indistinct conception, blotting the most important parts of it. If we knew what we meant by liberty, if we were always prepared with a clear and satisfactory definition of it, we should have no difficulty in discerning what is its proper place in political science. But we have accustomed ourselves to use the term so loosely that the thing henceforth pursues us like a Will-o'-the-wisp;

and wherever we meet with debate or agitation of any kind on public affairs we see, as a matter of course, a struggle between the spirit of liberty and its opposite.

Of course the word "liberty" may be taken in so large a sense as to justify this use: but we are concerned with the word only as a term of science, and in this large sense it is wholly useless in science. What makes it so delightful to poets, its unlimited generality, deprives it here of all value. When the poet sings

> O freedom is a noble thing !
> Freedom makes man to have liking, etc.,

it sounds very exhilarating; but inquire, and you will find that in that passage "freedom" merely means *not being in prison*. Now a word which may mean this, and at the same time a hundred other things wholly different, must be left to rhetoric and poetry where it belongs. In science, if it is to be useful, it must submit to narrower definition.

I cannot well advance further without coming to some conclusion as to the meaning to be attached to this word, and it is really worth your while to reflect for a moment on the use or abuse to which it is commonly subjected among us. By studying this word, better than in any other way, you may become aware in what confusion of thought we cheerfully and good-naturedly live, what sort of arguments are put forward seriously, and by what sort of arguments they are with equal seriousness answered among us.

Coleridge has a poem in which he says he had at the outset warmly approved the French Revolution, because he had always been an admirer of the free motion of the clouds across the sky, and of the free rolling of the waves on the surface of the ocean. This is poetry no doubt, but it is intended to have a serious meaning. What can that meaning be, or what can Coleridge intend to infer from the fact that the adjective "free" may in a certain context be applied to the motion of the clouds, and also in a certain wholly different context to the institutions of a state? In any case I should never have thought that the argument, whatever it may mean, was capable of being answered. Mr. Ruskin, however, boldly takes up the gauntlet. He undertakes to show that the clouds in the sky are not free, for are they not subject to the laws of gravitation, light, and heat? He infers, therefore, that there is no such thing as freedom, for that all things are subject to law. I should have thought that the conclusion to be drawn from this was that the French Revolution never did take place, or at least that it was not really a rebellion against law. Mr. Ruskin prefers to conclude that though the clouds obey law, the French have found out some way of shaking themselves free from the laws of nature; that though there *is* no such thing as freedom, the French have somehow made such a thing. Surely it is strange that two really eminent men should in all seriousness, nay, with solemn prophetic eloquence, discuss a most important practical matter in a style so utterly hollow. Here is another example. Shelley in his *Masque of Anarchy* draws a harrowing picture of the distress of the working classes in England about 1820. They are starving, he says, and one would have thought it was not necessary to say more, for surely nothing can be worse than starvation. Shelley, however, still feels something wanting. He is writing a political poem, and you cannot make a political poem any more than a political speech without bringing in liberty. He therefore boldly affirms that a man who is starving is not *free*.

> Nay, in countries that are free
> Such starvation cannot be
> As in England now we see.

So liberty is actually discovered to be something to eat.

But if we put poetry on one side and look only at the usage of the most sober and matter-of-fact writers, we shall see, I think, that the term "liberty" is used to describe wholly different conditions or states of affairs. Horatius and Leonidas keeping a position against the enemy are called champions of liberty, and so are Brutus and Hampden resisting arbitrary government. Surely the two causes are

wholly different. To resist the government of the
state, however justifiably, is an act wholly different
from resistance under the orders of the government
to a foreign enemy. If we call the first act a
maintenance of liberty we ought to call the other a
defence of independence. But liberty and independence ought not to be confounded, and in like manner
the word "patriotism," if we consider, is appropriate
only to the second class of actions and not to the
first. Again, decentralisation is often described as
"local liberty." Decentralisation, as we defined it
last week, is a certain relation between two kinds of
government. Where it exists the local magistrate
in performing acts of authority is not under the
dictation or tutelage of another magistrate at the
centre of affairs. Now observe that in other instances
liberty was a freedom from restraint enjoyed by the
subject in relation to the government : here it is a
freedom from restraint enjoyed by one government
in relation to another. The difference between the
two things is enormous. For freedom in a government may easily be equivalent to slavery in the
subject, since it is freedom to command, to prohibit,
to punish. But such heedless laxity has prevailed in
the use of this word liberty, that in many despotic
states, where liberty in the proper sense has been
unknown, a clamorous controversy about the ancient
liberties of the country has continued for centuries

together. So it was in the Holy Roman Empire of
the German nation. The liberties of Germany were
solemnly guaranteed by France in the Treaty of
Westphalia. Liberties! why, what liberties had
the subjects of Frederick the Great, or of those
Hessian princes who used to sell their youth as
mercenary soldiers to England and France? The
liberties meant are in fact that very despotism.
What France guaranteed was that the minor sovereigns should be independent of the emperor in the
exercise of their authority—that is, should have .
liberty to do what they chose with their people.

How then is liberty to be defined as a term of
political science? Can we give it a more special, a
more precise meaning, and can we do so without
wresting it out of the meaning it has in popular
parlance? If we can succeed in finding for it such
a meaning, at once definite, important, a meaning
which properly belongs to it, and also a meaning
properly political, we shall have enriched science
with a serviceable term which will probably be of
much use to it.

I say the meaning must be properly political.
The word "liberty" may be used quite legitimately
and yet in such a way that it does not belong to
political science at all. Think of Mr. Mill's essay on
Liberty. He spoke there of a certain oppressive
power residing in public opinion, and in opposition

to this he claimed for the individual a right to hold
independent opinions and to indulge personal tastes
and preferences in a greater degree than has usually
been thought allowable. Now it was quite legitimate
to use the word liberty so, but such liberty is not
political liberty. The phenomenon we study is the
state, that is, the community held together by
government. Government is a power of constraint
or compulsion exercised by means of punishment.
This power of constraint may in certain circumstances be oppressive ; in opposition to it liberty is
set up. Thus in political science the tyranny to
which liberty is opposed must reside in the government. If at the same time there exists another sort
of tyranny, which is exercised not by the government
but by public opinion, this fact is very interesting,
and may even indirectly affect the government and
the state ; but such tyranny is not in itself political,
nor is the liberty opposed to it properly political.

We · must look at government, and we must
inquire how government may use that power of
constraint which is inherent in it in such a way as
to infringe liberty.

Now let us for a moment consider the history of
the word "liberty."

In Latin it expressed properly a certain *status*
which was possessed by certain individuals in the
community but was wanting to others. It was not,

when used literally, a political term, but a legal term, for it expressed a relation not between the citizen and the government, but between some individuals who were not called citizens, and other individuals who were citizens. Metaphorically, in poetry or high-flown oratory, it might be used in a political sense, but when this was done it was done consciously. When the oppressed citizen was called a slave he was deliberately and intentionally compared to the degraded, squalid, half-brutal creatures who kennelled in the outhouses of Roman palaces or worked in chains on the estates of great nobles.

Now no such servile *status* exists in modern Europe; in England for many centuries, with the exception of a few negroes who in the eighteenth century might have been found in a few English houses, no slaves have been seen. But though the thing is quite unknown to us the metaphor founded upon it is constantly used, and we talk of liberty much more habitually than the Romans themselves did. This is a very curious fact, and seems to me to account in a great measure for the reckless vagueness with which we employ the word. Our liberty is a metaphor which has been, as it were, cut adrift; it expresses a resemblance, an analogy, which we can never test, because the phenomenon to which it points is entirely unknown to us.

Now what was the peculiarity of the *status* of the

slave in ancient Rome or in other countries in which
slavery has been allowed? Was it that the slave
was cruelly treated? Many slaves no doubt were
cruelly treated, and the *status* lent itself to such cruelty.
But many slaves, on the other hand, were treated
kindly, some were petted and treated affectionately,
but they were none the less slaves on that account.

When, therefore, we use the word slavery to express the condition of those who are subject to a
cruel or excessively severe government, we are not
using it in a very appropriate manner. For suppose
quite a different sort of government, one which is
mild and paternal but at the same time interfering,
one which decides everything and meddles in every
affair, so that the subject is absolutely deprived of the
use of his free-will and held, as it were, in leading-
strings. We shall want to call this too slavery. And
yet this condition is not only very different from the
other, but may chance to be diametrically opposite to
it. For as the mild government may be extremely
interfering, so on the other hand the cruel and brutal
government may interfere very seldom; or, in other
words, may allow an unusual and exceptional degree
of liberty. I will take two extreme examples to
illustrate the vast difference between these two kinds
of government.

Take first the government of the Tartars in Russia
from the thirteenth to the fifteenth century. Nothing

could be more ruthless and brutal. On the other hand, it interfered so seldom and so little that for the most part the Russian population were scarcely aware of its existence. The ruling horde lived within its own encampment, from which at times it issued on expeditions of plunder and devastation, but it was content in ordinary times if the Russian princes, the dukes of Moscow, or the burghers of Novgorod, made an annual pilgrimage to present their tribute to the great Khan. Thus in this government there was at the same time the greatest degree of cruelty and the greatest degree of liberty. Something similar may be noted in the Turkish Empire, where there is much cruelty but at the same time in some respects a re-markable degree of freedom is granted to the Chris-tian populations.

Now look at the other extreme in the Jesuit government of Paraguay. Here everything was mild, amiable, paternal. But at the same time such a complete control was established over the minds of the natives that their free-will was absolutely taken from them, and their lives reduced to an unalterable routine. It is said that all the most private acts that a man can do, the acts in which among us no one would allow the least interference, were performed in Paraguay according to a fixed rule and at the ringing of a bell. Was this liberty? It was just the system against which we exclaim most loudly when we are threatened with the introduction of it, and we cry out on slavery and protest in the name of liberty. And yet if liberty means merely the opposite of cruelty and oppression we must confess that it was liberty, for it was a government singularly free from cruelty and oppression.

One of these two inconsistent senses that may be given to the word liberty we must evidently discard. I think we had better discard the sense which puts it in opposition to cruel government, for the simple reason, if for no other, that we do not want a special term for this. Mild government is a simple and sufficient term for such a simple notion; it is mere waste of a good word to call it liberty.

Shall we then adopt the other sense? Shall we treat liberty as the opposite of over-government? By doing so we should keep sufficiently close to the original unmetaphorical meaning of the word. For it was the peculiarity of the *status* of the slave that he was under an *unlimited* government. The free citizen might be bound to obey an employer or a state official within certain limits fixed by law or by contract; but the slave had no reserved province of free-will except what his master chose to allow him; all his time and all his powers might be confiscated to the master's use. If then in any state the government makes a similar unlimited demand, intruding its authority into the most personal parts of human life,

I

allowing the subject no rest and no scope for free-will, it may very properly be said to make its subjects slaves, or to deprive them of liberty. Not only may we properly use this expression, but we constantly do use it; the word liberty used in this sense is familiar to us all.

Unfortunately we use it at the same time, and even more often, in a sense different from this, and different at the same time from the other senses which I have considered already. Liberty is commonly regarded as the equivalent of parliamentary government. The rights of parliament were the ancient liberties for which we contended in the seventeenth century, and which were our boast and privilege among the European nations in the eighteenth. Accordingly when we desire to know of any country whether it has liberty, it is our practice simply to ask whether it has a free parliament. If it has this, and by means of this a power of calling the government to account, or of changing it if it does not govern in conformity with public opinion, we say of such a country that it has liberty, and if not, not.

Now here is a use of the word which is familiar, and which in many cases at least seems highly appropriate. But observe that if we adopt it we must give up the other use of the word, which also seemed satisfactory, or again if we adopt the other we must give up this. For it will not do to assign to the same word two wholly distinct meanings at the same time.

Perhaps we do not clearly understand that the two meanings *are* wholly distinct. We can bring this question speedily to the test, for we have only to ask ourselves two things—First, Is a parliamentary government always contented to govern as little as possible? Secondly, Is an absolute government always ambitious of governing as much as possible? For if so, then the two meanings of "liberty" melt into one; a parliamentary government and an uninterfering government are identical, and therefore may both alike be called "liberty," as on the other hand an absolute government is equivalent to a meddlesome government, and both alike may be called slavery. Now I think the fact is not so at all. The two things have no inherent affinity or connection whatever. Many of the most absolute governments in history have been, as I said above, cruel but not at all interfering. On the other hand, popular government at some periods has shown itself restlessly busy and meddlesome.[1]

You will observe that there is no reason why this should surprise us, for on the one hand a despot has

[1] "Look only at the French Revolution. When it took its second or Jacobinical shape in 1792, breaking with Monarchy and basing itself decisively upon the many, did it become modest? Did it profess to regard government as a necessary evil, which it was all-important to confine within the narrowest province possible? Assuredly not. It interfered with everything and took possession of the whole man. It meddled with religion ; it turned France into a camp. In short, instead of diminishing it extended the province of government as much as it popularised its basis."—From the Fourth Lecture of the 1891 Course.

no peculiar temptation to interfere; on the other hand a popular government has no particular motive for refraining from interference. To the despot interference is laborious, while at the same time he gets nothing by it; his temptation would rather be to indolent negligence; but the popular parliament naturally feels an intense interest in those regulations of government which affect so powerfully the condition of the people.

Accordingly I think we may venture to say that what affinity there is is of the opposite kind, that is, that on the whole parliamentary government is tempted to do too much and absolute government to do too little. Surely what we witness in England must lead us to this conclusion, at least as far as popular government is concerned. We have lived in a period in which government has been growing continually more and more popular, and we see that each new reform bill is followed by a new outburst of legislative activity. We are not told that a reform bill is passed in order that we may be *let alone* more than in former times, but in order that we may be governed more than formerly, not in order that the governing apparatus may be held in check, but in order that it may be made tenfold more active and energetic.[1]

[1] "It was the pride of our country in the eighteenth century to lean less than other countries on legislation, and to believe in it less. At the time when we had a monopoly among European states of liberty, liberty was understood to mean this. It was a

Of course I do not raise the question whether this
activity is excessive; there are times when government has occasion to be very active. But assuredly
the temptation to excessive activity besets a popular
government, which is full of confidence, of fresh
interest in the matter of government, of party excitement, and of the consciousness of a mighty support behind it, far more than it can beset the languid officials
of absolutism in the midst of a silent passive people.

And De Tocqueville has observed in his examination of the absolute government of France before the
Revolution that in spite of all the pride and parade
of absolutism, that government was timid. Not only
is such a government inert from want of any interest
in action, but it is inert from timidity. Being separated
from the people it labours under a want of satisfactory
information, and is afraid to advance because it does not
know the ground. For the opposite reason, that is, be-

dislike and repugnance to artificial forms. When the continent
groaned under over-government, under an excess of restraint and
institutions, England was supposed to have succeeded in keeping
nearer—such was the language of the time—to the original pattern
of nature. We were said to be

　　　By forms unfashioned, fresh from Nature's hand.

But in those days we were not democratic. We had not yet seen
our first Reform Act. The franchise was narrow and exclusive.
　　"In the present century all this has been changed. Government has been put into the hands of many. At the same time
the old dislike of government interference has disappeared. The
ancient parties have disappeared, which were alike devoted to the
ancient constitutions, and another party, devoted to innovation
and the enlargement of the province of government, has risen to
ascendancy."—From the Fourth Lecture of the 1891 Course.

cause it knows the ground incomparably well, a popular government advances with the utmost confidence.

It appears, then, that these two meanings which we give at the same time to the word "liberty" are not, as we seem to think, much the same, but wholly different. Nor are they, if not the same, yet similar or cognate; so that a state which has liberty in the one sense is pretty sure to have it also in the other. No; there are two wholly dissimilar characteristics which a state may have; these two characteristics have no tendency whatever to appear together, they have even some tendency to hurt or neutralise each other, and yet we call them both liberty.

One of these is parliamentarism, that is to say—as for the present purpose we may describe it—an accountability of the government to the majority of the people. This may very well be called in popular language "liberty"; but I doubt if by calling it so we put the word to its best use. Here, again, the word is not particularly wanted; it is quite sufficient and satisfactory to speak of the accountability or responsibility of government. And if we decide to say liberty here we must find some other term for that other property of certain states which we have discovered to be wholly distinct. But for this the term liberty seems to me perfectly appropriate. All perplexity and ambiguity disappear at once if we consider liberty to be the opposite of over-government.

In ordinary parlance liberty does not mean happiness or comfort or freedom from hardship; it means
permission to do what you like.   It is not, therefore,
the opposite of misgovernment, for misgovernment
may produce these other evils, but does not, as misgovernment, destroy liberty any more than good
government does.   Good government and misgovernment are alike government, and as such necessarily,
as far as they go, abridge liberty; they differ from
each other not in this respect, but in the fact that the
one abridges liberty in a wholesome manner, while
the other does not.

Liberty, in short, in the common use of language,
is opposed to restraint: and as government, in the
political department, is restraint, liberty in a political
sense should be the opposite of government.[1]

Strictly and properly it is the opposite not merely
of over-government but of government itself.   Strictly,
therefore, there cannot be in a state perfect liberty,
for perfect liberty is equivalent to total absence of
government, and where government is absent there
can be no state.   Nevertheless it is quite admissible
to speak of liberty as that which some states possess
and other states want; only we must understand
clearly in what sense this is said.

Liberty being taken as the opposite of govern-

[1] I infer, from a pencil note of the author, that it was his
intention at this point to introduce some discussion of the Kantian
view of freedom as the end of law.—ED.

ment, we may say that each man's life is divided into two provinces, the province of government and the province of liberty. To the first belongs all that part of his life which is given up to authority, which is guided by a foreign will; to the latter all that part which he has to himself. Now in some states this part, which is abandoned to individual free-will and which is not invaded by government, is large, and in other states it is small. In the former class we say there is liberty, or the people are free; in the latter class we say liberty is wanting, or the people are not free. This is quite in accordance with the usage according to which we call some things "hot" and others "cold," not meaning by "cold" "entirely devoid of heat," but only "below the average of things in respect of heat."

We may say, then, that liberty is primarily the absence of restraint or the opposite of government; but in a secondary sense, which is also convenient, it is the absence of excessive restraint or the opposite of over-government.

When, therefore, we inquire after practical liberty in a state we must not ask whether the laws are good or bad, whether they are enforced by mild or by cruel punishments, whether they are enacted in a popular assembly where all interests are duly represented, or in some exclusive, secret, and interested conspiracy of oppressors. These questions are of

course all important. If a favourable answer can be
returned to them the country will perhaps be happy
and in a healthy condition. But shall we call it free?
It seems almost impossible not to use the word,
which seems expected and indispensable whenever a
people in a healthy condition is to be described.
And yet if the word is really to be taken from
rhetoric and poetry and made available for science,
we must confine it to one notion, and that a notion
different from any of these. If we do so, we shall
inquire not after the quality of the laws, whether
they are good or bad, but after the quantity of them,
whether they are many or few. The question, the
only question will be, Is the individual frankly let
alone? Is he permitted, wherever it is possible, to
do what he chooses? Is the number of state regulations, the number of restrictions upon free-will,
reduced to the lowest point? If so, the people is
free, even if their arrangements are bad, even if their
life is unhappy. If not, the people is not free, however
well governed and healthy and happy they may be.

I put this proposition purposely in the sharpest
language and expect to provoke the objection, " If so,
it is very doubtful whether liberty is a good thing."
Well! who said it was a good thing? The truth is,
we have a difficulty in handling a conception which
never shows itself but in the perorations of high-flown
speeches. Like some king who can do no wrong, Liberty

is disguised in a splendid robe of legal fiction, and if
she appears to do harm it is considered decent to say
that some one else was acting under her name. The
formula runs : " That is not liberty, that is license ! '
Oh ! yes, it *is* liberty. But like everything else that
is real, Liberty is only good in certain circumstances, \
and in a certain degree. There have been moments,
many moments, in history when it has been a price-
less blessing, when the highest minds have been
passionately devoted to it, so that the very word
Liberty has risen to the same sacred height as Virtue
or as Heaven, and become a worshipped ideal.

> Now high on waves that idly burst,
>   Like Heavenly Hope she crowned the sea,
> And now, the bloodless point reversed,
>   She bore the blade of Liberty.

But Liberty is not the universal ideal of every
place and age. In some states, we ought to be prepared to think, she may appear before her time or in
an exaggerated form ; and still more, we ought not
to assume that Liberty is the only and all-sufficient
object of all political striving. Above all, after having with due care defined the word and attached it
to a particular notion, we must not change our mind
merely to gratify the demands of poetry.

But we must not forget for what purpose we
entered upon this discussion. Our object is classification. I have analysed the notion of liberty to-day,

not for its own sake, but only in order that we may make use of liberty as a principle of classification. But the analysis itself has occupied me through the whole hour. It remains to apply to our classification the result we have arrived at. This will be the subject of the next lecture.

WE paused last week in our task of classification and devoted an hour to a different sort of task, to an exercise in the definition of terms. We inquired into the best and most convenient way of applying in political science the term liberty. But we did this with a view to classification. Finding in popular discussion that states are distinguished as having liberty or wanting it, and again as having it in a greater or a less degree, we wished to ascertain whether it would be possible to give precision to this popular classification and make it available for scientific purposes.

The conclusion we arrived at is this, that it is not convenient to use the word in the sense in which it is most ordinarily used. According to this ordinary usage, liberty is merely constitutionalism or responsible government. Where the government, as soon as it becomes unpopular, can be turned out, and another government commanding more popular support installed in its room, there liberty in its fullest form is said to exist, and some degree of

liberty is recognised where the popular discontent is
allowed to show itself through some recognised organ,
and is habitually treated by the government with
deference. This is responsibility of government, and
it is of course of the utmost importance. But it did
not appear to us either necessary or convenient to
appropriate to this the term liberty.

But we found another sense which is just as much
recognised in popular parlance, and which is also of
great importance, though it may be of not equally
great importance, in which the word liberty may
most conveniently be taken. What is the phenomenon
with which our science deals? It is government.
And government is a power of constraint or coercion.
Now, liberty in the simplest, most universal, acceptation is the condition of the person who is not
under such restraint or coercion. He who is under
government does as he is bid; he who does what he
chooses is at *liberty*. But further, no one is always
or altogether under government. Government does
not dictate to any one all his actions; it does not
take possession of the whole time, the whole property, or all the powers, of any one. What it
refrains from taking possession of, what it abandons
to the man's own free disposal, is his *liberty*. This is
the liberty of an individual. What is the liberty of
a people? Evidently it is that province in the life
of the people over which government assumes no

control, which is left to the voluntary principle.
For instance, if the government decides to refrain
from the attempt to regulate trade, by doing so it
adds trade to the province of liberty; as we say,
trade becomes free. On this principle, what makes
one people free and another not free? what is the
test of liberty and absence of liberty? There will be
no rigid test, and liberty in all cases will be but
comparative. But we shall say that a nation has
liberty where the province left to the voluntary
principle is comparatively large, and the domain of
government, or the domain in which authoritative
regulation prevails, is comparatively small, and conversely.

To sum up: it may be convenient to contrast
briefly the three chief political meanings of the word
liberty in popular usage :—

First, it stands for national independence. "This
is the case especially in ancient history and poetry,
as when we connect it with Marathon, Thermopylæ,
Morgarten, Bannockburn, and so on.

Secondly, for responsibility of government. This
occurs not only in ancient history, in the classical
stories of tyrannicide, but also in our own constitutional history, for the main object of our struggle
in the seventeenth century was to establish the responsibility of government.

Thirdly, it stands for a limitation of the province

of government. This meaning also is quite usual, but it has seldom been distinguished from the other. Look, for instance, at our own constitutional history. The responsibility of government is the principle most strongly asserted, but when the power of church courts is limited, when religious toleration is introduced and dissenting worship is permitted, when the Licensing Act is allowed to expire, and so the Press acquires freedom,—in all these cases we see government not submitting to responsibility but limiting its province.

I gave reasons for thinking that the word liberty is best applied when it bears this meaning, so that a people ought to be called free in proportion as its government has a restricted province.

Thus understood, liberty will appear to be a good or a bad thing according to circumstances. When it is complete it will be equivalent to utter anarchy, and that is not a condition which we have any reason to think desirable. Whatever in human history is great or admirable has been found in governed communities; in other words, has been the result of a certain restriction of liberty. On the other hand, when government is once established it easily becomes excessively strong. During a great part of their recorded history men have suffered from an excess of government. Accordingly they have learnt to sigh for liberty as one of the greatest of blessings, but in accustoming themselves to regard it so they have insensibly modified the meaning of the word. What poets and orators yearn for is not the destruction of government—though they are not careful to explain this, being accustomed to pre-suppose a government which is certain to be strong enough—but only a reasonable restriction of govern-ment. In taking the word "liberty" out of rhetoric and transferring it to science, we make, as I said, just the same correction in its meaning as in the word "heat." "Liberty" in the rhetorical sense would be in our language "a good deal of liberty," just as what is popularly called "heat" is in scientific language "a good deal of heat."

I now proceed to consider the different degrees in which liberty may appear in a state. You see that this may be otherwise expressed as "the different degrees of extension that may be given to the pro-vince of government." Here appears very clearly how different is this mode of treating political science from the dogmatic method.

The province of government has always been a favourite topic among teachers of politics, but they have commonly introduced it under the form of an inquiry. What is the legitimate province of govern-ment? And still more commonly in discussing particular cases of government interference it is argued that they are infringements of natural,

inalienable liberty; in other words, that the right
of coercion which belongs to government is a strictly
limited right, and also that it has the same limits
everywhere.

Now I do not say that we may not ultimately
arrive at the notion of some such moral limitation of
the competence of government, but I say that at this
stage we have nothing whatever to do with it. We
take now a naturalistic view of the subject.[1] The
human group, in struggling against the difficulties
that surround it, in resisting pressure from neighbouring tribes, or from an adverse nature or climate,
has recourse to the contrivance of government. By
this contrivance it vastly increases its power of withstanding attack or of executing such aggressive plans
as it may form. But the principle, once admitted
into the group, modifies it greatly and rapidly. We
desire to study the modification it produces. Now
much evidently will depend upon the amount of
government which is admitted, upon the dose of

---

[1] In 1891 the author's alienation from the "dogmatic" point of
view was more strongly expressed :—"It undertakes," he said, "to
lay down dogmatically what things government has, and what
things it has not, the right to regulate; or, in other words, how
wide the province of government by the nature and definition of
government ought to be.   From all such inquiries I am precluded
by the general principles which I began by laying down.   I treat
government not as a conscious contrivance, but as a half-instinctive
product of the effort which human beings make to ward off from
themselves certain evils to which they are exposed.   If then you
ask, How much government ought we to have? the only answer I
can give will be, You not only ought to have but you infallibly
will have as much government as is necessary for this purpose."

K

government which is taken. And to ascertain the amount of government is to ascertain the amount of liberty. Liberty, therefore, becomes important to us. But in this inquiry it does not concern us at all by what right liberty is restricted when government is introduced, or to what degree it is morally allowable to put restrictions on liberty. For the modifications produced by government will be the same whether the government is rightful or wrongful, and therefore our classification will be the same in either case. And this classification we can make at once, while the question of the natural rights of the individual against the government, or of government against the individual, the whole question in fact of the relation between politics and ethics, is not yet ripe for discussion.

But though we cannot yet say by what right government crushes the individual will, we may point out the cause which brings government into existence, and may argue that according to the intensity with which this cause acts will probably be the intensity of government. I put aside here all those states which I have called inorganic; in these of course government rests on violence and covetousness. It is the organic state that we consider, and in this the political principle is awakened and developed by the struggle of the society with its environment. The community is under a pressure which calls for common action, and common action calls for government. It is reasonable therefore to conjecture that the degree of government will be directly proportional, and that means that the degree of liberty will be inversely proportional, to the degree of pressure. In other words, given a community which lives at large, in easy conditions and furnished with abundant room, you may expect to find that community enjoying a large share of liberty; given a community which has to maintain itself against great difficulties and in the midst of great dangers, you may expect to find in it little liberty and a great deal of government.

The historical examples which may be cited in support of this general proposition lie on the surface, and in dealing with them I may be brief. Among European states, which has taken the lead in liberty, in which has government rested content with the most modest province? Evidently in our own state. But outside Europe we should all agree in pointing to the United States as a state which has from the beginning shown an equal devotion to liberty. Can any explanation of this be offered? A very tempting explanation offers itself at once. In those two states the population is closely akin. And so we say, it is the sturdy Anglo-Saxon race which on both sides alike of the Atlantic Ocean rebels against tyranny, and cannot live without liberty. But now these two populations have another common quality which it

would be equally plausible to allege. Both alike
have an excellent natural frontier. We live in an
island and are protected from the enemy by a silver
streak. And what the narrow channel does for us
is done for them by the broad Atlantic Ocean. Let
any historical student ask himself the question why
it was that in the seventeenth century, while the
development of England was steadily towards liberty,
France moved with equal steadiness in the direction
of absolutism. Assuredly in Louis XIV.'s reign the
dominant fact in France was the frontier. Louis
XIV. himself, as Ranke says, was regarded in his
own time less as a great conqueror than as the
fortifier of France, the man sent to give France a
satisfactory frontier. But the more he strengthened
the country against the foreign enemy, the more he
consolidated his own authority, crushed liberty, and
established absolutism.

I will cite in the second place the example of
Prussia and the Hohenzollern Monarchy. This
state took its present form in the early years of
the eighteenth century, under the reign of Frederick
William, the eccentric father of Frederick the Great.
That king established a peculiar form of absolutism
more rudely and brutally military than had been
seen in Europe before. He became almost a laughing
stock, yet now after a hundred and fifty years what
political experiment of the eighteenth century can

be named which has proved so strikingly successful.
How can this be explained? The Prussian population
was Teutonic, and it was also Protestant. Why then
did it turn its back so pointedly on liberty? Look
at the frontier. Frederick William's territory was
the least defensible in Europe. It consisted of three
masses wholly separate and without intercommunica-
tion; and we are able to show that this extreme
military disadvantage had been in a special manner
brought home to Frederick William I. in the early
years of his reign by the great war of the North.
His innovations were in a great measure an attempt
to profit by the military lessons he had learnt in
the course of that war from Charles XII. and Peter
the Great.

This generalisation illustrates two principles which
I would recommend you never to lose sight of in
trying to generalise upon history. The one is, never
be content with looking at states purely from within;
always remember that they have another aspect,
which is wholly different, their relation towards
foreign states. This is a rule which it is particularly
necessary to impress upon English students, for there
is no nation which has disregarded it so much as
our own. We have an inveterate habit of regarding
our own history as self-contained, and of assuming
that whatever has happened in England can be explained by English causes. So much so, that 1

think the English history still remains to be written which shall do anything like justice to the foreign or continental influences which have contributed to determine the course of English affairs. The other principle is, that we should be slow to allege mere national character in explanation of great historical phenomena. No explanation is so obvious, or suggests itself so easily. No explanation is so vague, cheap, and so difficult to verify. Why did the English gain freedom early? Any one can answer, because they are English, and it is the nature of Englishmen to love liberty. I call this a cheap explanation. It is easily given, and almost impossible to verify. It is the more suspicious, because it gratifies national vanity. For these reasons it seems to me that this explanation ought to be regarded in general as inadmissible.

To return : we see that intense government is the reaction against intense pressure, and on the other hand liberty, or relaxed government, is the effect of relaxed pressure. This is the general rule ; as a matter of course it will suffer many exceptions.

And now, liberty being thus defined and explained, can we use it as a principle of classification? Evidently states will differ through all degrees in the amount of liberty they admit. The only doubt can be whether the differences thus caused are such as to create a moderate number of well-marked

groups to each of which we may attach a characteristic name, or whether they are too small, gradual,
and numerous to admit of distinction or lend themselves to classification.   For of course it will not be a
sufficient reason for putting two states in different
classes, that in one of them government is in general
more disposed to interfere than in the other.

But it will be more satisfactory if we can observe
that some great and well-known department of affairs
is in one state subject to government regulation,
but in another state is abandoned to voluntary agency.
According to our definition, this is the very distinction upon which liberty depends.   Liberty prevails where many departments are thus abandoned
by government, and *vice versâ.*

I must again remind you that I lay down nothing
about any absolute limit to the province of government which may be imposed by some abstract
principle.   We all know that in the present age
it is usual to regard the interference of government
in certain classes of affairs as absolutely wrong
and inconsistent with civilisation.   Thus, though in
former times government used almost everywhere
alike to interfere with religious belief, or at least
religious worship—it cost us a struggle of about
half a century to obtain the modest degree of
toleration which was granted by the Toleration Act
of William and Mary — nothing now seems so

universally accepted as the absolute duty of all
government to grant a practically unlimited religious
toleration, The old restrictive legislation seems to
be commonly assumed to have been always utterly
indefensible.. This kind of dogmatism in politics
I do not understand. Nothing of course can be
more undeniable than that government restrictions
on such subjects as these are wholly incompatible
with the ideas that prevail in the present age, but
it seems to me very rash to condemn a system which
in other ages was well-nigh universal as if in those
ages it had been as indefensible as it would be now.
There is no limit to the right of self-defence. Government will assume, and no one can forbid it to assume,
whatever powers are necessary to save societies from
massacre and destruction. But in this case, you
will ask, how can it possibly have any concern with
religion; what dangers of this obvious kind can
possibly arise from allowing the most unbounded
religious toleration? In certain periods, it is true,
no such dangers are to be feared. But was this so,
for instance, in the days of the Crusades, or earlier,
in the age of the Arian controversy? It rather
appears to me that the great standing dangers which
government exists to avert take two forms. First,
there is the enemy in the neighbourhood, the next
tribe which is waiting just beyond the frontier. But
there is also an enemy less visible, less material.

I have before shown that religion has a great deal
to do with the origin and essential nature of the
state. States are composed of men who are in some
sense homogeneous, and not only homogeneous in
blood and descent, but also in ideas or views of
the universe. During very large periods of human
history men have refused to live together in the
same state who did not hold the same religion.
And within these periods, it seems to me, the
tendency was irresistible, so that toleration in such
times was impossible. It would have led to the
violent dissolution of society. It seems to me that
religious toleration, if it had been introduced pre-
maturely, would have caused those very horrors
against which we commonly regard government as
having been principally provided. Religion is of
course the extreme case. All other departments
which government has in exceptional cases arrogated
to itself will seem more admissible than this. Accordingly there is no more conclusive way of establishing
what I may call the relativeness of political truth
than by advancing that even religious intolerance,
which to the present age appears almost the un-
pardonable sin, was, in its own time and place, not
absolutely condemnable. It may be called the test
question upon which depends the choice between a
dogmatic and a scientific view of history. Those
who think toleration an absolute law allowing no

exceptions, must turn away from a considerable part
of the history of the world as if it were a bad dream.
What can they do with the Crusades or with the
Counter-reformation and the whole story of the
Spanish Monarchy? And yet I should like to meet
the man who would venture to tell me plainly that
it would have been safe to introduce toleration in
the great European states earlier by a century or
two than it was introduced; that, for instance, it
might have been introduced into England under
Elizabeth, or that Philip II. might have introduced
it into Spain, or the House of Valois into France.

But our business at present is classification, and
the immediate question is whether it would be
possible and advisable to arrange states in a series
according to the extent which they allow to the
province of government. We can measure this
province roughly by reckoning up the classes of
affairs of which government may claim to itself
the regulation. According to the view we have
taken, the class of affairs which originally and most
necessarily belongs to government is the defence of
the country against an enemy, together, of course,
with any offensive wars the state may undertake.
Where war is waged it is more necessarily than
anything else the affair of the state. Next after
this comes law. The repression of crime and violence
we see to be undertaken at an early stage by the

government. After law in this restricted sense
comes law in its larger acceptation. Distributive
justice, the function of composing differences and
enforcing contracts, is added in due time to the
more necessary functions of government. But now
we observe that as government develops in a state
another kind of development is also going forward.
When we compare the primitive with the more
advanced condition of society we see that they differ
not merely in government, but more generally in
what I have called specialisation. In property, in
industry, in occupations and pursuits, society becomes
more diversified. At first all property is in land,
and almost every citizen is occupied in the same way.
No special skills have yet been invented, there are
no arts, and labour has not been divided. Every
man, for instance, is equally a soldier. The time
comes when all this is altered: industry becomes
complex, manufacture and foreign trade are developed, capital accumulates, personal property
takes its place by the side of real, money comes
into use, and after money credit, arts and sciences
spring up, education and literature become important,
schools and universities are founded. This development is not in itself strictly political, and yet it
continually raises new political problems. For at
any stage the question may arise:—This new thing
that has appeared in the state, to which of the two

provinces shall it belong—to the province of liberty,
or to that of government? Is there trade? Then
ought government to regulate trade? Is there literature? Then ought every author to publish at his
own pleasure, or ought he to obtain a license from
government?

You see, I think, that we might arrange a series
of states according to the answer which is given to
these questions, and we might invent a nomenclature
corresponding to the different extent given in different
states to the province of government. German
writers use such a nomenclature. The state where
government is at a minimum is often called by them
the War-state, *Der Kriegstaat.* They speak also of
the Law-state, *Der Rechtsstaat,* the Trade-state, *Der
Handelsstaat,* the Police-state, *Der Polizeistaat.* On
the other hand, for states in which the province is
very large they have the expression Culture-state,
Der Kulturstaat. And you will see that if we adopt
a classification of this kind it will consist in the main
of two great classes, for the grand question will
always be, Shall we, or shall we not, adopt a material-
ist view? that is, shall we consider that the state is
concerned only with temporal objects such as order,
comfort, and the repression of crime? Or, on the
other hand, shall we allow to the state a higher
character? Shall we suffer it to concern itself with
the great ideals of humanity, with religion, morality,

science, and art? Shall we in one word admit the
Kulturstaat, or shall we not?

As I have explained, it is not my undertaking in
this course of lectures to give a dogmatic answer to
such questions. I confine myself to the classification
of states. But I have to notice the mighty drifts of
opinion which have prevailed on this very subject
during the last two centuries. Till the seventeenth
century if there was a universal opinion it was that
purity of religion was the principal object of the
political union. The state and the church were in a
manner identical. This view was but very gradually
given up. About the same time that it began to disappear we note the germs of a later controversy
about the limits of the province of the state, which
has disturbed the world almost as much. Toleration
was definitively admitted in England under William
and Mary. The very same period saw a series of
great wars commence for England, which, when we
examine their origin, are seen to arise out of trade,
and particularly out of the pretension which was
then common to all governments of regulating
trade. We are thus brought to the eighteenth
century, and it was not till the second half of
that century had opened that the idea began
to seize the minds of men that governments aimed
too high and attempted too much. In that strange
unrest which was the principal moral cause of the

French Revolution the feeling was certainly a principal ingredient that government had gone much too far, that mankind was greatly over-governed. In several departments at once,—in religion, education, trade, and politics,—the same cry arose; a demand for more simplicity, for less institution and greater confidence in nature. *Laissez-faire, laissez-passer*, was the watchword of this new school. This watchword embodies the principle I have once or twice mentioned— the principle that government is a necessary evil, and that its activity ought to be restrained to a minimum. In other words, it is the watchword of liberty in the sense which we have given to that word. It is, of course, a great question for political science whether this watchword ought or ought not to have succeeded; but, as I have urged, in laying down any dogmatic conclusion, the relativeness of all political truth ought by all means to be borne in mind. In each state the conditions of government are different. Population is large here, small there; this state is in an advanced stage, and that in an early stage of development. Is it reasonable, then, to expect that any dogma universally applicable can be laid down with respect to the extent which may be properly given to the province of government? The doctrine of *laissez-faire* once laid down in the eighteenth century had a great vogue; and yet the reaction against it in the nineteenth century

has been powerful too. Has it won on the whole,
or has it lost? To give a short answer to this
question would perhaps be difficult. On some great
questions, as that of religion, it has certainly been
completely victorious, so that most people at the
present day find it difficult to understand how so
many nations through so many centuries can have
believed that government had any concern with
religious worship. But in general I hardly think
the watchword itself, *Laissez-faire*, is popular now.
We know, indeed, that on the other great question,
that of trade, it won a great victory in England,
and that when, forty-five years ago, we adopted the
principle of free-trade, the advocates of it among
us devoutly believed that their reform would be
adopted before long all over the world. We know,
however, that this did not take place, and that by
many great states it is still almost as much as in
old times considered to be among the most important
functions of government to regulate trade.

In the main the tendency now sets in the most
energetic manner the other way, that is, in the
direction of state interference, and what I may call
establishment. Thus of late years the state has included education within its province. Primary education has been in the fullest sense established, all the
state's power of compulsion being brought to bear
upon individuals. Secondary education and uni-

versities have been vigorously remodelled by the intervention of Parliament. The same may be said of sanitation, and every day new demands are preferred in behalf of some new interest for the cutting of some knot by the trenchant hand of government.

But the best proof of the change is to be found in the prodigious activity which now prevails in politics, in the agreement of all parties that there is a vast amount to be done, that we have more work before us than can possibly be overtaken, This shows, not indeed that the province of government is increasing in all directions, but that in one direction it increases vastly, For all this activity is devoted to one kind of work, viz. legislation,

Looked at historically, the present activity of governments in legislation is very remarkable and abnormal. In other departments the action of governments is regarded with as much jealousy as ever, or more. There never was a time when they were more liable to censure for arbitrary interference in private affairs, or for severity of administration. In these matters we abide by the old tradition of liberty. But we make a distinction in favour of legislation. We think governments ought to be continually busy in passing important laws.

Historically, this is as unlike as possible to the doctrine of other periods. The state in other times, it may almost be said, was not supposed to be concerned with legislation. Communities had indeed laws, and at times, though rarely, they altered them; but the task of alteration hardly fell to the state.

To illustrate this I cannot do better than cite an example given by Sir H. Maine. Runjeet Singh, says he, was not only a ruler but a despotic ruler, if there ever was one; yet probably in his whole life he never performed an act of legislation. He was, as it were, the state in person, yet, as such, he had scarcely any concern with legislation.

In earlier times, the state, that is the power which issues commands and inflicts punishments, was hardly supposed capable of making law. It could conduct a campaign, levy a tax, remedy a grievance, but law was supposed to be in a somewhat different sphere. Law was a sacred custom; the state might administer, or enforce, or codify it; but legislation, the creating, or altering, or annulling of law, was conceived as a very high power, rarely to be used, and concerning which it was doubtful who possessed it. Laws are ὑψίποδες δι᾽ αἰθέρα τεκνωθέντες, "walking on high, born above the heavens." Often religion was called in, and commonly some degree of fiction was used to conceal the too daring alteration that was made.

On this point we have completely broken with the tradition of earlier times. I said the Germans speak of the Law-state; by this they mean merely the state which undertakes to guard rights; we want another name to describe the state of the nineteenth century. It is the Legislation-state. It has abandoned the exercise of many powers which states used to wield, but the power which states in past time were afraid to claim it uses with the utmost freedom and with indefatigable energy. It makes law and unmakes it, and alters it. Law it conceives simply as the opinion of the majority, founded upon discussion and reasoning. It is the Legislation-state.

You see that though I am able to suggest names by which states may be distinguished according to the province of state-action, I do not find that I can arrange states in a progressive series according to the degree of liberty. Liberty shifts its ground. Sometimes it appears in one department, sometimes in another, of human action. The state that favours liberty in some matters is found adverse to it in others.

Of course, however, we can discern in general two sorts of state, in one of which liberty and in the other government is chiefly favoured, and we can find in history examples of either sort in many different degrees. But the examples which are most obvious, and occur to the mind most naturally, cannot in our system be classified under this head. Nine out of ten of the oppressive and crushing governments presented by history are, in our nomenclature, simply inorganic, governments founded from the beginning on nothing but force. When, however, all these examples have been rejected, there will remain a small number of states which it is possible to arrange in a progressive series according to the intensity of government; or, in other words, according to the extent of the province it assumes.

LECTURE VII

You have listened to two lectures on the subject of Liberty. What are the conclusions to which we have been brought? Our first inquiry was, whether it is possible to classify states according to the degree of liberty which they admit. We found that the province of government, and therefore, according to our definition, the province of liberty, differs very greatly in different states, and that in some states liberty is very small and government very large, in others liberty is very large and government very small. But we also found that the differences are not merely quantitative, and that the provinces do not simply increase or diminish in extent, but often increase in one direction while they diminish in another. We did therefore arrive at a classification, but not quite such a classification as we expected; or rather we arrived at two classifications, only one of which can be said to be based simply on the principle of liberty. It will be worth while to recall briefly the difference between the two.

First, then, some states are intense and others lax,

i.e. in some government is strong and active, in others
forbearing and passive. And as a general rule it
appears that the energy of government corresponds
to the need of it, that is, to the difficulties with
which the community has to contend.

I quoted examples to show that where the frontier
is weak, government usually by way of compensation
makes itself strong. All the world understands that
in a camp there must be much more government than
in a peaceful trading settlement, for the simple reason
that an enemy is to be feared. A community with a
weak frontier has in this respect the nature of a
camp, and accordingly it creates for itself a strong
government. I may remark that other needs beside
that of defence against an external foe may conceiv-
ably produce the same effect. Anarchic instincts
within the community, an intestine discord between
families or sects or parties, may provoke the community to remedy the evil by creating an iron
government.

Governments then may be arranged in a certain
gradation of intensity or laxity roughly corresponding
to the difficulty of defending the state against destruc-
tive influences, external or internal ; the most striking
division being between the governments which in any
way assert authority over the mind and those which
do not. Where a government uses its power of
coercion to prescribe some religion or some education,

or to prohibit certain doctrines or speculations or certain associations for purposes of study or worship as dangerous, it separates itself strikingly from states professing tolerance. Only we must be on our guard against erecting tolerance into an absolute principle, any deviation from which would be a sin. The question is one of self-defence. If tolerance can be allowed in a state, so much the better; that proves that the state is strong. But the majority of states have not been strong enough to bear it, and have been obliged in self-defence to place restrictions upon it. The most Liberal states on the Continent find that they can scarcely tolerate Jesuitism.

However this may be, there are toleration-states, and an opposite class. Again, we might distinguish between states which impose military service upon all citizens and those which do not. Here, again, is a difference in the intensity of government caused evidently by a difference in the difficulty of defending the state; for such states as Germany, whose frontier is always exposed, adopt the principle of universal service, while England and the United States, which are not exposed to attack, do not.

Perhaps you may on reflection be able to distinguish other similar classes. And I think you will find it an instructive exercise to seek in history exemplifications of the great law we have been considering, that governments draw the reins tight when dangers

threaten the state, and that liberty flourishes where-\
ever there is little danger.

But, as we saw, this classification of states according to the degree of liberty is complicated by another
classification according to the kind of liberty. For
we find that different communities turn their attention
to different objects, and it is natural that government
in each should follow and conform to the inclination
of the community. Accordingly government will
lean now on one side, now on another, and, as liberty
is wherever government is not, there will be just as
many varieties of partial liberty.

We have now to observe that however far we may
go in devising classifications of this kind, we have
rather missed the mark at which we primarily aimed
in undertaking the inquiry. Our object was to give
scientific shape and precision to the great broad distinction, which is implied in the current use of the
term "liberty" as characteristic of certain states, in
certain phases of their development. But when we
speak—for instance—of English liberty, or trace the
consolidation of it in the constitutional struggles of
the seventeenth century, or the adoption of it by the
continental states since the French Revolution, we
most commonly use the word liberty in a sense different from that which I have thought it best to adopt.
True that since the seventeenth century we have
constantly considered the question of the extent of

the province of government, but the liberty of which
in the eighteenth century we had a monopoly, and of
which we still boast does not consist so much in the
contraction of the province of government as in a
peculiarity in the manner in which government is
conducted.   Let us begin by stating in general terms
in what this peculiarity consists.   Evidently it has
something to do with the power assigned to Parliament.   As in the first sense Liberty was opposed to
needless interference, so in this other sense liberty
is opposed to absolutism or personal government.
So far, then, it corresponds to Aristotle's government
by few or many in opposition to his government by
one.   But we never apply the word liberty to what
we distinctly recognise as government by a few.   The
English Parliament now represents a vast number of
people.   In the middle of the last century, when it
was still the only "free" Parliament, it represented,
we know, a number of people comparatively small;
but if that number had not been positively at least
considerable our country would never have claimed
in virtue of its parliament to be considered free.   On
the other hand, it has to be admitted that liberty,
taken in this sense, as in the other, is usually in
practice comparative rather than absolute.   It would
be a very extreme view to refuse to reckon England
among the states that have liberty on the ground
that universal manhood suffrage has not yet been

realised in England after so many Reform Acts; but
we recognise that her "liberty" is not absolute but
only comparative. A "free" Parliament must represent at least a good many people : but only if it
represents all—or, as in the ancient city-states,
actually includes all—do we say that there is liberty
absolute, taking liberty in this sense.

This remark shows that there is a theory underlying the positive facts which are expressed by
the word liberty when it is thus used. It shows
that we think we know why the Parliament should
have so much power, since we think it not fully
developed so long as it does not either represent or actually include all. This theory is commonly expressed by the word self-government, so
that liberty in this sense is often called self-government. Hitherto we have often spoken of government
as the badge by which the state is known. I have
considered the essence of it to lie in the imposition
of his will by one man upon another, so that A does
under fear of punishment not what A but what B
wills to do. This statement, you see, excludes such
a thing as self-government. But perhaps we may
imagine, between the case where a man does simply
what he himself wills and the case where he does what
another wills, a third case where he does that which
is neither simply his own will nor simply another's
will, but that which for a special purpose, viz. the

general good, he consents to have considered as his
own will.   This would be a sort of self-government in
its naked form.   The formula of it would be somewhat
as follows.   A at the present moment would personally
prefer to remain wholly inactive, but taking into account the danger which threatens the community from
the neighbouring tribe, and the necessity of vigorous common action in order to avert it, he, under
no constraint, freely elects and wills to march against
the enemy.   This, you see, is self-government, and if
such a system could be worked out it is perhaps conceivable that the operations of the state might be
purged of that taint of violence which from the beginning has corrupted them, and that such a thing
as government without coercion might come to be
regarded as possible.

Here, perhaps, is an ideal to attain which it
might be worth while to make some considerable
sacrifice.   For the purpose, you see, it would be
necessary that each individual citizen should be consulted in two distinct capacities.   First, he must be
asked simply what he as an individual wills and
chooses.   Secondly, he must be asked, as a member
perhaps of some universal assembly, what, taking
everything, the public good included, into consideration, he desires to be considered as his will.   This
would be self-government, or government without
coercion.   Is such a thing possible?   It is often spoken

of as if it were not only possible, but had been already realised. Thus it is common among us to say, On this subject the people has expressed its will, and that will is supreme. But you observe that the ideal I described is not attained so long as any one person is obliged to do the thing which, considering everything, he does not wish to do. Now, I put aside for the present that we cannot speak with correctness of the will of the people so long as the suffrage remains short of universal, and that when all the men have been admitted in order to ascertain the will of the people you must also consult all the women and all the children. This is a trifle. Besides this, if you would get rid of coercion the voting in your universal parliament must always be unanimous. For on this principle, what possible right can a majority have to bind a minority? I think no sufficient justification of this right of the majority has ever been given. A French writer has justly remarked that the right of an enormously large majority may be granted, but that it is almost impossible to defend the right of a small majority. Thus, if out of thirty millions 29,900,000 are agreed, we may talk of the will of the people as if it had been pronounced approximately, but it is quite otherwise when it is pronounced only by a majority of ten or twenty in an assembly in which 700 men represent 37,000,000.

Surely this assumption that in matters of legislation

the majority is to count for the whole, and the minority, even if it amount almost to a full half of the citizens, is not to count at all, is so enormous that we may at least be surprised to find it admitted, as it commonly is admitted, without discussion. But suppose we admit that in political science the majority may be taken to stand for the whole, still the word self-government—which might fairly be applied to a system of government in which no violence was done to individual wills—is not properly applicable to a system in which individual wills may be overridden freely so long as, taken together, they form but a minority of the whole. Such a system may be justified perhaps by convenience or by the difficulty of devising another, but it surrenders the ideal of a collective will of the people and of government without coercion.

Instead, then, of laying it down that there may be two kinds of government, the personal government of an individual, and the self-government of all the citizens, we should rather state that the opposite of personal government is the government of the minority by the majority. Though this latter is by no means self-government, it is none the less a system of the utmost importance. I do not see how it can be based upon abstract right; even to assert that the will of the majority is in all cases, or even in the majority of cases, likely to be preferable to

that of the minority would be very rash. All, I
think, that can be said is that the principle of giving
authority to the majority over the minority is simple
and easily intelligible, and, where the majority is
enormously large, approximately just; that it reduces
to a minimum the odium with which government is
naturally regarded; and that it is so far natural
that it gives authority to the section which, as being
the more numerous, would probably win if an appeal
were made to physical force. But in virtue of
all these advantages together we may say that the
principle of giving rights to the majority is perhaps
the greatest and most momentous practical invention
ever made in the department of politics. Only do
not let us resort to fiction, and when it is quite
sufficient to say that it is in many respects convenient to yield to the majority, do not let us say
that it is of course just to do so, or that of course
the majority is to be regarded as equivalent to the
whole.

This, I say, is the greatest practical invention,
though it is commonly regarded as if it were rather
a discovery than an invention, and as if it had
theoretical justice as well as practical convenience
to recommend it. Closely connected with it is
another great invention which deserves that name
much more evidently. In general we have to be on
our guard in political science against attributing too

much to conscious contrivance. Most political phenomena seem rather to have grown than to have been
invented. But the idea of the representative system,
which has wholly transformed the aspect of political
institutions, constitutes an exception. One of the
most fundamental facts which I have to put before
you is, that whereas both personal government and
government by majority are found in antiquity as
well as in modern states, on the other hand the
representative system was scarcely known to the
ancient world. This grand difference between the
ancient and modern world is closely connected with
that other broad difference which strikes our attention so instantaneously. That in ancient Greece and
Italy the state was identified with the city rather
than with a large territory,—this is necessarily the
first observation we make when we compare them
with modern Europe. But the second observation is
this, that though notoriously the ancients had what
we often call liberty, that is, government by majority,
—so much so that the modern movement in the
same direction which began in the eighteenth century
seemed like a revival of antiquity,—yet ancient
"liberty" assumed a form which it has been found
impossible to revive. The Ecclesia at Athens was not
an assembly of the representatives of the Athenian
community: it was, we may say, the community
itself. And we remark the same thing if we turn

from Greece to Rome. There, too, popular assemblies
met and conducted the business of the state. There
was the Comitia Centuriata, which was supposed to
have been founded by one of the ancient kings,
Servius Tullius; and there was the Comitia Tributa.
Between these assemblies there were great differences, but neither was founded on the representative
principle. Both alike were open to all citizens.
The Senate at Rome was of course in some respects
and at certain periods extremely influential, and
this certainly did not include the whole mass of
citizens, but neither was it in any degree representative.

We thus discover two grand differences between
the world of classical antiquity and the modern
world in respect of political development. Let me
now proceed to point out how closely these two
differences are connected together. It is by taking
note of this that we see what has been the precise
line of human evolution in this political department.
Both personal government and government by a
majority were known to ancient states as well as
to modern. But in ancient states, being city-states,
the introduction of government by majority implied
an assembly in which all the citizens should have a
place. The very idea of such an assembly, if it were
suggested to any modern politician, would take his
breath away. In modern states the utmost point of

progress is the creation of an assembly founded upon
universal suffrage, that is, a parliament in electing
which every citizen shall have an infinitesimal share.
But in Athens and Rome every citizen was himself a
member of parliament. Now why was this comprehensiveness of democracy possible to them, while it
is impossible to us? You see that it was possible to
them simply because they were city-states. In a
city-state the population will be small, and the
citizens will live near each other. In a city-state
such scenes may be witnessed as you will find
described near the beginning of the Acharnians of
Aristophanes. There you find described the summoning and the meeting of the Athenian Ecclesia
itself. In the market-place, says the poet, the people
are gossiping, and up and down you see them trying
to dodge the vermilion-dyed rope. Yes! there is
indeed a picture of universal suffrage. Every person
in the market-place has not only a right but a positive duty to take his place on the Pnyx; and that
no one might escape, a rope was drawn round the
market-place which should sweep the whole population bodily into parliament, and it was dyed that it
might at least leave a mark upon those who might
try to escape the duty.

But in a country-state, where the population
numbers 30,000,000 and is scattered over 200,000
square miles, how shall such a comprehensive de-

mocracy be introduced? Aristotle himself recognises
the difficulty when he asks—speaking of an overgrown city-state—Must not the herald that is to address such a multitude be a Stentor? Here, indeed,
is a practical obstacle. We see that to Aristotle it
must have seemed insurmountable. He could conceive government by many, but he could conceive it
only in a city-state. ⨯

But this obstacle has been surmounted by the
introduction of the principle of representation, which
has this grand advantage, that it is applicable to the
country-state. Being so applicable it opened out to
mankind the possibility of a new political development. For a long time the greatness of the ancient
world lay with an oppressive weight like an incubus
upon the moderns. The ancients, it seemed, had
done everything, and nothing remained to be done.
Literature, art, philosophy, all were theirs. The spell
was first broken perhaps by the maritime discoverers
of the fifteenth century, who first extended modern
knowledge clearly beyond the knowledge of the
ancient world. Among the superiorities of antiquity
was its superiority in politics. In the monotonous
world of feudalism, where government took always
much the same form, and that not a very high one,
it was remembered that antiquity had had splendid
states, renowned assemblies that had been controlled
by the eloquence of Demosthenes and Cicero. The

time came when the modern world was able to rival the ancient in this department too. It did not indeed revive the ancient " Polis," but it invented something analogous, so that at last it became in a position to add a second part to the Politics of Aristotle. It developed the country-state, and showed how this might be made capable of all the splendour, liberty, and glory of the Polis. And this it did by means of the representative principle.

You see, then, that the system which was thus introduced, and which has taken such deep root, is not only not in a strict sense self-government, but is removed from it by two degrees. Self-government strictly taken would be government in accordance with the wishes of the governed, but this is a system, in the first place, of government in accordance with the wishes only of the majority—a very different thing. But now, secondly, it is a system under which the people itself is not consulted at all, but only its representatives, and you know what a small number of representatives are consulted. Here in England, out of a population of some 37,000,000, the representatives in the House of Commons amount to less than seven hundred. Surely under this system the share of power assigned to the individual does not amount to much, even if we suppose the system very completely realised. Let us make the most extreme assumptions. Let us suppose in the first place that

the suffrage is extended to the utmost, so that almost
everybody enjoys it; secondly, that the Parliament
which results has the whole government in its hands;
thirdly, let us suppose that the province of government is enlarged to the utmost degree, that is,
according to our definition, that liberty in the state is
reduced to a minimum, yet even then what share of
power has the individual? He has, perhaps, a thirty-
millionth part in determining of whom this omnipotent
assembly shall consist. I am reminded of a remark
made by M. About, who says of the system as it
stood some forty years ago in France, where Parliamentary government was combined with rigid
centralisation and restless government interference—
he says that it was the pride of every Frenchman,
when he looked in his glass in the morning, to think
that he saw there the twenty-seven-millionth part of a
tyrant, but that he was apt to forget that at the same
time he saw the whole of a slave.

This representative principle, however, has taken
such deep root, and we have become so familiar with
it, that we perhaps have a difficulty in understanding
its prodigious importance or the extreme slowness of
its introduction into the world. Look, however, at
one of the largest and most palpable facts in history.
The older system, that of universal assemblies, came
to an end evidently in Rome. That singular revolution, which we call the fall of the ancient Roman

republic, or perhaps the fall of liberty at Rome, was in reality the fall of the city-state. It was followed, we know, by the rise of Imperialism, the establishment of an absolutism which grew ever more military. Century after century passed, experiment after experiment was tried, but one experiment appeared always hopeless, and that was the restoration of the old republic. Nor could anything of the same nature be devised. From that time no government had a chance that was not a form of absolutism.

Now, if you inquire into the reason of the impossibility of reviving the republic, you speedily discover that the old republican institutions of Rome were essentially civic. They were fitted only for a city-state, and a city-state Rome could never again be. The Comitia Centuriata might meet in the Campus Martius to elect the annual consuls, so long as it was not quite absurd to identify the citizens of Rome with the inhabitants of that city. But Rome had become the centre of a vast dominion, limited by the Rhine and the Danube. By this expansion the state had changed its whole aspect and manifestly outgrown its old institutions. But, perhaps you will say, in that case why did not Augustus introduce the representative system. If Rome had ceased to be a city-state, why did he not introduce into it the institutions proper to a country-state? You might as well ask, "Why did not Augustus discover America?" If, as we have

seen, the political philosophers of antiquity scarcely
realised that there was such a thing as a country-state,
can we expect the Roman politicians to have known
by what changes of machinery, by what reforms, a
city-state could be transformed into a healthy country-
state? For this was the problem, which has been
somewhat obscured to us by our habit of introducing
everywhere the terms monarchy and republic, liberty
and slavery. These terms are thought to explain
everything in politics; and so in the Roman Revolution we see the fall of a republic and the introduction
of a monarchy; the fall of liberty and the introduction of absolutism. This description misses the
essential feature of it. It was the fall of a city-state,
and along with that the fall of the institutions proper
to the city-state, and, in particular, of the universal
unrepresentative Assembly.

What would happen in government after the fall
of the city-state seems to have been a problem wholly
beyond solution by any political thinker of those ages.
No one divined that the country-state would be found
capable of so much development, and in particular no
one seems to have guessed that assemblies analogous
to those which had been addressed by Demosthenes
and Cicero would be seen, assemblies not universal
but at the same time large, assemblies founded on the
representative principle. To open this new course
and enter successfully upon it took much more than a

thousand years. The English Parliament, which is now regarded as the mother of Parliaments, dates, as we know, in its proper representative form only from the latter part of the thirteenth century.

But though the progress of this principle has been incredibly slow, it has been so solid that in the present age this principle and what flows from it occupy the very centre of politics. In England, from the thirteenth century to the seventeenth, parliamentary government did not make any marked progress. Parliament was always there, and at certain periods very powerful, but in those four centuries the principle of representation by no means developed all that was in it. Then came the revolutions of the seventeenth century, which I mention here, not for the purpose of discussing them, but only in order to mark their total result. Other disturbances, which in some of their stages were extremely wild and confused, had a remarkably happy termination in 1688. A settlement was arrived at which secured for a great country-state that particular form of government by majority which is based upon the representative principle. The representation of the people was, of course, extremely imperfect, but the authority of the representative assembly even in the greatest questions was established. A century followed in which for the most part England appeared to have a monopoly of what were called "free" institutions.

But since the wars of the French Revolution a system substantially identical began to spread itself over continental states : in 1848 it made solid progress : and now, if we judge liberty by largeness of suffrage, more than one continental state is in advance of England in liberty. A remarkable uniformity has been attained in the political constitutions of the globe through the universal prevalence of the representative system. As Aristotle's state, the Polis, has disappeared, so too Aristotle's popular assembly, the Ecclesia, giving direct power of government to the whole multitude of the citizens, has disappeared. Government by many is known now only in a modified form ; it means now government by a comparatively small assembly of representatives. But in this modified form it has received the highest honour which in the political department can be given to anything, for it is called by the name of liberty.

In the last lecture we were concerned with the notion of "Government by Many." Before we proceed to consider this further, in the modified form which it has assumed in modern states, we may conveniently examine more closely that "Government by One" which we are wont to contrast with it under the name of Despotism.

It is the custom to regard despotism as a sort of unmixed curse, as an incubus or nightmare, as a supernatural evil which, leagued with superstition, crushes the unhappy race of mortals in the dust. This doctrine is the counterpart of that which represents liberty as an unqualified divine blessing, equally desirable in all times and places. Now there is a sort of despotism as ghastly as this theory imagines; in inorganic states, where everything is founded on violence and conquest, such horrors are not rare. But we have nothing to do here with inorganic states. The forms of government with which we are concerned have grown up by a reaction of the political vital principle against some pres-

sure.   Among these forms is the government of one.
By the hypothesis it meets some want; and in some
cases it is obvious that one important want which it
meets is the want of protection for the people at large
against the tyranny of the few.   Thus Julius Cæsar,
as we know, began his career as the head of the
democratic party in Rome; and the Roman emperors
were the champions of the provincials against the
oppression of senatorian proconsuls, who had depended on the aristocracy.   Thus the English
supported their strong Tudor kings to be their
protection against the lawlessness of the armed
nobility.   Thus in the Dutch Republic, when the
people entered into politics, they threw up their
caps for the Prince of Orange, and raised the cry of
"Orange Boven" as the watchword of resistance to
tyranny of the burghers.   How, again, did the
French monarchy in the thirteenth century rise so
rapidly to despotic powers in the very country where
a century before monarchy had been exceptionally
insignificant?   It was by reaction against the tyranny
of feudal nobles, by the support of the Communes
who in all parts of France at once found that the
king was ready to give them aid in their struggle
against the seigneur.   Once more, look at the
strongest form of despotism which modern Europe
has known.   What has made Russia for so long a
time loyal to her Czars?   The desire of the mass of

the population to have a strong protector against
the Boyars. Witness the famous scene of the
accession of Anne. When the Boyars called Anne,
Duchess of Courland, to a throne to which she had
but a poor title, imposing upon her a constitution as
the price of their support, what frustrated their
scheme? The people rose in rebellion, knowing that
the weakness of the Czarina meant oppression to
themselves. They insisted that she should be
absolute, and it was like a charter to the Russian
people that she solemnly tore the charter that had
been extorted from her by the Russian nobles.

Examples such as these may awaken in you a
certain feeling of dissatisfaction with respect to the
popular political philosophy. What I said on liberty
will, I trust, have convinced you that we are scarcely
so strict as we ought to be in the use of political
terms. But those remarks left the citadel of the
popular philosophy unthreatened. They tended to
show only that it might be more conveniently
stated in other terms. They called only for the
alteration of a word. Put but popular principles or
popular government for liberty, which we found it
more convenient to use in another sense, and the
accepted theory would still seem as true as ever.
But what do you think of the view of despotism
which I have just suggested? The popular theory
certainly holds nothing in so much horror as

despotism ; in opposition to this, as the government
of happiness, it sets up democracy. It does not of
course like oligarchy, but it regards oligarchy, so far
as oligarchy is republican, so far as it involves debate
and discussion in an assembly, as less monstrous than
despotism, which it puts almost on a level with some
Mexican idol-worship. You see now that it is possible by the help of historical examples to give a
different account of despotism, according to which it
is not the worst government, but a contrivance for
escaping a sort of government more oppressive still.
Instead of being opposed to democracy it may, on this
hypothesis, be a rude form of it. That is, a great
population scattered over a large territory and
struggling against the oppression of great magnates,
being unable to organise concerted action over so
large a space, may collect all its power into the hands
of an individual, and arm him with a sort of iron
mace strong enough to crush any or all of the
enemies of the people. Such a power, compared
with an oligarchical Senate, would be rude and in ,
appearance brutal. It would strike hard blows and
use no refined artificial eloquence, but its rudeness
and coarseness would be democratic. The despot, so
regarded, would be only the demagogue armed with
power.

This has certainly been the character of some
despotisms, and in other despotisms we may trace

that they had this character at the beginning, and have only lost it by corruption. Before, however, we abandon as false the favourite contrast between monarchy and republic, and the doctrine, almost universally held, that democracy is a strong and almost extreme form of opposition to despotism, it will be well to examine the notion of despotism somewhat more closely. For we observe that the word does not merely denote the fact, but is supposed in some sort also to explain it. With the name is involved a sort of theory of the phenomenon. For through the whole accepted doctrine there runs an assumption that government is of two kinds, radically distinct, which may be distinguished as government from above and government from below. We keep constantly before our eyes two types of authority, unmistakably different, and these two types serve us as a practical guide which we feel sure can never mislead us. One is inherent authority, speaking in a tone of command and using force. This kind, when it is most favourably described, may be illustrated by that of a father over infants. In that one instance it is allowed to be good and lawful, but it is maintained that such authority, when claimed by a ruler in the state, cannot be allowed without degrading the citizens into infants, and ascribing to the ruler an inherent superiority which he cannot possibly have. The

other type is entrusted authority. In this the
ruler is really the servant, and the subjects taken
all together are the rulers. An obvious illustration
may be taken from the office-bearers of a club or
company, to whom a certain amount of authority is
granted merely in order that the wishes of the
society may be carried more promptly into effect,
but who do not presume to have any opinion of their
own; or at least, if they find themselves so far in
disagreement with the majority that they cannot consent to sacrifice their own opinions, they are expected
quietly to withdraw. This view of government,
which, since it was clearly set forth by Rousseau, has
been the ferment of the European revolution, is called
the doctrine of the sovereignty of the people. But
how old the theory of the two opposite types is, and
how deeply it has penetrated all minds, may be seen
from the popular use of the words republic and
commonwealth! One of those words translates the
other, and we might suppose neither could ever be
adopted as the distinctive name for any one form of
government. For surely, however forms of government may differ, they must at least all agree in
professing concern for the commonweal, and must
therefore, all be equally "republics." But no; this
name is given to states where an assembly rules and
where there is no monarch, because it is supposed
that the monarch does not necessarily even profess

to aim at the common good, but rules by inherent authority. That the kernel of the accepted theory lies in this distinction may be seen from the way it treats rulers like Cromwell and Napoleon. They, to be sure, were monarchs not less despotic than Charles I. wished to be, or than Louis XIV. was. Yet they are regarded quite differently, because we suppose that they acknowledged themselves to hold their power, absolute as it was, from the people and for the people.

Certainly the distinction, if real, is all-important, and indeed we should have a very terrible view of history if we were obliged to think that Louis XIV. and Charles I., and the long royal lines which in most European countries represented for a long period the same principles of government, ruled their subjects as a master rules a household of slaves, crushing them down by superior force. Assuredly no rhetoric or poetry could ever exaggerate the horror of such a system, but I can scarcely describe it without betraying how difficult it is to conceive such a system at work. Let us try to imagine Louis XIV. crushing down the French people by superior force! Clearly we cannot take the words literally! Even a slave-owner does not hold down his many slaves literally by the use of superior force, but by the threat of a superior force which he could speedily call in : for in a slave-holding country all the free population are banded

together to hold the slaves in subjection. Well then !
Louis XIV., if the French people had risen against
him, would have called in assistance from neighbouring kings to put them down? Bodies of police would
have been sent from Germany and from England to
restore order? You know that nothing of the sort
would have happened, and that the French people
could not have been led to suppose that it would.
What then would have happened? He would have
called in his soldiers. What? But I thought these
soldiers were themselves among the Frenchmen whom
he was to hold down. Surely one of his principal
difficulties lay in the fact that a large number of his
slaves were armed and disciplined. Surely if you
admit that Louis XIV. depended upon his army, it is
evident that his power too "came from below," just
as that of the modern ruler who says that he derives
his power from the people. The systems no doubt are
different, but in both cases the support is below, not
above. For as the modern ruler must yield if the
people do not support him, so must Louis XIV. have
yielded if the army had deserted him.

The truth is that the antithesis between government from above and government from below is
illusory. A despot governing by superior force as a
father governs infant children is an absurd conception.

What is true is this. A comparatively small
number may by superior concert and organisation

control a large number, and this small number may
have a chief at their head. Cromwell, for instance,
could not by his own personal strength control the
English nation, but by means of a trained army of
50,000 men who were devoted to him, he could easily
do so. But to get the services of this army he must
in some way have persuaded them. And if so he
must have been dependent on them, responsible to
them.

Indeed it seems strange that we should imagine
the monarchical of all forms of government to rest on
force, since evidently it is the only one of the three
Aristotelian forms which cannot possibly do so. The
many may of course easily rule by force, for they have
the superiority in force; the few may do so, for by
organisation and discipline they may render their
force practically superior; but the one cannot do so.
At the utmost we might conceive that in a very small
primitive clan some Achilles might for a short time
rule by sheer physical superiority; but if we tried to
describe such a heroic personal government we should
soon find ourselves driven to admit admiration, hope
of reward, and sense of public interest, as well as the
sheer intimidation before a superior force, to a place
among the motives of obedience.

In short, while the few and the many alike may
depend on themselves alone and use naked force, the
monarch cannot do so, but must necessarily persuade

somebody to help him, convince somebody that his
rule is desirable, and therefore must depend on somebody, be responsible to somebody. Therefore there
is no such thing as irresponsible monarchy, though
irresponsible oligarchy, and still more irresponsible
democracy, are quite possible and ordinary.

This would be evident to us if our minds were not
clouded with the dust of the old divine-right controversy. For that leads us to bring in the idea of a
supernatural Power supporting the monarch, without closely considering whether we mean that the
supernatural Power really does support him, or only
that some people erroneously believe this to be the
case.

It has always been taught that the law of duty is
enforced by divine sanctions, that what we ought to do
it is well for us to do, and ill for us to do what we ought
not to do. Religion, especially Christianity, makes
it in general a moral duty to obey the government.
Accordingly government necessarily enjoys the benefit
of this teaching, and is considered to be supported by
the Power that rules the universe. Usually, but not
necessarily, that Power has been regarded as acting
by supernatural means as well as by natural. So
far, then, government is regarded as supported by
supernatural power, but so far this applies to all governments alike, and not merely to monarchical governments. It has often been remarked that those well-

known texts of the New Testament were originally intended to apply, not to a hereditary monarchy, but to an elective imperialism. It is not monarchy only, but in general "the powers that be," that are said to be ordained of God. If this religious sanction has practically been enjoyed more by monarchy than by other forms of government, that, I take it, is only because all over Europe for many centuries monarchy has been the government in possession, "the power that is." Other governments equally, whenever they find it necessary, call religion to their aid; aristocracy, and still more democracy, try to represent themselves as the only right, just, religious form that government can take, and democracy particularly loves to be regarded as the practical fulfilment of the Christian ideal.

But the important thing is to note in what way religious sanctions strengthen government, when they do strengthen it. The monarch, I have pointed out, cannot rest on force, because superior force is just the thing which he most evidently lacks. And yet he especially uses a high tone, and seems to depend on an intrinsic superiority. Is this because Heaven actually interferes in his behalf with thunder and lightning? Not so; religion acts by faith, not by sight. It does not alter the actual proportion of force between the ruler and his subjects, but it acts upon the minds of the subjects. It forms in them an opinion concerning their ruler which they would not otherwise have entertained. Louis XIV. in the midst of the French was actually but a puny weakling, but owing to many influences, of which religion was one of the most important, they regarded him with awe. They probably did not believe, any more than we do, that any one disobeying him would have been instantaneously reduced to ashes by fire from Heaven. Only the prevalent opinion among them was that, taking all things into consideration,—the present and the future, themselves, future generations and the realm, the welfare of their bodies and the welfare of their souls,—it was expedient to render him loyal obedience. If so, you observe that Louis XIV. did not depend immediately upon support from above, but upon an opinion in the minds of his subjects below.

It may be replied : " True, the one cannot rule purely by force ; but as the few can prevail over the many by adding to force organisation, so the one can eke out his insufficient force by the help of fraud. The despot is an impostor falsely pretending to supernatural power, and maintaining his authority by means of superstition and deception."

Now in special circumstances and for a short time this may be just conceivable, as we see by the story of the Veiled Prophet of Khorassan. If not by supernatural power, yet by the pretence of supernatural

power, the one may succeed in being for practical
purposes more strong than the many, and so may be
independent of his subjects and irresponsible.

But such a bare possibility does not at all help us
in explaining the historical examples of despotism.
Let us bring Louis XIV. into court again. The awe
with which he was regarded had a strong religious
element in it, and we might admit that the religious
teaching which had fostered it was not quite true,
was tainted with superstition. But if there was
deception, Louis XIV. himself was not the deceiver.
The extravagant claims had not been put forward
mainly by him, nor by others in his pay. A doctrine
had sprung up in the French church and nation,
which had gathered strength through a long period
from many circumstances ; of this Louis XIV. reaped
the benefit. Observe, then, the promulgators of the
opinion which was so useful to him were distinct
from him ; they might change their opinion and pro-
mulgate another. He was therefore dependent on
them and to some extent responsible to them ; he
was under the necessity, if he would reign successfully, of carefully watching, studying, and humouring
the minds of those who taught the people to obey.
As Cromwell on his army, Louis XIV. was in a great
degree dependent on his bishops ; he succeeded on
the whole in carrying them with him in his contest
with the Papacy, but his whole reign would wear

now a very different aspect if they had chanced to side against him. As it was, while no despotism that modern Europe has known has been much more complete than that of Louis XIV., still few states have had so much unity of feeling or been so thoroughly organic as France was in his age. In that age the devotion of the French to their monarchs became a proverb, and it continued unshaken half through the reign of Louis XV.

The distinction I am trying to impress upon you is one which I have found to be of great practical importance. According to the popular notion despotism is a mere incubus, under the weight of which there can be no life or movement of any kind. Under its pressure there can be no play of interests, no political activity, no thought of the common good, but mere abject servility, sloth, and death. It is to be observed that despotism rather favours than combats this notion of itself, since the despot likes it to be supposed that he derives his power from above and prides himself upon his supposed irresponsibility. But to the historical student, I think, despotism comes to wear a somewhat different aspect. In the first place, he finds that it is just as dependent as any other form of government upon support from below. No despotism ever encounters him in the course of his researches concerning which he cannot with great confidence pronounce upon what interests, upon the

support of what group of persons, it leaned. The fancy
of two distinct kinds of government—one responsible
and one irresponsible, one from above, the other from
below—gradually vanishes from his mind. Secondly,
though he finds despotism in particular cases quite as
terrible, sometimes perhaps even more terrible than it
is popularly conceived, yet these cases appear to fall
under one class, the class of inorganic governments.
That is, when the despotism rests on the support of
some group foreign to the community, a horde of
conquerors, or a mercenary army, in these cases there
is often no limit to its tyranny. But when despotism
is organic—and this happens not so rarely—it is not
by any means the monotonous death-in-life we are
apt to suppose. The despot, like the Constitutional
Minister, has to reckon with public opinion. He
knows well what interests he must conciliate, what
classes he must not offend, what public wants he must
satisfy. Study the Tudors, study Louis XIV., study
modern Prussia. These despotisms are organic, and
therefore they exhibit all the movements and processes of organic life.

We may now, I think, reasonably draw the conclusion that the accepted distinction between monarchy
and republic or commonwealth is incorrect and ought
to be abandoned. These two latter words evidently
describe a state in which the good of the whole is the
object of government. Why then should they be

taken to denote any state which is not monarchical, as if a monarch, say Alfred or St. Louis, were necessarily, as such, an oppressor, and every governing assembly — say the Venetian Council or the Roman Senate in the time of Sulla—were necessarily well-intentioned ?

In our system "republic" or "commonwealth" are terms very suitable to describe what we have called the organic state. An organic state, we have laid it down, springs up by the effort of the social organism to resist a hateful pressure, that is, by a striving towards the common good or commonweal. Opposed to this are all those states which we have called inorganic, because they rest upon the violent effort of some group or section to coerce the community for its own advantage. I have had in view principally the case where this group is a conquering horde ; at a later stage perhaps I may discuss the inorganic state more in detail. This state is not necessarily monarchical. The government of the Mamelukes was an oligarchy. But since an army is governed by a general, and since the ruling group in such a state has the nature of an army, the government of an inorganic state is perhaps most commonly monarchical, being in the hands of the general of the ruling group, who is called Emperor, or Khan, or Sultan, or Khedive, or sometimes King.

This monarch is not really irresponsible, for he

depends entirely upon the favour of the ruling group. The great Turk himself, most despotic of despots, was often overthrown in a moment by a rebellion of the Janissaries. But with respect to the mass of his subjects he is wholly irresponsible, and it escapes their notice that a class of men exists without whose help he could do nothing. Accordingly in their imaginations he figures as a god upon earth, and he is glad enough to encourage a delusion which is highly useful to him. Here is the genesis of that poetical monster, the irresponsible king, ruling from above and supported on nothing below him, the Kehama or Almighty Man.

But the European monarch of Divine right does not really belong to this class, though he partly professed to do so. The Tudor monarchy, and that of Louis XIV., rested on a public need, was supported by public opinion, and did not for a moment profess to have anything else in view but the public good. But it did profess that for the measures which it might take for the public good it was not responsible to the people, but only to God. This was a fantastic theory, but we must not allow it to affect our opinion of what that form of government really was. What the government was is one thing, what it supposed itself to be quite another. James II. may have imagined himself not to be responsible to his subjects. This is a pity, but nothing can be more evident than that in so imagining he mistook the nature of his own authority. And if Louis XIV. himself supposed that his power did not rest on the consent of his people he was just as much mistaken, though his mistake was not exposed in the same overwhelming manner.

Perhaps, then, we may consider these conclusions as established. Firstly, all monarchy whatsoever rests upon the consent of some tolerably numerous group. This group will in most cases be a section of the community, though we may imagine a case where it lives apart and sends help to the monarch from another country. For instance it may be said that our government in India is supported, not by the help of any section of the Indian population, but by the help of the population of another country, namely England.

Secondly, there is such a thing as organic monarchy, which is at the same time despotic. This may be called a monarchical commonwealth or republic though it has no parliament. Such a despotism must rest on the consent, not perhaps of the people at large, but at least of that part of the people which takes an interest in public affairs; strictly speaking, it has the active consent of the political classes and the passive consent of the rest. The phrase monarchical commonwealth has often been used to describe a parliamentary government with a king at its head. I use it here, as you see, in a

different sense to denote a government which, while
it enjoys popular support, is absolutely in the hands
of the king or monarch.

You ask, perhaps, How can a nation deliberately
support a despotism, as though they were in love with
slavery? If their wishes are really consulted, surely
they will give their voice for a parliament. I answer,
Not by any means always. Often there are practical
difficulties which prevent the formation of a parliament such as the people would desire to see. Thus,
in Russia at the accession of Anne no assembly
could have been formed which would not have been
oligarchic, for Russia contained no class below the
noblesse out of which such an assembly could have
been taken. But the Russian people deliberately
preferred a despotic Czarina to such an oligarchic
assembly. More frequent still, perhaps, is the case
where the first need of the nation is guidance in war.
For the time all other objects are postponed to the
public safety, and all classes and interests unite in
supporting the chieftain who seems most capable of
conducting the nation to victory. If the exigency is
transient it will call into existence but a brief
dictatorship, but if it is a standing exigency, caused
by a weak frontier, as in Prussia, or by the national resolution to wage war persistently until a strong frontier
is gained, as in France, then it will call into existence a
dynasty of securely seated despotic monarchs. These

considerations explain equally the Russian Czars, Louis XIV., Frederick the Great, and Napoleon. Only it must be understood in all these cases that an organic despotism thus created is always liable to outlast the need that called it into existence. To dissolve it when its work is done is almost impossible ; it remains to encumber and curse for a generation or two the community it once saved. The corrupt survivals of organic despotism are often as bad as inorganic despotism itself, and increase in our minds the difficulty of conceiving that despotism can ever be a healthy, natural, and beneficial form of government.

I have been labouring all this time to make room for the true distinction between despotism and government by assembly, by removing an imaginary one. Government from above, it appears, is a chimæra formed by misconceiving the nature of an inorganic government which chances to depend on some small, scarcely visible, group of supporters alien to the community. Such government by an alien group, a mercenary or foreign band, is indeed despotism, and despotism of a kind very frequent in history ; but then it is inorganic, and therefore does not concern us here. Organic despotism may seem at first sight impossible, an incongruous conception, but I trust I have shown you that it is not so, and that the greatest, most civilised despotisms known to history are of this kind. Being organic, these despotisms rest on the consent of the people not less than parliamentary or republican governments. And now comes the question, In what respect then do such despotisms differ from government by assembly?

Undoubtedly the question is very bewildering, chiefly owing to a cause of mistake which is peculiar to political science and does not trouble the naturalist. How very trying it would be to the animal physiologist if the animals which he studies continually poured into his ears their own views, their own theories, of their own structure and organisation! The student of political constitutions and institutions can scarcely attend to the actual facts before him for the clamour of explanation, theory, representation and misrepresentation, which deafens him from the subjects themselves of his investigation. We have to go to the English parliamentary debates of the seventeenth century for information about the nature of parliamentary government; but who does not know how those discussions teem with legal fiction and obsolete theory? It is not an easy thing to detach the simple facts from all that incrustation!

We are told that by the English constitution the popular assembly reserved to itself the right of the purse. From this example the general principle has been deduced, as the essence of popular government, that no man is to be taxed without his own consent.

What a clumsy, helpless, grotesque generalisation ! In its modern meaning, by the way, it is quite erroneous. By taxation *we* mean the annual subscription upon which government absolutely depends. In the time of the Stuarts, government paid its way out of quite another fund, and only resorted to taxation in extraordinary cases. So that the power of the purse did not in those days mean, as we suppose, a power of paralysing government whenever government should take an unpopular course. But, apart from this historical error, what can such a principle mean ? What is there specially sacred about taxation that we should hold that a government may in other things act at its pleasure, only not venture to take money out of the pockets of the people. Evidently, when we generalise in this fashion, we confound together the end our ancestors aimed at with the means which in their need they seized because by chance they found them within their reach ; we waste upon a mere practical device, a mere accidental expedient of politics, the enthusiasm and awe that properly belong to great universal principles.

We are misled in another way, as it seems to me, when we lay it down that Parliament in England is the organ of legislative power, and the king or minister that of the executive power, and then proceed to describe the contest of the seventeenth century as a struggle by which the legislative asserted its independence of the executive. This, to be sure, is not so grotesque an attempt at philosophising as the other; but I cannot admit it to be at all true, though I cannot at this moment pause to examine it.

If it were true, those memorable struggles of the seventeenth century would evidently afford us little help in our attempt to find a general description of the difference between government by assembly and personal government or despotism, unless indeed we should suppose both forms to be corrupt. For we should have to assume, on the one hand, that in despotism the executive has swallowed up the legislative power, and, on the other hand, that in government by assembly the legislative power has swallowed up the executive.

I suggest—and perhaps in the lectures of next term I may take occasion to show in detail—that great caution must be used in generalising upon the revolutions of the seventeenth century. They make a most interesting, but at the same time a difficult, an intricate chapter of history, a chapter which the student is scarcely prepared to understand until he has mastered the whole doctrine of "fiction," and learned how large an allowance must be made for fiction in interpreting the contemporary record of any great political transformation. I suggest also that we shall get more light on the particular question before us from our own time than from a past age.

Of late, popular government has assumed in
England a peculiarly transparent form. Legal fiction
is reduced to a minimum, and the whole process is
laid bare, so that it has become really almost too
simple, almost too intelligible. We see the country
ruled by a statesman who bears the title of Prime
Minister, and we see him resting undisguisedly upon
the opinion of the majority. While this opinion
supports him, he is powerful; when it wavers, he
becomes anxious and timid ; when it declares against
him he makes no resistance, but lays down his office
without delay and is succeeded by the rival statesman
to whom prevalent opinion has transferred its loyalty.
Now, as I have shown at so much length, in organic
states a system substantially similar—within limits—
has always been pursued. For while in all states the
ruler has always leaned upon the favourable opinion,
upon the choice, of some group of supporters, in completely organic states the ruler has derived his power
from the favour of the community at large. It matters
nothing, so we held, upon what title the ruler may
profess to depend, what theory of his own authority
he may adopt or profess to adopt. He may maintain
that he succeeds to the post of ruler by the same legal
right by which a landowner succeeds to his estate, or
that he rules by divine appointment, either in the
natural sense, as we may say, that a father is divinely
appointed to govern his children, or, supernaturally,

as David is said in the Bible to have reigned as " the man after God's own heart." These theories may be true or false; in any case they can only be effective as arguments addressed to the community. They are reasons why the community should support the ruler who puts them forth. In themselves they have no power to support anything, but if they convince the community the ruler will stand. In that case we may say, using an abbreviated language, that he stands on such and such a title. In reality he stands and can stand only on the support of certain persons, who give their support for reasons which they regard as good. And if the state is organic, then the opinion that supports the ruler is the prevalent opinion of the community at large, or at least of the classes that take an interest in public affairs.

So far, then, despotism and government by assembly, even in its most recent, most frank, and candid form, agree. In what then do they differ? Surely in this, that in the modern system public opinion expresses itself and is ascertained by fixed rules and through certain recognised channels. The favour of the public is recorded, and at the same time measured, by a majority in the House of Commons; and a change in the favour of the public by a change in that majority.

This may be expressed in one word by saying that public opinion has an organ by means of which it makes, supports, and destroys the government.

This formula may be expressed more generally so as to apply equally to all states alike, those which are inorganic, and those (this point, it will be seen later, is important) which are only partially organic, or in which political consciousness is only partly developed. For we may say that in all states there is a government-making power. This name we may give to the group of persons, small or large, foreign or native, disinterested or selfish, upon whose support the government depends. In all states alike, then, this government-making power may have a recognised organ through which it habitually acts ; or again, it may be without such an organ.

Now, suppose it to want such an organ, what will happen at those moments when it changes its mind ? When the power on which a government has long rested becomes unwilling to support it any longer, and has no official way of expressing this change of mind, what must take place ? Evidently the state will be convulsed. The unorganised force will break forth chaotically. When Enceladus *fessum mutat latus*, all Sicily is shaken. This is what we call revolution. It is the chaotic outbreak of the government-making power, for which no organ has been provided.

Thus, it used to be said, and indeed it may still be said, of the Russian government that it is an autocracy tempered by assassination. The truth is that all autocracy, at least pure autocracy, is and must be tempered by assassination. If assemblies of any kind exist the government-making power may work through them and develop them into an organ for its action. But if there is a want even of germs or rudiments, then there is no remedy, and violent actions will infallibly be done. In two notable instances the ruler of a vast state, in which for special reasons no assembly capable of becoming an organ of the government-making power existed or could exist, has chanced to be simply a lunatic. I refer to Caligula and Paul of Russia. In both cases the imprisoned power broke out in assassination.

We have had no royal assassinations in England for four centuries, and when we had a king who at times lost the use of his reason he was treated with pity and respect, and reigned for sixty years. This is because the power here has an organ. We have also been in the habit of saying that in England we do not have revolutions. This, of course, is intelligible, but it would be almost more accurate to say that in England we have always a revolution. Hardly anywhere do governments fall more frequently or more suddenly than in England. Why, then, do we seem in comparison with most states so exceptionably steadfast and stable. It is not because we do not have revolutions, but because we have reduced revolution to a system and given it legal forms. We have always a revolution, and therefore, in a certain sense, we never have a revolution.

We have arrived then at a mode of stating the difference between despotism and government by assembly. I only offer it for the present as a suggestion. Before we can accept it there will be needed much more investigation and much consideration of the various historical examples of either system. As there is no question in political science more important practically nor more prominent historically than this, I shall spare no pains and no time necessary for elucidating it thoroughly. But I am glad to have been able in this last lecture of the present term to carry the inquiry so far as to arrive at least at a tenable hypothesis.

I close this course, then, with the following theoretic statement, which will be our starting-point when we meet again :—

1. Government rests upon force or coercion.

2. In most cases government is forced to assume a form more or less monarchical. In an army there is one commander ; in a law court there is either one judge or a small number.

3. One person cannot apply force or coercion to a large number except by receiving assistance from at least a considerable number.

4. Such assistance must be given voluntarily or

from conviction, though the motives of those who render it may be good or bad, selfish or disinterested, low or high.

5. It follows that in every governed community there must be not merely two things, the government and the governed, as we are apt to suppose, but three things, the government, the government-supporting body, and the governed.

6. What supports the government also makes it, and when it chooses to withdraw its support destroys it. The government-supporting body or power is therefore the government-making power.

7. This power may be in a particular instance entirely without organisation, or again it may be entirely unorganised as such. Louis XIV. was supported by a public opinion almost unanimous but entirely unorganised; Cromwell was supported by his army, that is, by a body organised indeed, but not organised avowedly for the purpose of supporting him.

8. In other cases the government-making power may be organised. In other words, some states have not only a government-making power, but also a government-making organ.

9. In such states there is an assembly which often appears to govern. In reality it usually does not govern, but makes, supports, and destroys the government.

10. In the former class of states there is no similar

assembly. The government stands apparently alone. It therefore easily represents itself and supposes itself to govern by an inherent force, or by supernatural or providential assistance. In reality it is supported by a power below, by a power not visible, because not organised.

11. This is despotism; the other is government by assembly.

SECOND SERIES

(Lent Term, 1886)

LECTURE I

THE vacation interrupted us while we were examining perhaps the most important of all the differences which are observed among states, the difference which in popular discussion is described as equivalent to the difference of light and darkness or good and evil. If we confine ourselves to pure matter of fact, this difference consists in the presence or absence of an assembly for political debate ; but when we attempt to define the precise function performed by this assembly, and so to measure the difference produced in a state, by having it or wanting it, we meet with difficulties.. Some of these difficulties we thought we had removed, and in the last lecture I was able to lay before you a theoretic statement of the difference between the two sorts of state, which appeared at least intelligible and conceivable. But a theory may be clear without being well-grounded, and the view I took of the political assembly differed from that which is currently accepted, and though consistent with some striking historical facts might appear at first sight inconsistent with others. The theory in short was presented and explained, but I have still to establish it.

Our science is intended before all things to be a guide to history. Now this particular question, the introduction of the assembly, and the increase of its influence, or in certain unfortunate periods its decline and disappearance, occupies historical students more than any other question. This is the chapter headed "Liberty," and though we thought it more convenient to use that word in another sense, yet we cannot help seeing that this and no other has been the question of questions since political debate began. In English history the standing topic from Magna Charta to the Reform Bill is the growth of parliamentary government; in French history it has been so since the Revolution and before the Revolution; the main problem is to trace the causes which gave despotism the advantage over parliaments. Ancient history deals with the disappearance of kingship, and the establishment of government by assembly in city-states, then at a later time of the mishaps that befel government by assembly, and of the restoration of personal government. The medieval history of Italy, reviving the city-state, presents a somewhat similar series of occurrences. Everywhere we meet with this contrast between the assembly and the person. It should be our object, therefore, to furnish an account of the difference which might throw a broad light over the whole field of history. I was obliged to confess that my theory did not seem at first sight to be much confirmed by the history of the Stuart controversy, and that it was necessary to read that chapter of history with much caution. And yet no chapter surely is more memorable or momentous. We cannot be content to leave the subject in a condition so unsatisfactory to historical students. It will be no waste of time if we linger over historical occurrences so exceptionally important, suspending our theoretic exposition for the sake of them, and taking special pains that what stands out most in history should receive the fullest light from theory. I intend, therefore, to devote two or three lectures to English constitutional history in order to remove the difficulties which hamper the theoretic description of parliamentary movement.

Let me begin by recapitulating the theory. First, we put aside all inorganic states, and attend only to such states as evolve government by a vital process, in which therefore government, of whatever kind, answers a public need and is supported by public feeling. We find that among such states, too, the difference in question exists. These, too, fall into two classes, those which have an assembly and those which have not. Now the theory says that the assembly is an organ by which the government is created and supported or destroyed, and that such an

organ forms itself in one class of states; but that
there are other states which want the organ, in which
therefore government rests upon a support more or
less hidden—some support it must in all cases have
—and can only be changed violently if the public
feeling should demand a change. The former class
have great freedom of debate and reform, but great
security from revolution; the latter know no alternative between immobility and revolution, because they
want the organ of reconstruction. Now here is a
theory which at first sight does not square with the
great historical facts of the seventeenth century. It
is held that, by the Revolution of 1688, England
succeeded after many struggles in establishing
parliamentary government, and fairly left the other
kind, personal government, behind it. Yet assuredly
it was not determined by that revolution that
Parliament has the power of creating and destroying
governments. The utmost that was claimed was
a power of setting aside a ruler who showed an
extreme contempt for his engagements. Only in
extremity and on the ground of self-defence could
the parliament destroy government, and even then
the new government created itself by the operation
of a fixed law of succession, and Parliament only
ventured of its own power to associate with the
new monarch her husband and cousin. Yet before
it could use these powers, which fell so far short

of a power of creating and destroying government,
the state was shaken to its centre; and it was held
that in so acting Parliament did not fulfil a
normal function, but only called into play an extreme power reserved to it for the preservation of
the state.

Evidently, then, it will cost me some trouble to
reconcile the theory I have suggested with facts
which seem so much at variance with it. But the
theory is a key which fits the lock of our present
system much better. Now that the minister rules,
and that he rests on the support of a parliamentary
majority, sinking at once when that majority fails
him, Parliament may perhaps be said to have, at
least among other functions, the function of creating
and destroying government. At any rate such a
statement is not open to the same objections as occur
to us against a similar statement applied to the
English Constitution of the seventeenth century.
Our present system is one thing, our old constitution
quite another. I propose, therefore, in the present
lecture to speak only of the former, leaving the
latter for another occasion. To-day the question
simply is whether the theory gives a satisfactory
account of the function of Parliament in England at
the present time.

For of course we are aware that quite a different
account is current. The rise and fall of governments

according to the oscillations of the parliamentary
majority cannot of course be denied, but it is not
usual to represent them as the effects which Parliament exists to produce, rather as incidental consequences which follow from the discharge by Parliament of other functions.   What are these other
functions? Parliament, we are told, is the *Legislature*.
Blackstone will inform you that there are two powers
in the state, the legislative and the executive. The
executive power, he says, resides in the King, but
is exercised by him through responsible Ministers.
The legislative power, on the other hand, resides in
King, Lords, and Commons acting together. This
is the formal statement. But if we are content to
recognise facts, we must add that the personal share
of the King in legislation has fallen out of use, every
Act passed by the two Houses since a particular date
in the reign of William III. having received the
royal assent without opposition or delay. This power
of the Crown, then, having dropped and being manifestly incapable of revival, it follows that the
Legislature is now not King and Parliament, but
Parliament alone. Parliament consists of two Houses,
but in the present discussion I do not think it will be
necessary to consider the Houses separately. At the
present day, under ordinary circumstances, legislation
by Parliament practically means legislation by the
House of Commons : for simplicity, therefore, I shall

speak as if Parliament consisted of the House of
Commons alone.

Now if this is a true account of the English Constitution, a very tempting generalisation presents
itself. We see the personal element prevailing in the
executive, the assembly appropriating the legislative
power. Now what is the difference between these
two powers? They seem to us contrasted much
in the same way as theory and practice or as
principles and details. In legislation, we fancy, the
principles of government are laid down, then the
executive carries these principles into effect. And
we can readily understand that the first task wants
an assembly, but that the second is better done by
individuals. In our experience of societies and clubs,
we meet with a committee or general meeting which
in like manner legislates, and then with the active,
precise, and punctual secretary, who translates the
wishes of the meeting into act. Reasoning in this
way, we arrive at a theory of government which
seems very plausible. Government in reality, we are
disposed to think, is a very simple thing, and wants
only a little common-sense and honesty. Let the
citizens—or, in a modern state, their elected representatives—meet and consider on what general plan
they wish to be governed. As soon as a majority
of them has decided on this plan they may disperse.
But they must leave behind a certain number of

individuals, whose business it shall be to put into execution what has been resolved, supplying from their common-sense any necessary details that may have been forgotten. Thus in a rational civilised government, the execution and administration of the laws will be assigned to individuals, while the alteration of them, the repealing of those which appear unsatisfactory, the creation of others which may seem advisable, will be in the hands of an assembly. If, however, honesty is wanting, or if barbaric manners prevail, this simple arrangement is liable to be disturbed. An individual avails himself of the advantages of his position, of being always on the spot, of superior knowledge, of access to the funds, and gets control over the assembly, intimidating or bribing its members. Sometimes he procures that it shall wholly cease to meet for formal business. Thus creeps in the other type of government, the personal. It is in reality not another type, but a corruption of the one true type; and the corruption consists in this, that the two powers, which should be held distinct, have been confused together, and the one has encroached on the other. Absolutism consists in the encroachment of the executive upon the legislative power.

Now what objection can be made to this explanation of the matter, or what need can there be of resorting to a far-fetched one when this simple one is at hand?

I will point out to you a historical fact which forcibly suggests that all is not right with this theory. In the middle of the last century it had great vogue through the authority of Montesquieu. Thirty years later there commenced a period which is pre-eminently the constitutional period of the modern world. America made a constitution for itself, and speedily France followed its example, constructing for itself four different constitutions in fourteen years, first a Constitutional Monarchy, then a Republic without a President, then a Republic with a President (called a First Consul), lastly an Empire. Both in America and in France the constitution-builders had the English Constitution before them, and studied to reproduce its main outlines. They held that in England the King had the executive and Parliament the legislative power. What was the consequence? In both countries they drew the conclusion that the Ministry ought not to sit in Parliament. Accordingly to this day in the United States the Ministers do not sit in Congress, and in France, when the first Constitution came into operation in 1791, the Parliament was called the Legislative Assembly, and in this Legislative Assembly the Ministers did not sit.

Now it is certainly true of that French Constitution that it was ruined by this peculiarity. By the want of a link between the Government and the Parliament, the two powers were ranged in mortal

P

opposition to each other, and within a year the system sank in blood. In America there has been no such failure, but a system has been created which, good or bad, is not the English system, and works in quite a different manner. And nothing is more obvious than that the whole fabric of English politics, as we see it, would fall at once if the principle of excluding Ministers from Parliament were introduced. Can we imagine, then, that a theory of the English Constitution can be sound from which this principle seemed both to the French and to the Americans to follow by logical necessity?

Let us consider why they drew this conclusion. They reasoned thus. The function of Ministers is to administer. Their power is executive. But the function of Parliament is legislative. Ministers therefore have no natural place in Parliament, and if the great danger to be feared is a confusion of the two powers, how could such a confusion more easily and necessarily begin than by allowing Ministers to sit in Parliament?

Now I think the force of this argument cannot be denied. Nevertheless it is not quite conclusive. For we may meet it thus. Ministers certainly, as Ministers, have no place in Parliament, and a place cannot be given to them without danger. But, on the other hand, it is practically very advantageous that they should have seats, and the advantage on the whole greatly outweighs the danger. Nor is there any positive breach of principle in allowing them a place, for it does not follow because a man is a Minister and has executive power, that he cannot also be a representative and have legislative power, especially if by the contrivance of re-election the consent of his constituency be obtained. Thus the English system may be represented as founded on a due distinction between executive and legislative power, but as including also a very happy practical adjustment by which the two powers are prevented from falling out of harmony, or coming into collision with each other.

Let us resort again to the club or society for an illustration. Such a society may have a paid secretary who is not a member of the committee, and has no vote on it. But this secretary would attend the meetings of the committee, nay, he would be regarded as more essential to the meetings of the committee than any committee man, and it would be held absurd to discuss the affairs of the society and refuse the advice of the person necessarily best acquainted with them. Now the English system adopts this principle of practical good sense. It does not exclude from parliamentary debate the very men who have the best right by their official knowledge to take a share in it. It attains this end, not indeed by allowing them to be present and to speak but not to vote, but by allowing them to represent constituencies at the same time that they hold ministerial portfolios.

So the English system may be represented, and in this way it may be defended. But the defence is hollow, and the representation ludicrously unlike the reality. According to this statement the Ministers as such have nothing to do with Parliament. They only happen by great good luck to be there. It is a kind of club where they pass their evenings. They are present under a sort of disguise, not as Ministers, but as members for Tiverton or Midlothian. Happening to find themselves there, and hearing matters discussed upon which they are well informed, they cannot help giving their opinion, and this opinion is naturally heard with respect; but the decision of the House is no affair of theirs, or rather their responsibility extends only to one vote out of six hundred and seventy. Can there be a wilder misrepresentation of the fact?

We allow ourselves to be misled by the form. It is true that the Prime Minister or Chancellor of the Exchequer sits in the House of Commons only as representative of some borough or district, and that his office confers no seat. But nothing can be more untrue than that in the House of Commons he acts not as Minister, but only as member for a locality. On the contrary, it is as Minister that the First Lord of the Treasury leads the House, and the Chancellor of the Exchequer opens the budget. Their executive function is not ignored in the House, but makes the foundation of all the proceedings, the plot of the whole drama. Properly speaking, indeed, the English parliamentary session ought not to be considered as a series of legislative debates at which the Ministers give the benefit of their official knowledge. Such a description misses the principal feature. It is a series of conferences between the executive government and the representatives of the people.

The mistake, then, of those legislators who in France and America tried to reproduce the English Constitution did not consist simply in this, that they overlooked the expediency of allowing the Ministers to be present and take part in the debates. They overlooked that the essence of the English system lies in this, that the Ministers are present and take the lead not in another character but as Ministers, and that the whole business of Parliament is to talk to them and to be talked to by them. Here lay the great failure of Mirabeau. It had been his ambition to dominate the French Revolution as he had seen the elder Pitt dominate the politics of England, *i.e.* by combining in one person the characters of a commanding popular orator and of a great administrator; but no such combination was possible to a Minister who was either excluded from the assembly, or was only allowed there in disguise ; it required a Minister leading the House as Minister.

But if all this is admitted it seems to me to follow that the whole theory which would make Parliament the special organ of legislative power falls to the ground. For the essence of the institution appears to lie rather in some sort of negotiation or parley with the executive power.

It is true of course that a new law cannot in general be made except by a bill passing both Houses of Parliament, for I will not insist on the fact that a certain amount of law comes into existence in another way through the decisions of the judges. It is true also that the executive power is wielded by the Ministers in their respective departments. Parliament *has* legislative, and the Ministers *have* executive power, but it is not true that parliamentary power is correctly described as legislative, or ministerial power as executive, for parliamentary power is executive as well as legislative, and ministerial power is legislative as well as executive. In fact the distinction of legislative and executive, though theoretically perhaps unobjectionable, appears practically to have been quite disregarded in assigning the powers of the Crown or Ministry, and of Parliament.

What is the principal business of Parliament? To grant money for the annual expenses of administration. If you examine the plan according to which the parliamentary session is arranged, you will see that everything is made dependent on this main task, which extends over the whole of it. It is still possible to mark the traces of the old system, according to which legislation, instead of being the work of parliament, was the concession extorted from the Crown as an equivalent for the money granted. The session, as I said, is a conference or negotiation; the parties to it are on the one side the government, on the other side the representatives of the people; these arrange the terms of a bargain according to which certain sums shall be granted and certain grievances redressed. The redress of grievances is legislation, but the grant of money cannot properly be called legislation. At least if the word legislation be so loosely defined as to make it include the levying of a sum of money in one year for the use of government, it ceases to have anything distinctive, and therefore can no longer be distinguished from executive power. Thus the main or principal business of Parliament is one which cannot be properly described as legislative. The truth is that a circular argument influences us here. We have grown accustomed to call granting money legislation, because it is done by the body which we call the Legislature. But if you still fancy that it might be possible to frame a definition of law and legislation that might include the granting of taxes, let me ask you this: if it takes legislation to grant a tax, does it not take legislation to make war? Surely it is absurd to maintain that the former act is more of the nature of a law than the latter. But in England when war is to be made it is not made by Parliament but by the Ministry. You will observe that I do not raise the question whether it is reasonable or unreasonable that parliamentary power should be necessary to raise the smallest tax, but not necessary to declare the greatest war. I inquire only wherein the difference consists between parliamentary and ministerial power. Now I think you must admit one of two things. Either granting taxes is not legislation; but in this case the principal power that Parliament possesses is not legislative; or making war is legisla-tion; but in this case the Ministry, too, have legislative power.

The theory I am discussing would represent the Ministry and Parliament as having each respect-ively its province of affairs in which the other has no right to interfere, whereas the very essence of our constitutional system lies in the negation of this, and in the principle that the Ministry and the Parliament have absolutely the same subjects of interest and occupation. The difference is strikingly brought before us by a remarkable letter written by Napoleon to the Abbé Siéyès at the time when he was meditat-ing his *coup d'état*. No one, he says, can have greater respect for the independence of the legislative power than he; but legislation does not mean finance, criticism of the administration, or ninety-nine out of

the hundred things with which in England the
Parliament occupies itself. The Legislature should
legislate, that is, construct grand laws on scientific
principles of jurisprudence, but it must respect the
independence of the executive as it desires its own
independence to be respected. It must not criticise
the government, and as its legislative labours are
essentially of a scientific kind there can be no reason
why its debates should be reported.

You see at once that he has in view a system
precisely opposite to the English. With us whatever
the Government does becomes a subject of discussion
in the House. No appointment can be made, no
circular be issued from any government department,
but it is liable to be canvassed in debate. And when
a Minister is thus called to account he does not rise
in his place and ask Mr. Speaker whether it is orderly
in a legislative assembly to mention or discuss matters
which can only concern the executive power. On
the contrary, he renders his account with anxious
humility, and we have seen powerful governments endangered by such incidents as that one Minister had
returned a rough answer, another had jobbed an
appointment, a third had evaded a statute. Parliament, in short, is interested in everything that the
Ministry can do. Its resolutions, its votes of censure
or of confidence, in which it does not even pretend
to legislate, are regarded as just as important and

perhaps even more interesting than its ponderous achievements of legislation.

And now look at the Ministry. Does that confine itself to exercising executive power ? Really I must apologise for raising such questions. Who does not know what a clamour is raised whenever a new government takes office, how we ask what will they do ? what is their programme ? have they really a policy ? or do they really mean to face Parliament with no policy at all ? Policy ? what is this ? It commonly means the introduction into Parliament of a number of bills; in other words, it means legislation. What we call the policy of a government is scarcely at all its exercise of executive power ; a Ministry which confined itself to that would be said to do nothing. Imagine how it would be received should a Minister in reply to the appeals of the House say that he was and would continue to be industrious in his office, that that was his policy, and that as Minister he could have no other policy, for as Minister he had only executive power ; in his legislative capacity he had no more responsibility than other members of the House, and that his policy as Member would consist in faithfully representing the interests of his constituency.

The truth is that the Ministry, and the Ministry as such, has legislative power in a far higher sense and greater degree than Parliament. It has the task of initiating, designing, and working out the details of almost all important legislation. Nominally, of course, no Act can pass but by the will of the majority of the House. But consider under what conditions this power is exercised. In almost all important cases the bill is brought forward upon the responsibility of the Ministry. Now the Ministry, it is understood, has a majority in the House, otherwise it would not be a Ministry. In important cases, therefore, their consent is secured beforehand—at least it is known that if the Parliament refuses an important bill they by the same act expel the Ministry from office. For a Ministry in dealing with an important bill will stake its own existence upon ·success. It will allow the House a certain freedom in dealing with its minor provisions. Some things the House will be permitted to alter, but in its main parts the House must take the bill or be prepared to dismiss the Ministry. Now by the very nature of our system the House will not be prepared to do this, for to dismiss the Ministry means at the same time to install the opposite party in office : but by the hypothesis the majority of the House are favourable to the Ministry and adverse to its opponents ; they have been sent to Parliament to support the Ministers and to oppose their opponents. Now, if by legislative power be meant a free power of deciding what shall become and what shall not become law, can it be said that the House of Commons standing in this relation to the Ministers possesses in itself and apart from them much legislative power? With respect to any given proposal it has little freedom. Its one substantial power is that of turning out the Ministers with whom in the main it agrees, and substituting in their place other Ministers with whom in the main it differs. Such a power as this, instead of being called a power of legislation, should perhaps be rather called a *veto* on legislation, and a *veto* which it is not easy practically to use.

To sum up, then, it is said that Parliament has legislative power but not executive. In reality it has but a certain veto on legislation, which it exercises under great difficulties, and a certain power of altering the minor details of bills. But besides this it has a most formidable power of oversight and criticism upon the proceedings of the executive. Again, it is said that the Ministry have executive power, but not legislative. Executive power they have, but only under the strict and jealous control of the House; legislative power they have in a far greater degree than the House, so much so that the House has ordinarily only so much legislative power as the Ministry consent to allow it. It may be said, in short, as in execution the Ministry is afraid of the House, so in legislation the House is mortally afraid of the Ministry.

The source of error has been that technically our Ministers are also members of the House; this has led us to imagine that in legislation they do not act as Ministers but as members ; but there can be no greater mistake.

The result of all these considerations is to show that that tempting image of Parliament as representing the general meeting of a society, and the Minister as its paid secretary, who carries into effect the wishes expressed by the members, is utterly misleading. The Minister is not the servant of Parliament, but its king. He does not carry into effect the wishes of others, but his own wishes. It is a sort of high treason against the state when the Minister gives up his own view in deference to Parliament. If he must give up something, it is his duty to give up, not his view, but his office.

But now, if the Minister is king, not servant, of Parliament, what is Parliament? The remark I just made will suggest the answer. Parliament is king-maker, and at the same time can deprive its king of his office. It cannot dictate what he shall do ; on the contrary, he dictates to it. But it can bid him retire, and it can put another Minister in his room. And this is its main function. In legislation, as I have urged, its power is more nominal than real. But it is really true that the Minister is such because Parliament wills it, and ceases to be such when Parliament wills it.

There is something very singular—I imagine

unique—in the unceasing interest with which in England we follow the proceedings of Parliament. What would become of conversation among us if there were no Parliament? We should all be struck dumb. This is often explained by saying that the Englishman is a political animal, and King Louis Philippe used to say that the French would not have so many revolutions if they could learn the English habit of talking politics after dinner. But the cause is more special. Mr. Woodrow Wilson, in his interesting volume on the American constitution, entitled *Congressional Politics*, remarks that no one in America reads the debates of Congress. Not a few there are, he says, in America who read the English debates, but none who read the debates of Congress. Surely this is not because the American is less political in his tastes than the Englishman. Surely the reason is this, that Congress is only a legislative assembly, but not an assembly that makes and unmakes the government. For such is the fact. The President in America is chosen for four years by popular election; he chooses his Ministers, who have no seats in Congress, and are not, as a general rule, dependent on its vote. But this being so, the session of Congress is not, like the session of · our Parliament, a drama. There is no important action in it.

We may see, then, in what we ourselves feel the

importance of Parliament to consist. Why do we
read the debates? Simply to see whether the
Government is likely to stay in or to go out. We
follow the session with precisely the same interest
with which we follow a boat-race, and the successive
division lists show us whether the Opposition is or is
not gaining upon the Government. We may no
doubt occasionally feel interested also in the fate of
some particular bill, but what fixes the attention of
the whole nation with unflagging eagerness upon the
proceedings of Parliament is this, that by our system
no important bill can fail without bringing the
Government down with it.

It seems to me, then, that the theory I have suggested is fully confirmed by our system as it is now,
and also that the other theory might have been seen,
even in the time of Montesquieu, to be incorrect. I
do not assert, however, that in the time of Montesquieu it would have been possible to discern the king-
making power of Parliament. The present system
was then only in embryo. Godolphin and Walpole
were not such kings as modern Ministers are, nor
were they in the same degree dependent for their
position on Parliament. Even those who, near the
end of the eighteenth century, devised the Constitution of the United States seem not to have
been aware how much the king's power had declined—that, for example, his veto had perished,—

nor how much the Minister was taking the king's place.

The eighteenth century phase, as well as the seventeenth century phase, of our Constitution must be reserved for separate treatment.

LECTURE II

I DREW last week a distinction which may have struck you as somewhat subtle. It is commonly held, I said, that Parliament rules, and the Minister is but the servant of Parliament. Not at all; the Minister rules, and is the king, not the servant, of the nation and the Parliament alike. But Parliament makes him king, and can unmake him. A distinction without a difference, perhaps you say. If Parliament can dismiss a Minister at pleasure, it is evident that it can force the Minister by the threat of dismissal to obey it,—it is evident that the Minister will execute the will of Parliament in order to retain office.

But there is all the difference in the world between a representative and a delegate. We recognise this in the case of members of Parliament. The member is sent to the House of Commons to speak the mind of his constituents. Does that mean that he is not to speak his own mind? Not at all; he represents the constituency not by giving up his mind to theirs, but by having the same mind.

Q

Accordingly we think that if the representative holds conscientiously an opinion different from that of his constituents, it may or may not be proper for him to retire, but it cannot be proper for him to set .his own opinion aside and adopt slavishly that of his constituents. In other words, by becoming their representative he becomes in no sense their servant, and it is his duty in all cases to do what he himself thinks right, not what they think right.

This is true in a still higher degree of the Minister. He has the same mind as the Parliament; that is why he is Minister; but he has not borrowed their mind. They choose him, not because he is pliant, not because he has no opinion of his own, and will readily conform himself to any view that may become prevalent among themselves. They choose him for the very opposite reason,— because his convictions are, or at least seem, exceptionally strong, because they can count upon him that he will have the energy and force of one whose heart is in his work. It has always been recognised as a corruption of the ministerial system when the Minister has waited on the good pleasure of the House, when he has been ready to take back his plans and bring them up again amended, to say to the House :

> The piece, you think, is incorrect ; why, take it !
> I'm all submission ; what you'd have it, make it.

Why is this a corruption? Why ought this not to be? If the House were sovereign and the Minister but its secretary, such conduct would be reasonable and natural, as we hold it to be in the secretary of a society. But it is not so. The Minister is indeed chosen by the House, but he is chosen to rule, not to serve; the House does not dictate to him, but commissions him to dictate to itself. Perhaps the word Minister may contribute to mislead us; for does not Minister mean servant? But I need hardly remind you that the Minister is not Minister to the Parliament, but to the Crown. On the whole, then, the English Minister is a ruler. If he is dependent upon others who can make and unmake him, so is every ruler, as I showed in a former lecture. What is singular in his position is only the curious refinement of machinery by which the government-making power is enabled to exercise its function at pleasure and without delay.

In a great number of states this power, though it exists, for it must exist in all states, has, as I showed, no organ. It is therefore only called into action by extreme pressure, and then it acts with spasmodic violence. But I have propounded the theory that generally where we see an assembly taking a leading part in public affairs, we are to regard it as the organ of the government-making power, and I now consider myself to have shown this theory to afford a sufficient explanation of one prominent example. In this instance we see that the organ has a peculiar mode of action, viz. that the ruler is deposed by failing to get a majority in the assembly upon an important question. But as this system is very peculiar,—only found in England and some European states, which in recent times have adopted it from England,—and yet the political assembly is by no means uncommon, you will ask, in what way does the government-making organ usually perform its function? Putting aside for the present difficult cases which may require special investigation, I must try to show that the theory is widely applicable by pointing to some simple mode of action which in the ordinary constitutional or re-publican state supplies the place of this refinement. And I think I shall find this easy.

In the English system the truth has to be detected under disguises and bewildering misnomers. The ruler is not called ruler; oh no! he is a Minister, he has received Her Majesty's commands to form an administration. The ruler is not appointed by Parliament; heaven forbid! the ruler succeeds by hereditary right; still less can he be deposed by ·Parliament, for indeed no power on earth can depose him! It is only by obstinately disregarding these assertions and fixing our eyes resolutely upon the facts that we discover that the person called Minister, that is, servant, would be more properly called magistrate or ruler, and that he is virtually, though not nominally, appointed and also dismissed at pleasure by Parliament.[1]

Now in other states a direct course has been taken. The rulers have been actually elected by the assembly. This has been the method of appointment. Deposition was more difficult. How bring to trial a man who at the moment was in possession of all the power of the state? The difficulty has been met by a simple expedient, that of choosing the magistrate for a short term only. Misconduct in a ruler, even extreme misconduct, may be endured if the people have a security that it will soon come to an end. Thus in the eighteenth century, when our American colonists

[1] "You must begin by distinguishing two great developments which have taken place in modern England, the development which has given so much power to the representative assembly, and the other which has given so much power to the Minister. You must consider also that he wields this power in accordance with the rules of the party system. These things are wholly distinct. Parliament might have gained supreme power and yet the Minister might not have taken the place of the Crown. And again, these things might have happened without the establishment of that strict party system which we see, under which the leaders of Parliament and holders of ministerial departments are persons who agree in opinion on the great questions of the day.

"With us these three things go together, and it is the sum total of them that makes the English Constitution of the present day : (1) the decision of all questions by the vote of a representative assembly ; (2) the unbounded power of a ministerial cabinet combined with the nominal maintenance of royalty ; (3) the party system. And all these things have reappeared in some Continental states, e.g. Belgium and Italy, with the difference that the party system has not there worked with the same regularity, a number of cliques taking the place of the two great rival parties which have commonly confronted each other among ourselves."—From the Seventh Lecture of the 1891 Course.

tried to reproduce the substance of our English Constitution without the legal fictions in which it was
wrapped up, they created a President who should be
chosen by popular election.   They might have
entrusted the choice of him to Congress, and some
think they ought to have done so, but they considered
that as he was to be the king of the whole people, and
to lean on universal consent, the whole people ought
to take part in his election.   So much for the appointment of the ruler; for his deposition they provided a
method of impeachment, but as they did not consider
this sufficient they decreed also that the President
should hold office for four years only, so that the
citizens of the United States might have the assurance
that the worst reign in their annals should not be
much longer than that of James II. in England.

The history of what is called liberty in the Athenian
and Roman republics shows in full the development
of this system.   Out of hereditary kingship we trace
the growth of a system by which popular assemblies
elect their rulers for a term of one year.   This is
common to the constitutional history of Athens and
Rome, but the Athenian system has some peculiarities
which require a special explanation.   I will dwell for
a moment on the Roman system in order to show you
how easily and naturally our theory may be applied
to it.

The assemblies at Rome were called *comitia*.   They

were three in number, but of the three one was in the
historical period effete; the other two had certain
differences upon which it is not necessary here to
dwell. By the side of these assemblies was a sort
of council, neither popular nor representative, but
similar to our ancient Witenagemot, or to our modern
House of Lords, called the Senate. Power in the
strict sense of the word may be said to have been
confined to the popular assemblies; what the Senate
possessed was described in Latin as *auctoritas*, that is,
a high kind of influence, which on certain subjects
was allowed to have the force of law. Now when we
compare these assemblies to our Parliament we see
that their main function is one which among us is
formally performed neither by Parliament nor by
the constituencies, that of electing magistrates. In
Roman politics and in English alike popular election
is a very prominent topic, but the offices which are
filled by election are quite different. In England we
elect members of Parliament, but in Rome, as I said
last term, every citizen might be called a member of
Parliament, and the Senate was not strictly elective
at all. Elections were held at Rome for those offices
which we call executive, for the Ministry, in short,
though the Romans more correctly called them the
Magistracies; and to make these elections was the
main business of the assemblies.

At Rome, then, much more evidently than in

England, the assembly was the government-making power. In legislation it had much the same share as we have seen that our Parliament has. As with us, the active and constructive part of legislation belongs to the Ministry, so, or rather still more, it belonged at Rome to the magistrates; to the assembly in both states remains the passive part, the right of ratification. But to make the government, which here is virtually the function of the assembly, was there its function avowedly and technically. So much so that the word *comitia*, which is the name of the assembly, is also the recognised Latin word for an election.

The assembly made the government then; did the assembly also unmake or destroy it? No. But in that period of Roman history about which we have full information, the magistrates were elected for the term of one year only. The consuls, or secretaries of state, the prætors or judges, the ædiles, or commissioners of public works and police, the quæstors or junior lords of the treasury, the tribunes or guardians of the poor, all the magistrates except the censor, whose office was often in abeyance, had an annual term. Accordingly, their power of doing harm was strictly limited. Their competence was indeed extremely ample. The magistrate's edict decided many things without appeal. For example, the whole system of legal procedure seems to have depended absolutely upon the will of the prætor, whose edict, issued at the commencement of his term, might subvert all received usage. But, in Lord Camden's phrase, it was only "a forty days' despotism." Time speedily undid any possible mischief, and the consciousness of this limitation tamed and humbled the ambition of the magistrate.

Of the process by which this system grew up we have but imperfect information. But the traditional statement that, after the expulsion of Tarquin, the Romans resolved to abolish monarchy and to set up a republic is probably not very accurate either in form or in fact. I have already argued that the distinction of monarchy and republic is unreal, and, if it were real, it was probably quite unknown to the primitive generation that expelled Tarquin. The story itself, moreover, suggests that the change made was not sudden or abrupt but gradual, for we are told that after the flight of Tarquin a member of his family, Collatinus, held the consulship, and that a second revolution was required to rid the city of him. Just so, after the fall of the Bourbons in 1830, a younger branch in the person of Louis Philippe held the sceptre for eighteen years. Now, when we look closely at the story we find that there is absolutely no reason to suppose that the first magistrates appointed after the flight of Tarquin were consuls holding office for one year. For the story of the establishment of the consulate is but a vague tradition without chronology. The later Romans when they read of consuls could scarcely avoid thinking of annual consuls such as they were themselves accustomed to. But it seems most probable that there was no such cataclysm as the tradition describes, that there was no sudden abolition of the office of king, no sudden creation of the annual consulate, but a gradual decline of royal power such as has been witnessed in England. After Tarquin, Collatinus seems to have succeeded by hereditary right. Whether or not he was called consul, it is probable that his term of office was not yet limited. Then perhaps by a series of changes the monarchy shrank up into the annual consulate of later times, which indeed in form and ceremonial always continued to resemble monarchy. If so, we may see that the development consisted in two things—first, in making the office elective instead of hereditary ; secondly, in reducing the term of it to a single year.

It seems, then, that our theory is confirmed by the example of ancient Rome as well as by that of modern England. In describing shortly the constitutional development of ancient Rome we may henceforth reject the unmeaning formula that monarchy was abolished and a republic set up. Henceforth we shall prefer to say that a government-making organ was developed, and that in order to make room for its action the

monarchy was made elective and restricted to an
annual term.

And when, later, what is called the republic de-
cayed and monarchy (so-called) revived, it may be
seen that this process was reversed. Augustus caused
himself to be elected consul year after year. In
other words, the revival of monarchical power was
marked by the abolition of the limited term. Other
offices also the Emperor held in a similar manner
year after year, and on coins the tenth year of an
emperor's reign is expressed by the words "tribune
ten times."

I return now, as I promised, to English constitutional history, in order to examine that earlier
phase in which, though certainly the modern Minister,
chosen by Parliament to rule the country and deposed
by Parliament at pleasure, did not yet exist, still
we had a parliamentary government, and resisted
despotism with most conspicuous success. What
greater triumph has constitutionalism ever had than
the Revolution of 1688 ? Yet in 1688 Parliament did
not assert that it existed in order to make and unmake governments, but only at the utmost that in a
desperate extremity Parliament might venture to
interfere in a slight degree with the fixed law by
which the succession of rulers in the state, like the
succession of proprietors on a landed estate, was
regulated. Constitutionalism, then, it would appear,

may exist without any government-making organ, yet it is in this organ that our theory finds the essential feature of constitutionalism. This objection I will now deal with.

I begin by admitting very freely the facts upon which the objection is based. This is not always done. That Whig view of our history which has been fashionable since the time of Hallam and Macaulay exaggerates the importance of the Revolution of 1688 so much, that many of us, I think, suppose that the present ministerial system has prevailed ever since that date. We fancy that the abeyance of royal power dates from the disuse of the royal veto in William III.'s reign, and Macaulay traces the rise of the party system to the same period. I take quite a different view. It seems to me that royal power was not weakened by the Revolution, that William and Anne were just as powerful sovereigns, in some respects more powerful sovereigns, than their predecessors. I do not discover any symptoms of decline in royal power till about the middle of George II.'s reign, and even after this the Monarchy had a period of revival. Party principles began to prevail, in my opinion, at the accession of the House of Hanover, but for a long time after that they were materially different from the party principles of our own time. Altogether the modern system, so far from being traceable back to the

Revolution, that is, to the seventeenth century, is scarcely to be discovered even in the eighteenth, and has taken shape in the main since the first Reform Bill.

The constitutional development of modern England has not been a single movement culminating in the Revolution, but two distinct movements of which the one belongs mainly to the seventeenth century, the other partly to the eighteenth and partly to the nineteenth. The result which has been attained by these movements I have already described. A very powerful government has been created, and by the side of it a government-making organ highly sensitive and working with peculiar ease. This government is called a Ministry, and it is held together by a Monarch, who is called the Prime Minister. But it is the later, not the earlier, development which has given this character to the Prime Minister and to the Ministry. I must take some pains to point this out.

We have seen great Ministers in our own time, but surely, so perhaps you may say, there were great Ministers in the eighteenth, in the seventeenth, ay, in the sixteenth century too. In what were the Pitts, or Walpole, or Marlborough, or Clarendon, or Strafford, or Buckingham, or Burleigh, or Wolsey, so decidedly inferior to the Ministers of this age that they should be put in quite a different class? Only in one point, but then this point is all-important,—in exclusive dependence upon the Parliament, as the organ of public opinion.

The change has been gradual. The Minister is now dependent solely upon the Parliament and the people. There was a transition-period, which may be said roughly to cover the whole reign of George III., when popular influence was extremely useful to a Minister, and some Ministers for a short time depended exclusively upon it; but in that period the support of the Crown was equally, and for the most part more essential, and only such Ministers held a secure position as enjoyed, like the younger Pitt, the favour of the Crown and the people together. But if we ascend beyond this period, beyond the elder Pitt, the first Minister of public opinion, we come to an age— and still we are distant seventy years from the Revolution of 1688—when the Minister rested on the Crown and not on the people or the Parliament, when he was still in fact as well as in name His Majesty's Minister. Such were all Ministers in England till William Pitt the elder forced the gates of power by the help of the people in the year 1757. In that old time the Minister was not necessarily at all less great or less prominent and shining than now. He might outshine at that time the king who made him as much as now the Parliament who makes him. In France under the absolute king, great Ministers, Richelieu, Mazarin, Fleury, were more usual even than in free England. This is because kings, where they have as much power as .they will, are often enough glad to devolve the burden of government, either wholly or in part, upon a wise man. But this is at their pleasure, and the greatest Minister under that old system, a Marlborough or a Burleigh or a Wolsey, cannot properly be called a ruler or monarch, since his power depended upon the caprice of an individual, who, moreover, was always at liberty in particular cases to reject his advice.

I would advise any one who would understand how little the Minister was dependent on Parliament and how much on the Crown, even long after the Revolution, to study in Coxe's *Life of Marlborough* the change of Ministry which took place in 1710. It was then that Godolphin went out and Harley came in. You will see how completely the decision lies with Queen Anne. The Queen wants an adviser; that is all. Godolphin has served her for eight years, but they are no longer on such agreeable terms as formerly. She no longer feels the same confidence in him. She begins to wish to hear other advice. It is rumoured that she talks to Harley in private. Then the Duke of Shrewsbury is appointed Lord Chamberlain. Shrewsbury to be sure is not of the opposite party; still the appointment looks a little odd, and Godolphin does not like it. Thus suspicion grows, and the breach between Queen and Minister ·

widens until at last he receives a letter from her in
which she tells him. that she means to put the
Treasury into other hands, but that she will give him
a pension of four thousand a year, and that he may
break his staff instead of returning it to her, which
will be "more easy to us both." From first to last
scarcely a word of Parliament, or of public opinion,
though no doubt it was true even then that a
sovereign of moderate prudence was attentive to the
changes of public feeling, and that Godolphin might
have held office longer, but for the agitation produced by Sacheverell's trial.

Well then, in what sense was England a constitutional country in Queen Anne's reign, since the
Minister is merely an adviser, dismissed as soon as
sovereign is tired of him? And yet Queen Anne had
helped to expel her own father for violating English
liberties, and was at this very time keeping her
brother out of his inheritance in order to protect
the English people against arbitrary power.

My answer is in one word this: Parliament was
not then avowedly a government-making organ, and
the doctrine that the ruler of the country could be
dismissed and another appointed in his place by
Parliament would have been rejected with abhor-
rence. But yet we need neither deny that England
was already a constitutional country, nor need we
abandon our theory and seek for some new definition

of constitutionalism, for the power claimed then by
Parliament, and asserted decisively at the Revolution, was of the same kind, though much more modest
in degree. Not an unlimited power of making and
unmaking governments, far from it, but still a certain power in certain circumstances of making and
unmaking governments was asserted by Parliament,
and it was in virtue of this power, and not of some
other power, for example legislative power, possessed
by Parliament, that England might be called a constitutional country.

Very irresolutely in words, but without any
practical hesitation, Parliament had deposed a king.
By doing so they had asserted a right of destroying
the government. They had been just as reluctant
to assert the right of creating a government; it had
been their intention to allow the rule of succession to
operate in filling the vacant throne. Mary was to
succeed James precisely as if he had died or
abdicated. But they had been hurried farther than
they intended, and had been forced to make William
king.

Whatever then it might profess, Parliament was
really to a certain extent a government-making
organ. No doubt only in an extreme case, but still
in a certain case, where the King departed from all
the traditions of his office, it could depose a king.
And within very narrow limits it could choose a

king. Not that it professed for a moment to make the Crown elective, or dreamt of asserting a power of putting Halifax or Danby or Churchill in the vacant seat of James II. But it could venture to confer royalty upon one who, both by birth and marriage, was a member of the royal house, when he had rendered an inestimable service to the state.

The unmaking and making of governments is at all times a serious matter not to be taken in hand lightly. Under the modern system it is indeed always in a certain sense in hand. No sooner does a new government take office than we begin to watch the division list in order to see whether it is likely to be turned out again. Yet even now, when the government‑making power of Parliament is so supreme and its machinery works so easily, government would be felt to be impossible if no margin were allowed to the Ministry, if on the slightest pretext the support of Parliament were withdrawn from them and their majority deserted them. In Queen Anne's time it may be said that Parliament had the same power, but that the reluctance to use it, which even now is traceable, was immeasurably greater. Modern constitutionalism means that a government in England falls in no long time after it has begun to be unpopular; constitutionalism in Queen Anne's time meant that a king who incurred dislike and disapprobation, going beyond a certain point, could and would be dismissed by Parliament, and that the Crown would be given at the discretion of Parliament to some other member of the royal family. The difference no doubt is great, but it is still only a difference of degree. Compared with despotic states, England under Queen Anne may be said to belong to the same class as England under Queen Victoria.

Even now, as I have said, the true function of Parliament, as the government-making organ, is somewhat disguised. Parliament still professes to be a legislative body, a money-granting body, almost anything rather than a government-making body. In Queen Anne's time the disguise was so deep and impenetrable that it would not have occurred to any one to speak of Parliament as a maker or destroyer of governments. Only twice in a century had it ventured to destroy a government. It had destroyed that of James II., and earlier that of Charles I. ; but of its treatment of Charles I. it had afterwards bitterly repented. It had repented, too, of the revolutionary governments which it had set up in the place of his. It had also on two occasions created a durable government in England. It had made William king, and it had conferred the Crown on the heir of the Electress Sophia. During nearly two-thirds of the Stuart period Parliament had been in pretty constant session, and had worked industriously ; yet only in these rare cases, and then only on the plea of absolute neces-

sity, had it pretended to be a government-making
organ.

Nevertheless, in real importance these few exceptional acts far outweighed a whole century of granting taxes and redressing grievances. A single
successful precedent like the Revolution of 1688
altered the whole character of government in England.
Shall we say it made government *responsible?* Let
us remember the conclusion at which we arrived last
term. All monarchical government is responsible,
for all such government must rest upon the consent
of some body of persons, and this consent must in
some way be earned. Under the Tudors, when the
power of Parliament was inconsiderable, government, as we have seen, was responsible, and
supported by public opinion, so much so that it was
able to dispense with the support of an army.
What new thing then was introduced by the
Revolution of 1688?

Our theory supplies the answer. States are of two
kinds. In some states the power that supports the
government is latent and has no organ; in such
states the responsibility of government is, as it were,
a secret. Those who are in fact able to control the
government are not conscious of the power; the
government assumes an air of irresponsibility, declares itself to rule by divine right, and in every
way studies to conceal its own dependence. In the

other class of states the power that makes the government has an organ through which it can act with regularity and legal formality. Where this organ exists the responsibility of government cannot be concealed. It is not more real than in the other class of states, but it is not merely real—it is also evident and undeniable.

England passed into this class of states at the Revolution of 1688, through which it was shown, not that government could be brought to account, but that it could be brought to account with legal formality and through a qualified organ. Many kings had been brought to account in England— Edward II., Richard II., Richard III., Charles I. Their fate had proved sufficiently, if any one doubted it, that one man cannot with impunity tyrannise over thousands. But those revolutions had been lawless and terrible, and had disquieted the conscience of the nation. Most of all had the last revolution, that which overthrew Charles I., appeared lawless, precisely because it had tried to observe the forms of law. Parliament had been set in motion, but it was a sham Parliament, a Parliament mutilated by the soldiers. Accordingly a violent re-action had followed, and the paradoxical doctrine of the irresponsibility of monarchy had found favour for a time. England still belonged to the class of states in which there is no government-making organ.

It passed out of this class of states at the Revolution of 1688. Then was discovered a way of destroying and creating government sufficiently legal and formal to satisfy the conscience of the nation. This time it was found possible to use Parliament as a government-making organ without monstrous perversion and abuse. A revolution was made which after ages could look back upon with satisfaction, approval, and pride, to approve which has ever since been the principal point of our political orthodoxy.

In one word, then, our present England is widely different from the England of Queen Anne, but yet they belong to the same class of states, and may both alike be called constitutional as contrasted with despotic, because both alike have a government-making organ in Parliament. The difference is that under the present system Government, that is, the Ministry, rests solely upon the active support of Parliament, and falls as soon as that support is withdrawn; whereas under the old system the Government, that is, the King, rested on the passive support of Parliament, and only fell when Parliament was roused into active hostility. We may say, perhaps, that under the modern system it requires the action of Parliament to support a ruler, whereas formerly it required the action of Parliament to overthrow him.

LECTURE III

WE are engaged in an attempt to classify a multitude of things which we regard as living organisms, viz. states. As living organisms these things may be expected to have the characteristic of passing into each other by almost insensible gradations. For life works in this way. When we deal with inorganic things or with abstractions, classification is a comparatively simple matter, because here the differences are large and plain. The geometer has no difficulty in describing the difference between a triangle and a parallelogram, and is in no danger of mistaking one for the other. Nor is the chemist in danger of confounding air with water or nitrogen with oxygen. It is otherwise with animals and plants. Here you have innumerable small variations. Some individuals are widely different from each other, but the distance between them is filled up by a number of intermediate forms. And since everywhere in the domain of life we find development at work, we are not surprised to find here not only organs, but rudiments of organs that have not yet come fully into play, and survivals of organs that have become useless.

Political philosophers in earlier times did not much apply these physiological conceptions to states. They distinguished classes of states by very plain, inelastic tests, and, as a natural consequence, they conceived historical revolutions, when states have changed their form, as much more abrupt and cataclysmal than history shows them to have been. In the last lecture I gave you an example of this when I spoke of the fall of monarchy in primitive Rome. Historians have described this as if the shepherd warriors who clustered round the shrines of the Palatine and the Capitoline had been familiar with the Aristotelian classification of states, and had on a particular day resolved, in consequence of events which had thrown a strong light on the disadvantages of monarchy, to discard that political form and to adopt another form, that called republic. I remarked that nothing of this sort seems really to have happened, that monarchy was perhaps not consciously abolished at all, nor a republic consciously set up, but that the monarchy dwindled by a gradual process, so that after a certain lapse of time, perhaps after a hundred years, it became natural to say that monarchy had ceased to exist. And I remarked that just in the same gradual way when the republic in its turn declined, monarchy was restored by a series of small alterations between the time of Marius and that of Augustus.

If such is the general character of political develop-ment we must be prepared in the classification of states to find a great many transitional forms. By the side of states in which the organs are fully developed we may expect to find others in which the organs are rudimentary, and if this is true in general it will be true of the particular organ we have lately been considering, the government-making organ. We have laid it down that some states have this organ and others want it. The former we may call despotic states, the latter we might perhaps call constitutional. But we may now proceed to lay it down that in many states this organ is imperfectly developed, in some perhaps so imperfectly that a question may be raised whether it exists at all. Such in general, then, is the view I take of England at the end of the seventeenth century. It is a constitutional state, but imperfectly developed. The government-making organ is dis-cernible, but it is only half differentiated.

If this were so, nothing would be more natural than that it should be misunderstood and misdescribed at the time. It is by comparing Parliament as it then was with the same Parliament as it now is after the further development of a century and a half that we have arrived at our conception of it. But this comparison the philosophers of the seventeenth and eighteenth centuries were not able to make, and therefore they were liable to misconceive the essential function of Parliament—the rather because the comparison of other states gave them no help. Imperfectly developed as the English Parliament was, it was far in advance of any assemblies of estates that could be found in other countries.

Again, nothing was more natural than that the process of differentiation should be exceedingly slow, drawn out over more than a century. Development in a large country-state is always slow and difficult, and England was hampered also by its connection with Scotland and Ireland. The wonder rather is that the differentiation was possible at all than that it should be accomplished slowly. From the thirteenth century to the sixteenth Parliament had already existed without becoming a government-making organ, and in other countries assemblies not essentially different had also existed for centuries without developing in this manner.

But as the English Parliament is the classical example of a Parliament, it seems to me worth while to arrive at a clear conception, not only of its function, but also of its history and of the stages of its development. I took some pains in the last lecture to describe the degree of development which it had acquired at the beginning of the eighteenth century, and before that I had described it as it is in our own day. I will proceed to fill up the outline of the history by tracing through what stages it arrived at the condition in which the eighteenth century found it, and then through what further stages it developed itself into what we now see. You will understand that I shall attempt nothing like a continuous history, that I shall content myself with marking epochs, with distinguishing phases.

In the seventeenth century the growth of Parliament occupies the foreground of our history as it had never done in the three earlier centuries during which Parliament had existed. In the sixteenth century we find Parliament subservient to the Crown. Then in the latter part of the reign of James I. it gathers vigour and aggressive spirit. Against Charles it becomes rebellious, plunges into a war in which it proves victorious, but is itself at the same moment overcome by the military power. The country falls under the yoke of imperialism, until the military power in its turn is broken by intestine division. At the Restoration, King and Parliament are once more confronted with each other, as they had stood at the moment when the Civil War broke out, the whole period of discord being as far as possible cancelled and forgotten. But after a time a second struggle takes place between the second son of Charles and the Parliament, a struggle not unlike that in which Charles himself had engaged, but shorter and less tragic; and whereas the former struggle had ended first in the complete victory of Parliament and then in its defeat and surrender, this later one, conducted with more modesty and circumspection, ends in a solid and decisive victory for the Parliament.

These are the superficial facts which every one knows. What the total result of the long controversy was is not so generally understood, but I have already considered this question in a summary manner. I proceed now to inquire through what stages and in what way this result was attained by the struggles of the seventeenth century.

In the first struggle, that of the reign of Charles I., we see an audacious experiment, but one which by universal consent ended on the whole in failure. Parliament undertakes to make and un-make governments. It sits in judgment on the King, it abolishes the kingly office and establishes a new kind of government. But so disastrously ill does the experiment turn out that in the next generation the whole nation repudiates it, and for a time the prevalent opinion is not only that a wrong method had been chosen, but that actually a wrong object had been pursued, and that Parliament should not pretend in any way to make and unmake govern-ment—that government ought to be irresponsible. This failure is partly retrieved by the second struggle, from which it appears that Parliament may after all pretend to a certain power of making and unmaking government, if only this power is used with due caution.

So far, then, it appears that the first struggle had been successful only in proposing a question, and had failed altogether to find the true answer to it. But was it such a complete failure? Did Parliament at the Restoration fall back to the position which it had occupied when the civil contest began, and replace the Stuarts upon the almost imperial throne of the Tudors? We must not suppose this for a moment.

The system established after the Restoration in 1660 was wholly different from that which had preceded the meeting of the Long Parliament in 1640. It seems to me that the view of English history which has been made fashionable by Macaulay underrates the importance of the Restoration, as it in some respects overrates the importance of the Revolution. At the Restoration, as I understand the matter, and not at the Revolution, the English monarchy and system of government took the form which they retained throughout the eighteenth century.

Of course I could point to many changes which date from the Restoration. But in a large view of our history the Restoration takes its character, not from these minor changes, but from one change of capital importance which it introduced. It is the epoch from which we may say that *the permanence of Parliament* dates.

Before Parliament could become an effective government-making organ it was necessary that it should become a fixed and permanent feature of our body-politic. Now, it acquired this character at the Restoration, and we may say that herein consists the solid enduring benefit which the nation gained from its struggle with Charles I.

At a much earlier period, under the Plantagenets, Parliament had, it is true, already had this character. Professor Stubbs will tell you that in the fourteenth century Parliament was usually convened every year, and often more than once in the year. I should be led too far if I inquired into the early centuries of Parliament, and therefore I must content myself with remarking that this had ceased to be the case under the Tudors. Take down the records of Parliament, for instance, under Queen Elizabeth; inquire how often in that reign Parliament was summoned, and how long the session of it lasted; you will certainly perceive that the Parliament of those times was not only less powerful, but was a wholly different institution from the Parliament of our age. Parliament now has a permanent unity and a continuous history; it is a living thing; it is so, politically speaking, in a higher degree than anything else in England; so much so that I often complain that in the eyes of historians it eclipses everything else, and that in recent times what is called the history of England is often only the history of Parliament. But Parliament now meets every year, and sits half the year. Now, look at the Parliament of Queen Elizabeth. It met, I think, about ten times in a reign of forty-five years, and each time its session lasted about a month, or two months. The whole time during which Parliament sat was perhaps a year and a half in forty-five, and between these sessions, so short and few, there occurred intervals of three or four years.

Now, I say that such a Parliament could hardly be called an organ at all. It could have no policy, no systematic action, no corporate character. Such an Assembly was less like our Parliament than like the States-General of the old French Monarchy. France, too, had sometimes grand meetings of the Estates, and it is not to be supposed that these meetings were unimportant. But they only occurred at long intervals — perhaps once in a reign, or three or four times in a century. Accordingly, it could not be said that the States-General formed any part of the French Constitution. In the ordinary routine of French political life the States-General had no place whatever. Its function was neither to govern nor to control government. It was called in exceptionally when there was need of some fundamental change, of

a new remedy for some new evil. As for the last
time in 1789, so in earlier centuries, when the state
was at a deadlock, when men were at their wit's end,
they called out for the States-General.

The English Parliament under Elizabeth met no
doubt oftener than the French States-General, but
still scarcely often enough to deserve to be considered a part of the ordinary machinery of the
state. We often say now that England is governed
by Parliament; in Queen Anne's time it might have
been said that England was governed by the Crown
and Parliament together; but in Queen Elizabeth's
reign it would not have been natural, I think, in
describing the government of England to mention
Parliament at all. Not exactly that Parliament was
subservient, but that, in general, Parliament was not
there.

Does not the Church service put before us this
phase of England? In the Litany, the work of
Cranmer, all the institutions of the country are
passed in review in a series of petitions, but Parliament, in our view incomparably the most important,
is not mentioned. When he has prayed for the
King, the Royal Family, the Lords, and others of the
Privy Council, the Magistrates, and all the Nobility,
Cranmer is satisfied. If the Divine blessing rests on
these it is enough, all is well.

The Prayer-book has no doubt a form of prayer

for the High Court of Parliament to be used when it
is in session.   But here, too, the words chosen to
describe its function seem to apply not so much to a
governing or government-making body, such as the
modern Parliament is, as to a constituent assembly
called together exceptionally to make fundamental
changes.   We pray that *all things may be ordered and
settled by their endeavours upon the best and surest founda-
tions.*

When we have realised this old condition of
things, and then turn to the Restoration period, we
see, I think, in a moment what result had been
attained by the struggle between Charles and the
Parliament.   The ambitious experiment of the Parliament to set itself up without disguise as a government-making organ has failed; but a great step has
been made.   Not yet a government-making organ,
but Parliament is henceforth really an organ.   The
most prominent feature of the middle period of the
seventeenth century is the two Long Parliaments.
First came the Long Parliament of the Rebellion,
which sat for thirteen years before it was dissolved
by Cromwell, and met again after the fall of the
Protectorate.   And this was followed by the Long
Parliament of the Restoration, which sat for seven-
teen years, though during that period it suffered
some long adjournments.

The great idea of that generation, which is to be

S

clearly distinguished from the dreams, idle or pre-
mature, in which it occasionally indulged, was to give
Parliament permanence and solidity. From being a
comet, occasionally and rarely crossing the political
sky, Parliament is to become a fixed star. It
begins by declaring itself permanent, and after
the Restoration one of the first steps taken was to
pass a Triennial Act, of which the object was to
guard against a revival of the old system, and to
prevent the King from trying to dispense with Parliament for considerable periods. And though the
particular arrangement made by that Act did not at
that time prevail, yet the idea which suggested it
prevailed. The Long Parliament of the Restoration
imitates and, as it were, ratifies the Long Parliament
of the Rebellion. The permanent Parliament takes
its place from that time forth among English institutions, and with a certain interval in the closing years
of Charles II. and in the reign of James II., an
exceptional, revolutionary period, we have had it ever
since.

But this Parliament of the Restoration, though in
strength and firmness as superior to that of Queen
Elizabeth as a man is to a child, is still weighed
down by the failure which had brought it under
the yoke of the army, and had at last compelled
it to humble itself once more under the monarchy.
Then begins a second revolutionary period which

covers ten years, from 1678 to 1688. It is a second
struggle with the monarchy, in which, so long as
Charles II. lives, the monarchy on the whole has the
better; but afterwards, through the perversity of
James II., the Parliament is enabled to win a victory,
which in great part effaces the memory of the former
defeat. At the Revolution of 1688 our system arrives
at a point which seems like a triumphant consum-
mation and close of all development, and has proved
so to this extent, that all later development has been
so gradual and easy as to disfigure history with no
new revolutions, and scarcely even to leave a trace
on our constitutional law. For though, as I have
pointed out, the modern system is quite different
from that which was established at the Revolution, it
has been found possible to make the alterations
without legislation.

In the period following the Revolution our state
is what is called a limited monarchy. The King is
subject, as it is said, to constitutional checks. There
are some things which he may not do. From the
point of view of law the question would be, What are
these limits to the royal prerogative? But from our
point of view the question is rather, How are the
checks made operative? or in other words, What will
be done to the King if he transgresses the limits?
And the answer is, That will be done which was done
in 1688. In short, Parliament will depose him and

set up another king. To this extent, then, Parliament, which had become, in consequence of the struggle with Charles I., a fixed and permanent organ of the state, is made by the Revolution of 1688 a government-making organ.

The result was a position of stable equilibrium which lasted a long time. A remarkably convenient *modus vivendi* had been established between King and Parliament. It was agreeable to both parties; it ensured the public tranquillity; it was so generally liked that in later times, when further alterations were needed, it became the custom to conceal them by means of fiction, and up to the present day we have not ceased to believe that we are living under the Revolution system. In reality, however, that system has been left far behind.

I have described the modern system of government by a Minister, which has taken its place. How this grew up I may trace in the next lecture. Meanwhile I may say something on the manner in which the intermediate system, the system of limited monarchy or limited parliamentary power, practically worked.

The books say that after the failure of the attempt made by the old monarchy to rule by prerogative, it fell back upon a system of government by influence, and that this system for a time worked successfully. But they leave the origin of this system somewhat vague. It was admittedly prominent in the reign of

George III.; in that reign attention was drawn to it, it was named and described, it was analysed and denounced. But it had certainly prevailed long before; and my view is that it came in soon after the Restoration—as soon after as the necessary consequences of that event came to be understood. It was at the Restoration, I said, that Parliament began to be a permanent, fixed organ of the English state. I add now that Influence is simply the new weapon to which the Crown had recourse in this changed state of things; that as the Crown used prerogative so long as the Parliament was but an occasional assembly, it naturally fell back upon influence when Parliament gained the strength that comes from permanence.

Influence is a general name for all the different means of persuasion which the Crown by its greatness, splendour, wealth, and patronage could exert upon individuals. It could be brought into play as soon as the individual came within its reach or contact. Now, when Parliament became permanent the Crown had this compensation, that Parliament also came within its reach, and so became subject to its influence. The country gentlemen and noblemen who in former reigns had lived for the most part in the country, and only attended Parliament for a month or two once in four or five years, began now to be regular inhabitants of London for part of every

year. They were thus brought into the neighbourhood of the Court, and Charles II. had thus an
opportunity of trying in England the experiment
which was succeeding so wonderfully on the other side
of the channel in the hands of his cousin Louis XIV.
—that of turning the governing aristocratic class into
courtiers.   Under Charles II. accordingly the Court
comes more than before into prominence; the
pleasures and vices of the Court, the King's charm of
manner and conversation, are a favourite topic of the
historians of this reign.

Influence on its worst side is bribery.   In George
III.'s reign the great complaint of the reformers is
that the Crown has the command of so much wealth,
the appointment to so many posts, the bestowal of so
many pensions, that he becomes a sort of Corruptor-
General, as Bentham calls him, to the whole community.   Accordingly, the cry of that age was for
an economic reform which should diminish the King's
fund of bribery.   Now, the question has often been
discussed, When did the bribing of members of Parliament first begin?   Clearly not in George III.'s reign,
for the outcry against corruption was quite as loud in
Walpole's time.   But as clearly not in Walpole's
time, for in the reign of William III. there was not
merely an outcry, but already a strong and systematic
party movement against this very corrupt influence.
The agitation which produced the Place Bill and the

Triennial Act arose from the observation, which was already made, that members of Parliament were exposed to an overwhelming influence, and that no constituency could hope to be long faithfully served by its representative, tempted as he was by the bait of pension and place. And so we arrive at the Revolution. But the Revolution certainly did not create the evil, and when we look beyond it we find that the Long Parliament of the Restoration was so much exposed to corruption that it was called *the Pensioned Parliament:* a tradition indeed says that the first Minister who bribed members of Parliament was Clifford, who managed the finances in the Ministry called the Cabal.

Now, it may be said of the Cabal that it was the first Ministry which deliberately adapted itself to the new state of things created by the Restoration, for the earliest Minister of Charles, Clarendon, notoriously did not do this, but adhered to an obsolete system.

And thus you see that historically government by influence did really begin at the time when Parliament began to be permanent.

It is by putting together these two things,—the limited control exercised by Parliament over the Crown, the secret influence exercised by the Crown over Parliament,—that we acquire a conception of the eighteenth-century phase of the English Constitution. The foundation of it was laid, I said, at the Restoration. Then Parliament becomes permanent, and then the monarchy, recognising gradually the importance of this new feature, meets it with the new and redoubtable weapon of influence. Charles II.'s reign is in some parts very similar to a reign of the eighteenth century. But the system is not firmly established until it has undergone the fiery trial of 1688. What we call the Revolution was rather the warding off of a revolution. It did not so much introduce new things as confirm and save from violent destruction what had been introduced before. When this storm had been once weathered, the vessel glides into port. There begins a long period of constitutional tranquillity. In the eighteenth century it seemed as if Englishmen could never grow weary of contemplating the perfection of the system they had devised, and it was at the same time the "envy of surrounding nations." Very strange in truth it was to see so much liberty and yet so little turbulence, a prodigious commercial development, a commanding military power, an onward march in the van of nations,—all this with so much order and security, with such easy and happy retention of old forms and time-honoured institutions.

The secret lay in this play of action and reaction between the King and the Parliament, in the sort of modesty with which either behaved to the other, in the sedulous concealment of power which both prac-

tised. The Parliament had claimed and exercised
the formidable power of making and unmaking kings,
and the Monarchy assuredly had taken the lesson to
heart. Yet the Parliament was as far as possible
from presuming upon its power. On the contrary, it
studiously professed and took the greatest pains to
prove that it had never either exercised or intended
to exercise any such power. The King had not been
deposed—he had abdicated; or if there had been some
irregularity in the proceedings of 1688 they were not
to be drawn into precedent, and Parliament acquired
from them no new right. At most Parliament had
but followed the instinct of self-defence and used
that ultimate right which belongs to every living
creature in extreme, but only in extreme, circumstances. And in this modesty there was nothing
hypocritical, as we may see from the fact that the
success of the Revolution did not redeem the Rebellion
from discredit. What republican feeling had existed
in the country died out, the Church gained in strength,
and dissent, especially political dissent, lost its hold.
The country remained throughout the century
steadily monarchical ; and in George III.'s reign the
most influential writers, such as Hume, inclined even
to the Tory view of the seventeenth century controversies.

On the other hand, the Crown showed a similar
modesty in its bearing towards the Parliament. It

would seem to have made the deliberate calculation that it could best preserve its substantial power by withdrawing somewhat from public view. It had become aware that in its splendour, wealth, and patronage, in the profound loyalty and reverence of the people, it possessed a fund of indirect power, of influence, which, well husbanded, might last for centuries. But in order to husband it wisely the Monarchy must practise reserve. It must as little as possible appear in opposition to Parliament, but must rather endeavour to throw upon Parliament the responsibility of its acts. It must manage Parliament, and again in the management of Parliament not the Crown itself but only its Ministers must appear. As yet the apprehension had not arisen that a time might come when the Ministers would usurp the power of the Sovereign. *Now* the Minister speaks through the Sovereign; when we say the Queen wills, the Queen appoints, we mean the Minister wills or appoints; but in those days the Sovereign spoke, or could, if he chose, speak, through the Minister. But on the relation of King and Minister I shall speak more at large in the next lecture.

We say now, the Sovereign reigns, but does not govern. In the present century this has gradually grown to be the case. But the very opposite seems to have been the scheme or intention of the Revolution Monarchy. It seems to have designed to govern

without reigning, that is, to give up the appearance
of power in order to preserve the substance of it.
This it could do by means of the Minister so long as
the Minister continued really to be the King's
Minister, as through the eighteenth century in the
main he did. And this may suggest to you how we
ought to regard that famous surrender of the royal
veto which began in the reign of William III.
This is usually treated as a mark of the decline of
royal power. I confess it does not strike me so. I
see in it rather an evidence of the King's consciousness
of power, but at the same time of his inclination to
conceal his power. In a letter to Lord North,
George III. expressly says that though he will never
consent actually to resign the right of the Crown to
dissent, yet he hopes he shall never be driven to the
necessity of using that right. Just so : the veto fell
into disuse not because the Crown was not strong
enough to maintain it, but because the Crown was
strong enough to do without it. The Kings of the
eighteenth century calculated that so long as their
own Ministers took the lead in the proceedings of
either House, and so long as either House was full of
courtiers profoundly anxious, both from loyalty and
from desire of honour and of promotion, to win the
favour of the Crown, they had ample means of
defeating any measure that might be disagreeable to
them, and could scarcely be driven to use a power so

invidious as the *veto*, which would draw the Monarchy forth from behind the veil under which in this period it chose to conceal itself.

Such was the mutual arrangement between King and Parliament. It was calculated to work well and to last a long time. But it was more admirable in practice than in theory. To explain and justify on abstract principles that Revolution which had led to such a happy settlement was always found difficult. And that is just the reason why I am obliged here to give special attention to it. I am concerned here with theory, and when I lay it down that Parliament exists to create and destroy government, I have to explain why one of the most successful of all parliamentary systems carefully renounced all such claims for Parliament. I do so by laying it down that the organs of the body politic develop themselves slowly and gradually, and that at the Revolution the government-making organ did not suddenly come into mature existence, but only that an old institution in that crisis began to take the character of a government-making organ and naturally endeavoured to conceal the usurpation by embarrassed and unsatisfactory argument.

I HAVE represented the Parliament of the Restoration
as a government-making organ half developed, and
have compared it with the Parliament of our own
time, which is fully developed. But this representation will not be satisfactory till I have considered
the striking difference that exists between the two
Parliaments in another respect. The modern Parliament is not merely more fully developed than that
of the eighteenth century,—it directs its controlling
power upon another object. At the time of the
Revolution it was grappling with the King; now it
does not trouble itself about the Sovereign at all, but
grapples with the Minister.

I have remarked the stammering and hesitating
manner in which, at the time of the Revolution,
Parliament asserted its right to make and unmake
government, and have laid it down that this hesitation was only the natural mark of imperfect development. What should we expect then? Surely to find
the hesitation disappear as development advanced.
If at the Revolution nothing more was asserted than

that self-defence, which will justify almost anything, may justify Parliament in deposing the King, it might be predicted that, as time went on and the good effects of the first audacious experiment were seen, after the Crown had reconciled itself to a more modest tone and the Parliament grown accustomed to a prouder tone, the theory and practice of Parliament alike would grow more decided. The Revolution would be treated as a precedent, in spite of so many protests that it was never to be drawn into precedent. It would be argued that the power which Parliament might use in the last extremity it might clearly resort to in order to prevent such an extremity from arising,—that in short the Crown had become practically elective. We should expect, therefore, to see the royal power in the eighteenth century gradually dwindle, until at the end it should become a mere presidency with a short, perhaps an annual, term, as I supposed the Monarchy at Rome to have dwindled down to the consulate.

Now this did not take place. The tide which had been rising in the seventeenth century, which had flowed and ebbed, and then flowed again against the Monarchy, now changed its direction. The theory of government-making power which had been timidly sketched at the time of the Revolution was not developed further, but laid on one side and forgotten. No further attacks were made upon the Monarchy considered as an institution. It was left in possession of all its power. But gradually the result which had been aimed at in the stormy movements of the seventeenth century was attained by a circuitous route. ·Few chapters in political history are stranger than this development, in which an elaborate and subtle plan might seem to have been executed by a whole nation through a whole century, and yet it would be difficult to show that any plan was formed, or that any generation in the eighteenth century foresaw what system it was preparing for the nineteenth. So gradual was the development, and so much was it disguised at every step with legal fiction, that even now, I think, it is by no means clearly understood.

I suppose the common impression is simply that at the time of the Revolution an ingenious expedient was adopted. The national mind being puzzled by sophistries concerning divine right and passive obedience, certain enlightened statesmen saw the necessity of waiving a question which was too metaphysical for the popular understanding, and hit upon the contrivance of substituting in all discussion the name of the Minister for that of the King; that they said, We will admit that "the King can do no wrong" provided it is admitted that the King by himself can do nothing; we will admit that he is irresponsible, provided it is allowed that every act of

his must be countersigned by a Minister who *is*
responsible; that in this way the Monarchy was
shelved, with all its mystical pretensions, and a plain
Ministry, with which Parliament could deal freely,
substituted in its place. And so it is supposed that
though at the Revolution the Crown was left in
possession of all its theoretical pretensions, yet those
pretensions were then deprived of all serious meaning, and therefore, though theoretically there is no
dwindling of the Monarchy in the eighteenth century,
yet practically the Monarchy withered up and became
effete at the beginning of it.

This is a kind of legend or myth by which the
popular mind explains to itself the fact that the
Monarchy has now lost all effective power. To
imagine that such a change can have taken place
without any revolution, and by mere imperceptible
gradations, is difficult, and as no other revolution can
be found, the popular mind clutches at the Revolution
of 1688. And the vague hypothesis is supported by
one real fact. As I have pointed out, since the
Restoration, but most decisively since the Revolution,
the Monarchy adopted the policy of retiring from
public view, and of throwing as much responsibility
as possible upon Parliament. In particular, they
dropped the veto. The effect is that the kings of
the eighteenth century appear in history with less
strongly-marked features, more like each other and

more conventional in their language and bearing, than those of the seventeenth. . This conventionality may easily be mistaken for a loss of power. At the same time it is easy to point to powerful Ministers in those times, some of whom are contrasted with Sovereigns of less striking ability, and this is held sufficient to prove that the power which the Crown is supposed to have lost had passed to the Minister. Add to all this that the change which this theory supposes to have been complete in the eighteenth century did undoubtedly begin in that century,—that at certain moments of that century the Crown really was powerless and Ministers did rule by the same popular support as the Ministers of our own time,— and we shall see out of what ample materials the legend has been composed.

That it is a mere legend, I think it will not be difficult to show you. Kings may look featureless in history, and yet may have wielded great power. And certainly those who lived in the eighteenth century under these somewhat featureless kings did not complain that they had too little power, but more commonly that they had too much. There are certain exceptions, which I shall consider later, but, as a general rule, we may say that the eighteenth century, like the seventeenth, is occupied with a perpetual struggle to curb the exorbitant power of the Crown. In the middle of George III.'s reign a

T

resolution was proposed in the House of Commons that "the power of the Crown has increased, is increasing, and ought to be diminished." Nearly a century after the Revolution this resolution was proposed, and it might have been proposed at many other moments, both earlier and later. Pass in review the kings of this period. William III. was the great statesman of his age, dominating the politics of Europe ; and how powerful he was felt to be at home, in spite of his doubtful title, appears from that agitation for Place Bills and Triennial Acts which marks his reign. Anne, personally, was not strong, but her insignificance serves to set in a stronger light the power of the Monarchy in her time. She by her own will turned out Marlborough ; she contributed the largest share in that memorable change of policy which brought about the Treaty of Utrecht. George I. was a competent statesman, but certainly somewhat featureless. Both he and his successor retire in history behind Walpole their Minister. But, as I have said before, this is no proof of any decline in the Monarchy, unless you think that the French Monarchy declined, instead of gaining enormously in power, under Richelieu and Mazarin. Nevertheless, in the latter years of George II., I do perceive symptoms of decline, and from that time forward I note that new causes are at work from which the Monarchy suffers. But, as yet, these symptoms are rare and intermittent. For the greater part of George III.'s reign the Monarchy was, as all contemporaries thought, rather too strong than too weak.

It appears then, in the first place, that the decline of monarchical power, which has certainly taken place now, cannot be traced back to the Revolution, but at most only to about the middle of the eighteenth century. Now, let us consider the rise of the Minister and the encroachment of the Minister upon royal power. The Revolution had nothing to do with this. Macaulay does indeed think he can trace our system of party government back to the reign of William III., but he is thinking of another feature of our modern system, not the effacement of the Sovereign by the Minister,· but the agreement in opinion of the Ministers among themselves; and even so his view seems open to question. I have referred already to the change of Ministry which took place in 1710, that is, twenty-two years after the Revolution, and have pointed out how dependent Godolphin and Marlborough seem to be even so late upon the caprice of the Queen. Will you say, Walpole was a Minister of the modern type? Let us ask ourselves precisely what this modern type is. Powerful Ministers and Ministers holding office for a long time are no symptom of a declining Monarchy. I rather think that under despotism powerful Ministers holding office securely are more usual than where Parliament is strong. It is in despotism that we find the Wolsey, the Burleigh, the Richelieu, the Mazarin, the Kaunitz, the Hardenberg, the Metternich, the Bismarck. What we inquire is, not when Ministers began to be powerful, but when they began to be powerful against the Sovereign, to hold office not at his pleasure but at the pleasure of Parliament. Now the Revolution, I think, had no influence in bringing this about.

Very far back in our history the Parliament has occasionally dictated to the Sovereign what Ministers he shall *not* consult. Almost as far back as the beginning of Parliament is the beginning of the practice of controlling the King by attacking his counsellors. Buckingham, Strafford, and Danby are obvious examples of it in the seventeenth century. Such a practice proves only that the state is organic and has real vitality, that public opinion is alive. It is no evidence that the Monarchy is declining, or that the Minister is taking the place of the Monarch. The case is different when public opinion dictates to the Monarch, not only whom he shall *not*, but whom he *shall*, consult. Still more, when this is done, not once in some moment of extreme party struggle, but again and again—when it is done so often that the Minister ceases to be in any true sense the Minister of the King, and begins to be the nominee of the Parliament. In England we see that this has taken place. It is understood now that the function of the Sovereign is only to interpret the will of Parliament in the choice of a Minister, that for the most part this will is unmistakably clear, and that at the utmost the Sovereign can only hesitate between two names, and even within these narrow limits ought not to indulge a personal preference. The question then is, when and in what way the Sovereign parted with the power of appointing the Minister, when the Minister became independent of the Sovereign.

Now, I have said already that this did not happen at the Revolution. If, in the last years of William, when his position was materially weakened by the death of Mary, some signs of the approach of such a change may be discerned, they led to nothing. It was a transient phase, not a decline, but only a momentary depression of the Monarchy. But I say further that I cannot perceive that the change was even an in- direct consequence of the Revolution. The current theory requires that we should consider it a further step taken by the same enlightened party which had made the Revolution, as if this party, having decided in secret council that the superstitious populace would not endure to see the Monarchy directly attacked, dexterously changed its policy and determined, leaving the Sovereign alone, to secure for Parliament the nomination of the Minister. I find that no such party existed, and that no such plan was ever formed. I find that there was no desire in any large or influential party to reduce the Crown to a mere pageant, and accordingly that no party was likely to imagine any such contrivance. I find that half a century passed away after the Revolution before the King began to perceive that he had not full liberty in the choice of his Ministers, and when this happened it was the result of circumstances which were only very remotely connected with the Revolution.

According to me, the first distinct indications of the growth of a new system, in which the Minister would be independent of the Sovereign, appeared in the last fifteen years of the reign of George II., and are connected with the rise to power of the elder Pitt. The immediate cause of them was not any conscious design of weakening the Monarchy, but rather the working of the very peculiar system of party that came in with the House of Hanover.

Party principles were first adopted by the government of George I., but we must be careful not to imagine that the party principles then adopted were the party principles of our own time. Under George I. the Whigs came in, and the Tories were excluded, just as in our time the Ministry is all of one colour, either Liberal or Conservative. But the modern doctrine is that the Government ought to reflect the changes of feeling that take place in the public mind— that when the nation is in a Liberal mood it ought to

be governed by Liberals, and by Conservatives again
when its mood changes. No such fancy ever crossed
the mind of a politician in the reign of George I.
The doctrine which prevailed at that time was, not
that the nation ought to be governed by Whigs and
Tories alternately, but that it ought to be governed
by Whigs always, and by Whigs alone. The argument—you will find it most distinctly stated in
a paper which Lord Chancellor Cowper handed
in to George I., printed in Campbell's *Lives of
Chancellors*—ran thus:—The House of Hanover derives
its title purely from the Revolution. It must therefore rest for support on those who sincerely approve
the Revolution. Now, previous sovereigns, William
and Anne, have regarded both parties, Whigs and
Tories alike, as faithful friends of the Revolution
settlement. But though the Tories have professed in
a half-hearted way to approve the Revolution, yet it
is impossible they can be sincere. The Revolution is
evidently inconsistent with Tory principles; if Tories
profess to approve it, this can only be because they
are unwilling to exclude themselves from office and
from the favour of the Crown. And though for the
most part the system of dividing the favour of the
Crown impartially between the two parties was
applied not unsuccessfully by William and Anne,
yet in the last years of Anne, the unsafeness
of such a policy has been made manifest. The

wild reversal of English policy at the Treaty of
Utrecht, and the alarming revival of the party of the
Pretender, are only the natural consequence of
allowing the Tories to have a share in government.
The new dynasty therefore must take a new course in
this respect. It must no longer endeavour, as William
and Anne had done, to be impartial between the
Whigs and the Tories, or to play off one party against
the other, but must frankly and once for all declare
for the Whigs, its true friends. As for Tories, the
King must not persecute them—on the contrary he
must be a true father to all his people; but he must
not allow them to hold office.

It was under this form that party government first
grew up in England. The Crown declared itself
Whig, and this system prevailed till the fall of
Walpole. I think it was a more dangerous system
than that which it replaced. It drove the Tories
into the Jacobite camp, and probably it is largely
responsible for the two Jacobite rebellions which
mark this period. But it had another less direct
effect, which I think was never contemplated. It
gradually weakened the Monarchy. Under it the
King became a sort of ward under the guardianship of
the Whig party. And henceforward if he wished to
change his counsellors, it was not easy for him to do
it. For the Whigs had only to close their ranks, to
adopt the tactics of a Trades Union, to impose their

terms on the King by threatening a strike, and the King was in danger of a checkmate. He had alienated the Tories by treating them as rebels. Henceforth he could not throw himself into their hands. He could only appeal from one section of the Whigs to another, and this thrust the Whigs might parry by taking pains to efface sectional divisions in their body.

This came to light in the year 1745. The Pelhams then in office proposed to give William Pitt a place in the administration, but the King refused his consent. Upon this the whole Pelham connection resigned office together. Thereupon the King sent for Carteret and Pulteney, but these found it impossible to obtain the support of other public men. They were forced to restore the seals of office into the King's hand, and the King was forced to reinstate the Pelhams. Here, I take it, begins the decline of the Monarchy in England, for I imagine that no English king had been treated so before. Yet I see no reason to think that the Pelhams acted so from an enlightened intention of carrying the Revolution further, and reducing to a lower point the power of the Crown.

Before the end of the same reign another great occurrence tended to raise the Minister at the expense of the Monarch. This was the ascent of William Pitt to supreme power on the shoulders of the people— one of the most memorable events of the eighteenth

century. But it is an event which cannot be brought
into any connection with the Revolution, nor represented as a further development of the principle of it.
It is an event of a wholly different order. The
Revolution had been a triumph of Parliament. If
Parliament had now forced George II. to take William
Pitt as his Minister, this might have been regarded as
a further encroachment of the same kind. But it
was not Parliament that advanced William Pitt;
just here lay the newness and strangeness of the
event. It was not Parliament, but the people outside
Parliament. And so George II. said to him, "You,
sir, have taught me to look for the sense of my
people elsewhere than in Parliament;" and Glover, in
describing the state of the nation at the beginning of
his first administration, says, "You saw a strange
division in the country : William Pitt and the people
on one side; King, Lords, and Commons on the other."
There was no indication here of the further advance
of the principles of 1688. Something quite different
was at work. The growth of commerce and wealth,
I suppose, had quickened intelligence and was causing
the people to outgrow its institutions. Public opinion
had come into existence, and the rising tide chafed
just as much against the House of Commons as
against the Crown.

George II. was the first English king who was
conscious of a paralysis creeping upon the Monarchy.

When some one praised the English Constitution in his hearing, he said, "It was a good Constitution for the people, but not a good one for the King." When George III. revived royal power he did not, as is often represented, kick against the Revolution. He only rebelled against this new usurpation of the Minister which had been introduced by the Pelhams fifteen years before. And throughout his reign you will find him steadily insisting on one principle, that the Minister shall be *his* Minister. On the whole he is successful. The disturbed period before 1770 ends in the Ministry of Lord North, who is emphatically the King's own Minister, and who holds office for twelve years; the second short period of disturbance ends in the Ministry of the younger Pitt, also agreeable to the King, which lasts eighteen years; and after Pitt's death the other side can only hold office about a year.

The party that had humiliated his predecessor is held by George III. at arm's length. The party of the Pelhams, directed after the retirement of New-castle by Rockingham, and after Rockingham's time by Fox, and known in this reign simply as the Whig party, can only at long intervals during this reign force its way into power. The King will tolerate them for a moment if he sees no alternative, but always under protest. They are not his Ministers, and it is his fixed opinion that he has the right to appoint Ministers at his pleasure. Accordingly he receives them sullenly, watches them narrowly, and struggles, if he cannot appoint the whole Cabinet, at least to have representatives on it, some Thurlow or Ellenborough. And then he waits for his opportunity, which commonly arrives in about a year, dismisses them, and once more chooses a Ministry for himself.

For about half a century George III. was able to keep our system at this point. But under George IV. and William IV. the Minister's independence of the Crown grows again rapidly. Canning forces himself on George IV., and if it cannot exactly be said that Earl Grey forced himself on William, it is at least true that the share of the King in his appointment, compared to the share of the people, was as one to a hundred.

In the middle of this reign, in 1834, it finally appeared that the King had lost the power of appointing the Minister. William IV., tired of the Reform Ministry, seized the opportunity of Lord Althorp being called to the Upper House to make, as he said, "a new arrangement," dismissed his Ministers, and sent for Sir Robert Peel. Then it appeared how our Constitution had insensibly altered. The problem proposed to Sir Robert was insoluble. There was no more skilful manager of the House of Commons. But no skill could convert a minority into a majority. The House did not dispute the King's right to appoint his own Minister, they treated that Minister with all due respect; still when he unfolded his policy to the House it failed to obtain the approbation of the majority.

Now I hope you will not content yourselves with remarking that the principles of liberty were by this time too far developed to allow the House to acquiesce in any appointment the King might choose to make. We want to know precisely what alteration had taken place. Let us inquire, then, if a similar appointment had been made in George II.'s reign instead of William IV.'s, in what way would the Minister have avoided the same fate? Pelham or Newcastle stood surely as much in need of a majority in the House as Sir Robert Peel; how then could they be less dependent on the House?

My answer is this: We are accustomed to think that a statesman must have a majority before he can become Minister, but in the eighteenth century a Minister had a majority because he was Minister, and acquired a majority by becoming Minister. You may think I am hinting at bribery, but no! We must learn to understand in what way members of Parliament in those days regarded the Minister. The explanation flashes upon me when I read the speech of the elder Pitt on the Repeal of the Stamp Act. In answering Grenville he said, "The gentle-

man must not tell us that we passed the Act ourselves, and are therefore as much responsible for it
as he is. No! we took it on his credit as Minister."
And then he went on to say, "I wish the House had
not this habit. But so it is; even that chair, Mr.
Speaker, looks too often towards St. James'. When
I was in office it annoyed me that no one would
make any objection to the war. Night after night I
came down and said, Is any gentleman against a war?
No one would avow it; at last a gentleman who has
since gone to the other House (Sir F. Dashwood—
Lord Despenser) said he did not like a war! I
honoured him for it, and was sorry when he left us."

How this passage brings back the old state of
manners and feelings! You see with what profound
deference the Minister was regarded just because he
was Minister. The chair itself looks towards St.
James'. We often overlook this; surely Macaulay
overlooks it when he describes the unbounded
personal ascendency of Pitt during his war administration. You see Pitt himself did not think it was
from any awe of him personally that the members
were dumb, but from reverence for his ministerial
functions. So far from being proud, he is annoyed
at it.

The truth is that in those days a parliament was
still distinctly felt to be a conference between the
representatives of the people and the Sovereign,

present by his Ministers. Whatever the Sovereign
might propose was received with profound deference.
And it had not yet entered the mind of the representatives that they were entrusted with the government of the country. They were in the habit of
thinking that it was the business of the King to
govern the country. When therefore he was pleased
through his Ministers to explain what measures he
intended to take, they scarcely considered that they
were either entitled or qualified to judge of their
general expediency; they took them on the King's
credit; only they held themselves bound to consider
these measures as they affected the people, their constituents. If they pressed hardly upon the people,
took too much out of the subject's purse, or endangered any of his liberties, Parliament must inter-
vene, but scarcely otherwise. In general, therefore,
the Minister had a majority as a matter of course.
His majority was secured by the loyalty of the
people to the Crown.

But again, when I compare Sir Robert Peel with
Pelham or Newcastle I see another great difference.
Sir Robert is sunk up to the neck in great legislative
plans. The country has just been through a sort of
revolution. The Reform Bill has been passed, and
every institution of the country is being overhauled
in succession. A new poor law is to be carried, the
colonies are convulsed by the abolition of slavery, the

Irish Church is threatened, municipal reform is at
hand, financial reform is urgent. In Pelham's time
nothing of the kind! Scarcely any legislation in
that age was either offered by Ministers or required
of them. They neither had nor needed to have any
policy in the modern sense of the word. The old
institutions of the country continued for the most
part to suffice the people. Government in those days,
in short, did not mean legislation. It meant keeping
order, administering the laws, and very often waging
war.

I have already remarked how exceptional and
strange is the prominence of legislation in our time.
The immediate cause of it evidently was the vast
convulsions that followed the French Revolution.
When peace came in 1815 everything had changed
throughout the Empire, and the demand for new
legislation in every department was such as had
never been known before.

Now it was just at this time that without any
violent change, imperceptibly yet irresistibly, the
Minister rose to the head of affairs and became
dependent on Parliament instead of the Sovereign.
I believe that the effect was produced in a great
degree by this extreme and unprecedented prominence of legislation. And it was aided by the complete decay of royal influence which had taken place
during the long reign of George III.

That profoundly deferential and devoted feeling towards the government which we have remarked in the reign of George II. was partly based upon the immense wealth and patronage of the Crown. The Rockingham Whigs succeeded in greatly reducing this, and I imagine that the immense growth of the nation in wealth and population during the latter half of the eighteenth century caused the importance of the Court to dwindle insensibly. In the comparatively small, simple, and rustic society of the earlier time, the Court had been an object of immense magnitude, and the King seemed capable of buying up the whole community, as Cosmo de' Medici corrupted all Florence. All this imposing magnitude was lost in the crowded, commercial, manufacturing England of George IV. Parliament did not cease to be loyal, but the members ceased to be courtiers either in feeling or interest. They considered now with perfect coldness and impartiality the proposals which the Minister put before them.

And these proposals now for the most part concerned vast questions of legislative reform, questions in which large classes were interested, questions in which the Crown was not specially interested. In legislation the Crown had rarely since the Tudors taken a leading part. Dealing with foreign powers, making war and peace, or suppressing rebellion and maintaining order, this had been the province of the

U

Crown. Legislation had usually been a department in which the King rather presided than took the lead. In a peace of forty years, filled with the most momentous legislation, the King naturally fell into the part of a silent president, and his power of appointing the Minister became useless to him. It was now the main business of a minister to legislate, to legislate not on the succession to the Crown, or on the pretender, or on tests and abjuration oaths, or other matters in which the King was interested, but on workhouses and factories, and banks and tariffs and navigation laws,—questions on which the Crown could only be neutral, and on which the Minister could not advance a step without the support of a majority. And so in 1834 the King might appoint Sir Robert Peel, and Parliament made no objection to the appointment, but in the next year Sir Robert himself was obliged to confess that he could not govern. By an inevitable change, against which it was vain to struggle, the Minister had ceased to be the King's Minister, and had become the Minister of the Parliament.

I have wandered further perhaps than was necessary from theory. All that for my immediate purpose was absolutely necessary was to show that our system during the seventeenth and eighteenth centuries was not inconsistent with the theory of a government-making organ, but that it shows the

organ imperfect and in course of development. In
the seventeenth century Parliament was assuming
the character of a fixed organ, and asserting very
timidly a government - making power ; in the
eighteenth, as I have now shown, during a long
period of apparent calm, a further development was
prepared. The Minister became practically independent of the Sovereign, and dependent on the Parliament. The fact is simple and obvious enough, but
I thought it worth while to linger on the details, both
because they are not clearly understood, and because
the development was much more casual and accidental, much less necessary than is commonly supposed.
I have shown you that it was not a necessary result
of the growth of the "spirit of liberty," but a very
peculiar result of very special circumstances. It
follows, I think, that we ought not to consider a
Minister of the English type conducting legislation
and administration at once, and rising and falling at
the pleasure of Parliament, to be necessarily the
normal and only proper result of political development.

Nevertheless he is an extremely clear illustration
of the working of government-making power. So
long as Parliament dealt with the King it could assert
this power only hesitatingly, with many reserves and
qualifications. Dealing with the Minister it takes up
a bolder position. And so in modern England, more

clearly than in any other state, we see embodied the working of the great process which must go forward in every organic state,—government supported by the consent of an influential group in the people, and sinking when that consent is withdrawn.

LECTURE V

OUR long inquiry into the nature and function of political assemblies has led us to give, as it were, a new version of Aristotle's division of states according to the number of rulers. Some states, says Aristotle, are governed by one, some by many. Modern writers, in applying this classification, seem often to decide that a state is "governed by one," or "governed by many," according as it has or has not some person bearing the title of King. Perhaps it might seem frivolous to urge against this statement that even at Athens there was a person bearing the title of King, for one of the Archons had the title βασιλεύς, as at Rome a certain priestly functionary had the title *Rex*; but at any rate the modern world has produced many examples of kingship maintained in all its state and magnificence by the side of the most influential political assemblies. Take England—I will not say now—but England in the eighteenth century; the King was not only there, but had still great powers; and yet in the eyes of Europe, England seemed governed by an assembly. How is the Aristotelian classification to be applied to such a state? Are we to say it was governed by one or by many?

Again, there are States which have no King, in which, nevertheless, some one functionary is as prominent as the King in such a "monarchy" as England. Such was the Stadtholder in the Netherlands, who having been practically King for the greater part of two centuries, at last after 1815 actually assumed the title. Similarly, there was once a Protector in England, a First Consul in France, and there is a President in the United States. What are we to say of such States? Are they governed by one or by many?

Again, we surely ought not to take the word "one" too literally. If the government is divided into a number of departments, but within each department it is in the hands of one man, such a state ought not to be simply regarded as an example of government by many. This remark will apply to such a state as ancient Rome. There, to be sure, was found neither King nor President. There were two consuls, and in a rank just below them a number of magistrates, each supreme in his own limited province. Are we to say that Rome was governed by many because there were two consuls, or because the functions of government had by degrees been distributed among a number of officials? Rome at least was largely governed, I should say, by individuals, not by assemblies.

The fact is that in almost all states the one and the many may be discovered side by side, though in some the one, and in others the many, are more prominent ; and it rather appears that public affairs are in some way divided between them. In what way then ? I have suggested that, in most cases at least, the function of the Assembly is not properly to govern, but that another description ought to be found for it. Sometimes we find the Assembly electing magistrates, sometimes criticising their conduct, passing votes of censure or want of confidence, sometimes rejecting or accepting laws. The business they transact seems very miscellaneous, but it is not quite so miscellaneous as it seems. For if those votes of censure, those votes by which a proposal is rejected, lead to the retirement of a ruler, and the replacement of him by another ruler, then they are equivalent to elections. And it will appear that what is attained in some states by short terms of office and frequent elections is attained in others by the rule which makes the tenure of office dependent on the support of a majority. In all these cases alike, then, the principal function of the Assembly proves to be not government, but the making and unmaking of government.

Thus we regard the proposition that government may be in the hands of one or of many as not much confirmed by history. We say rather, government is ᴐ mainly work for individuals, not for assemblies. The difference between a so-called republic like ancient Rome, and an extreme monarchy like Turkey, is not that assemblies in the one do the work that an individual does in the other, but it consists in this—first, that in one the individual is chosen and frequently changed, in the other he holds office for life and then transmits it according to a fixed rule; secondly, that in the one there are several governing individuals, in the other only one.

I must call your attention again to the ambiguity that lurks in the word "many." "Many" may mean an assembly, or it may mean a number of persons acting separately. In the former sense we say, government is not work for many, but in the latter sense it is not only true but important that some states are governed by one and some by many. Both for its own sake and for the sake of removing more completely the ambiguity, it will be worth while to dwell for a few minutes on this kind of government by many.

Among the large differences between states which it is the object of these lectures to set forth there is one which I have not yet mentioned, perhaps because it was so obvious. I have indeed remarked that when a state grows large it is obliged to have two kinds of government, local and central, whereas when it is small this distinction is not called for. I might

have laid it down more generally that some states
have a simple, some a complex or highly developed,
organisation. A state which is small and consists of
primitive people, where life is uniform, where occupation and property are all of one kind, where there is
no variety of business, requires but a simple government. One man can be general and judge, and sometimes also teacher, of such a simple community. But
as population increases and industry becomes multi-
form, the government of one in the strict sense
becomes impossible, simply because the powers of one
man are limited. One man cannot understand
everything, nor find time to attend to everything.
Accordingly an alteration must be made, but it is an
alteration in machinery only, not in principle.
Instead of government by one there is introduced
government, not properly by many, but by a number
of ones.

In England the King used to preside in the law-
courts. One of these courts is still called the King's
Bench, another was the court of those Common Pleas
which Magna Charta forbade to follow the King, and
fixed at Westminster for the convenience of the
people. Now the King not only does not, but could
not, do the work of a judge. Why? because through
the increased complexity of society law has become
complex. What is the remedy? To suit a complex
state of affairs we make, as it were, a complex King.

Judges are created who represent separately a single aspect of the kingly office. The different powers of the King are distributed among a number of individuals.

Sometimes we surprise this development in the act of taking place. Thus in England the Lord Chancellor, who represented the principle of change or development in jurisprudence, was for a long time supposed not to require any special learning. He was to use his natural sense of right. But we are told that in Charles II.'s reign Sir Antony Ashley Cooper, the first Lord Shaftesbury, who held the seals without being even a lawyer, became aware that equity had reached a point when it could no longer be handled by the cleverest amateur. Specialisation had advanced another step. Henceforward the Chancellor must be a lawyer.

In England, as I remarked before, it is our custom to alter things but to leave their names unaltered. Accordingly this great process of differentiation by which the functions of government have been distributed among a number of individuals has been somewhat veiled. The King is still supposed to do everything. It is he who legislates "by and with the advice of his Lords and Commons in Parliament assembled." It is he who governs, by the advice of responsible Ministers. It is he who judges, through the mouth of Chancellors and Chief Justices. Now in other states the same process of differentiation has

gone on without the same attempt being made to
conceal it. Look at early Rome, where, as I have
already said, the Consul appears, not as a republican official who has been put in the place of the
King, but as the King himself, diminished by a
series of encroachments and deprived of his title. It
seemed to me that the earliest consuls may perhaps
have ruled for life and have been taken exclusively
from the Tarquin family. But it is written most
distinctly in the history that their functions were
gradually distributed in just the same manner as we
have seen the kingly functions distributed in England.
For we are told that at a certain date the office of
prætor, and at a certain other date the office of
censor, was created. The prætor was a judge, the
censor had certain high financial duties beside the
function of a Registrar-General. It appears that at
first all these functions were performed by the Consul.
Like the English King he was at first judge, but the
function was taken from him, not as in England, by
a fiction that he pronounced the law through the
mouth of another, but avowedly. When these sub-
tractions of power have taken place, the Roman
Consul appears for a long time chiefly as a military
commander, but in the last years of the republic he
loses this character too. ,War is now committed
chiefly to proconsuls and proprætors, and the Consul
in Cicero's time was a sort of civic dignitary.

In Rome this distribution of the functions of government was concurrent with the growth of popular power, with the triumphs of the principle of popular election. In like manner in England the same distribution has been concurrent with the growth of Parliament. Since the time of the Stuarts governmental departments have been steadily growing in number and distinctness. I have spoken of the judicial department. In like manner the military department has formed itself, has differentiated itself from the naval department, and both have grown to be independent of the Crown. The number of Secretaries of State has largely increased. A department of local government and another of education has been formed. All this development has been contemporaneous with the development of parliamentary control over government. But observe now that the one development is wholly distinct from the other, independent of it, and proceeds from different causes. The distribution of the functions of government is made necessary by the growth of the community in magnitude and complexity. It is not an effect of the advance of popular principles, and it would take place none the less if there were no advance of popular principles. This remark is confirmed by history.

Some European states grew large and complex at a time when they were still under a despotic government. This is especially true of France, which in the earlier part of Louis XV.'s reign was the most civilised state, and in wealth, commerce, and colonies was still running an equal race with England, yet was under a government which was absolute and almost Byzantine. Was then France really governed by the person called Louis XV.? Did he invent and issue laws, sit in law-courts, command armies and fleets? Of course he did not. He did not even exercise the general control which, if he had been an energetic man, would have been within his power. His personal government was perhaps almost as null as is that of the English Sovereign now. Yet France was under an absolute government.

The explanation is that the King's functions had been distributed among a number of officials. France was governed by a First Minister, a Chancellor, a Comptroller-General, a Minister of War, a Minister of Marine, a Minister of Police. Under these heads of departments intendants governed the provinces. But these officials in their several departments were, under a weak king, practically absolute. This shows us how despotism may take two forms. It may be completely in the hands of one man, but this is only possible where the state is small and simple. Where it is large and complex, and almost all modern states are of this kind, despotism tends to be distributed, not properly, as I said, among many, but among a number of ones. A clumsy name has been invented for despotism so distributed. It is called bureaucracy, and this is practically the chief form of despotism known to the modern world. The Assembly being absent, or if not absent insignificant, bureaucracy is none the less despotic because it divides power among many hands.

Government, then, according to this view, is usually personal, usually individual, but it may be collected in the hands of one person or distributed among many.

But by the side of government—so we lay it down—there must exist in every state another power not less important, a power creating government.

Now as we regard the state as a vital organism, we expect in every limb of it to find gradual development. As we consider government itself to take a distinct shape only gradually, as we trace it back through embryonic forms of priesthood and paternity, so shall we expect to find the government-making power in every stage of imperfect development, and we shall not be surprised to find it occasionally wholly unorganised. No chapters of history, therefore, seem more easy to understand than those which show us nations and communities devoid of any organ for the making of government, but perplexed, alarmed, and at a loss, when they are confronted

with the problem of changing government, of bringing government to an end, of creating a new government. We remarked of laws that, whereas to make
· a law seems to us extremely simple, in other periods
it has been held that laws must come from heaven
and cannot be made by men. The same may be said of
governments. Men have been thankful to find themselves under government—they have understood the
duty of obeying government; but when by some chance
government disappeared and a new one was needed,
or when, from being a blessing, government, through
the perversity of the ruler, became an intolerable
incubus, they have stood bewildered and dismayed.
They have looked up into the sky for intimations, or
listened to the birds who had access to the sky, or
consulted the entrails of sacrifices on which the deity
might have deigned to write his will, or asked the
advice of prophets. This perplexity is the growing-
pain, the impulse of development, in the political
organism. It indicates the want of an organ. In
such a state the organ of government has been
already formed, but the government-making organ is
still to form.

During the long period of waiting for the growth
of this organ, while the making of government is
still regarded as an insoluble problem, a provisional
solution is discovered which is sufficient for ordinary
cases. A bad king indeed can only be removed by

violence, but the demise of the Crown that occurs in the course of nature is remedied by the rule of hereditary succession. As in property so in government, the son may be regarded as a sort of equivalent. to the father, as the father over again. A difficulty indeed arises when sons are wanting, still more when there are absolutely no descendants. In some states this difficulty is smoothed away by lawyers, who devise a complete scale of succession. But other states have found it insoluble, and have been reduced to a pitiable condition of dismay by a failure of direct royal heirs. Slavonic states in particular have shown themselves unable to admit the fiction of inheritance beyond a certain point. In Poland the whole system of hereditary monarchy broke down with the failure of the line of Jagela, and in Russia the extinction of the line of Rurik introduced a period of terrible convulsions and wild popular hallucinations arising from this cause.

But now a further development takes place. The ruler has been in the habit of summoning assemblies for various purposes. In ancient times the citizens have been summoned to take the field as soldiers, and before the march began have been addressed and appealed to by the ruler on some public matter. After his address the chieftains have been permitted to give their opinion, and the crowd to express assent by clamour or dissent by murmur. In more modern times the ruler has found himself compelled to apply for money to the representatives of his people, and in return to listen to their complaints.   In either case the Assembly is a germ capable of much development. The murmur or complaint may be developed into opposition, and opposition into rebellion. Opposition observing certain forms may acquire a legal character, and in course of time even rebellion, considered as a developed form of opposition, may become in certain circumstances legal too.

And thus by slow steps the Assembly advances to the assertion of a government-making power. The earlier steps of such a process we studied in the English Revolution.   But we found that in England after the Revolution the development did not proceed, as it were, in a straight line, but from accidental causes, which we partly traced, followed a most extraordinary circuitous course.   This later English development is exceptional, and therefore theoretically the less instructive.

The normal[1] process is rather that which I imagine to have taken place in ancient Rome.   After asserting a government-making power to be used only in extreme necessity, the Assembly would begin to assert that something short of extreme necessity

---

[1] On this word I find a pencil note giving an explanation of the meaning attached to it by the author, " Normal because name corresponds to reality."—ED.

would justify the use of it, and next that in order to avoid the risk of such extremities the ruler's power should be limited to a term of years; then that the Assembly should take part in naming his successor. Gradually the term of office would become very short, and the free choice of a successor would be claimed by the Assembly. They might also control his power by giving him a colleague, and so at last two consuls would take the place of the King.

But now observe that, by the side of this, another development will almost always take place. The population is growing, wealth and arts are growing; almost necessarily therefore government is becoming a burden too heavy, a task too difficult for one man. Its functions begin to be distributed; military duties begin to be separated from judicial duties or duties of police. By the side of the consuls will now appear prætor, a censor, quæstors. Where this distribution of functions takes place in a state in which the government-making organ has not yet appeared the result, is bureaucracy, and the King may easily maintain the external show of undiminished power, the new officers passing as his delegates or mouthpieces. But what if it take place where the kingship has already been diminished to a consulate, has become elective and annual? In this case the new officials may easily appear side by side with the King or Consul, and almost on an equality with him. And in such a state

the original unity of government may almost disappear. Monarchy quite passes away, and its place
is taken by a number of magistrates, all nearly equal,
and none of them very imposing.

Meanwhile the Assembly has been growing in importance, and may at last completely eclipse in the
eyes of the world a government which has thus
dwindled. At Rome this would have happened to a
greater extent than it actually did if the government-
making assemblies, the comitia, had been scenes of
grand debate. This was not so. The debating
Assembly at Rome was the Senate, and this was
not a government-making Assembly. At Athens it
took place. There by the side of the Ecclesia, the
officials, who had once been great, dwindled till they
almost disappeared. The consuls and prætors of
Rome never lost their imposing dignity, but the
Athenian Archons became wholly unimportant.

In these circumstances it may appear as if the
State were actually governed by the Assembly, and
not by the officials. The Assembly is seen energetic-
ally occupying itself with public affairs, and is far
more prominent than the officials. If we use the
word "govern" without precision, such a state may
be said to be governed by the Assembly. But as I
have now shown, the occupation of the Assembly in
many instances is not really government. In Rome
it was almost exclusively the election of magistrates.

The stormy activity of our Parliament in the seventeenth century had for its object to overawe the government, and to assert a power in extreme cases of destroying it. And in the nineteenth century this Parliament appears not so much to govern as to choose and support the Ministry that governs; and though at first sight our Ministry appears to be but a part of the Parliament, on closer consideration it is seen to be substantially distinct.

So far we have not found a clear case of government by many. Are we then brought to the conclusion that there is no such thing? Are we to say that not only often, but always, where an assembly, of the citizens at large or of their representatives, appears to govern, the government is really in the hands of officials whose quiet activity is overlooked in the tumult of popular debate? No; if we said this, we should go too far.

I have referred several times to the experience we all have of the management by societies and clubs of their larger affairs. In these management, direction, seems to fall naturally to the Assembly rather than to the Official, to the Committee rather than to the Secretary, who appears as an agent or servant rather than as master of the Committee. Why should not a similar system, which seems so natural in all corporate action, prevail also in the greatest of all corporations, the State?

It would be surprising, I think, if it had not in some cases done so. Nevertheless there is a material difference between the position of the State and of any private society that exists under the protection of the State. We laid it down that government is strong and strict in proportion as the pressure upon the community is great, and that the pressure most commonly encountered is that from enemies and neighbours. The government of an army in the field is stronger and more monarchical than that of a quiet township. Now the State is always, compared to the private corporation, in some degree what an army is to a town. The private corporation is within the State, and protected by its laws. The State is in the presence of enemies and rivals against whom it must protect itself. It is easy to discern in history the working of this cause, which has led states to be discontented with the lower form of government. I will cite one or two examples from recent times.

In the first form which our American colonies gave themselves after their secession from England, they constituted themselves into a confederation without a President. The system did not work. In 1789 they substituted for this confederation the United States, placing at the head of it a president, and choosing for their first president the best general they had. And it may be observed in the subsequent history of the union that a great general is always thought to have a right to the presidency. America has had three wars. Each war has brought out a distinguished general. Each of these three generals, Washington, Andrew Jackson, and Grant, was afterwards president for two terms.

In France, after the fall of Louis XVI., republican feeling was so strong that they could not tolerate the thought even of a president. Their first Republic therefore had for an executive a directory of five. The number was found too large, and the express object of the Revolution of Brumaire was to introduce a more personal executive. For five directors three consuls were substituted, and of these three one was made infinitely more powerful than the others. In the second French Republic, that of 1849, and in the third, that of 1875, a president was created.

Only in Switzerland do we now see a Republic which is practically without a president, and Switzerland is placed by the guarantee of the great powers beyond the danger of war.

But, in the course of history, it has often happened that a community, owing generally to an isolated position, has found itself practically out of danger from enemies. Its territory, mountainous and barren, or surrounded by deserts, has offered no temptation to invaders. It has remained for a long period unassailed. Such a community is in the same condition as a private society; it needs very little that can properly be called government. Here the Assembly will undertake actually to govern, and it may do so with success.

Such, perhaps, was the case with some of the Germanic tribes before their migrations began. The popular Assembly may have been almost all the government. The old Saxons are said to have had no kings. Such for the most part has been the case with Switzerland. In the feebleness of feudalism a country so difficult of invasion was exceptionally safe, and it has never been driven by necessity to any strong form of organisation.

Somewhat similar is the case of the United States. Here I should not say, as I have said of England, that the assemblies do not govern but create the government. The government there is not created by the assemblies. It is the people, not Congress, who choose the president. On the other hand, legislation is mainly in the hands of Congress, which is not, as in England, controlled by Ministers; the Senate, too, seems to have a real share in the executive government. We are to remember, however, that of all great states the United States is that which is under least pressure. Internal pressure is diminished by being divided between the State governments and the Federal government; external pressure is averted by the comparative isolation of the country. Probably the system would have suffered much modification

before this time had it been exposed to more searching trials.

In some other cases the experiment of government
by assembly in the presence of enemies has been
tried, and has ended in failure. Poland is the most
conspicuous example of this. Here no real executive
or governing power was tolerated until it was too
late. At the last moment an attempt was made to
remove the elective monarchy and to substitute a
more stable institution, but it was frustrated by the
partitioning powers.

I have left to the last the case of Athens, the city-
state so glorious in the history of culture,—Athens,
which outshone for a time every other Greek state,
and which, if its prosperous period was not long,
at any rate only fell with Greece itself. I certainly do
not venture to say that in Athens the Assembly did not
govern. We may indeed, perhaps, consider that it had
the rudiments of a system like our own. Those orators,
who in succession gained the ear of the Assembly until
they were supplanted by some rival, may perhaps be
regarded as rulers made and unmade by the Assembly.
But if so the system was very loose, and, on the other
hand, the Assembly itself performed functions which
in almost every other state have fallen to officials. It
conferred with foreign ambassadors, decided upon war
or peace, devised the measures by which war was to
be carried on. And all this it did in the midst of

foreign enemies, under pressure such as almost everywhere else has led men to tighten the reins. Assuredly
nothing in all history is so strange as that enormous
Ecclesia, that permanent monster-meeting, actually
governing a state, actually steering it through difficulties and dangers.

That such a system did not positively fail is
wonderful. But it cannot fairly be said to have
succeeded. We are to note that this system has no
share in the bright and dazzling period of Athenian
history. It did not win Marathon and Salamis, nor
write the plays of Æschylus, nor nurse Socrates,
nor build the Parthenon; it was not the system of
the age of Pericles. So long as Pericles lived the
personal element prevailed. Athens, says Thucydides,
was a state ruled by its first citizen. Pericles was
king, not servant, of the Assembly. He even studied
the pose, cultivated the proud reserve, of a king.
When he went to the Pnyx, we are told, he was used
to pray to Zeus that he might not say too much. It
was not till after his death that the system of government by many became fully developed, and at his
death most manifestly began the decline of Athens.

My conclusion is that, as a general rule, where a
state is subject to any considerable pressure, government by assembly is not found practicable, the reason
being that such an assembly has not promptitude or
decision enough to deal with pressing dangers. If it

were adequate, government by assembly might be
better, and perhaps even the attempt to govern by
assembly in difficult times might have a most stimulating effect upon the community.   So much the
exceptional case of Athens may be quoted to prove.
Under that system the Athenian intellect became
miraculously acute ; it may almost be said that every
Athenian was a statesman.   But Athens cannot be
quoted to show that government by popular assembly
may be adequate.   For wonderful as the experiment
was, it assuredly failed.   The orations of Demosthenes
seem written to show that the government was not
adequate, and to explain why Athens lost her independence within a century after the death of Pericles.
In the Philippics and Olynthiacs you have the best
commentary upon the fall of Athens ; you see that it
fell because in times of pressing difficulty and danger
a popular assembly cannot govern.

LECTURE VI

THE One and the Many — in popular language Monarchy and Republic—I have treated perhaps at sufficient length. There is another pair of contrasted words not less familiar to us, of which hitherto I have said little, Aristocracy and Democracy. By this time we have acquired a considerable store of categories. States organic, states inorganic; tribal states, theocratic states, states proper; city-states, country-states centralised or decentralised; federations strong or weak; states where government has a large province, states where it has a small one; states which have a government-making organ, states which have not; states where the power of government is in one hand, states where it is distributed. But are not some states also aristocratic and others democratic? It is time to consider this question.

Hardly any question is more discussed in the present age than this contrast of aristocracy and democracy, and like all similar questions it is discussed without the least regard to precise definition. The cry is, Who cares about names? Who wants

pedantic verbal distinctions? We all know too
well in practice, the one side will say, the cold
inhuman arrogance of aristocracy,—the other will
say, the vulgarity and envy and coarseness of
democracy.   The question is not of distinguishing
them nicely, but of sweeping away the one or the
other.   These lectures must have been delivered quite
in vain, if at this stage it is still necessary for me to
argue that after all definition is urgently necessary,
and that without it political discussion must needs
degenerate into that interminable brawl which may
be profitable enough to aspiring politicians, but can
be of no profit to the commonwealth.

When I spoke of the power by which the government in a state is supported, I pointed out that this
power may be the whole people, but may also be only
a part, and even an extremely small part, of the
people.   It is now evident that states will differ
greatly in character and complexion, according as
they rest in this way on a broad or a narrow
basis.

But again, states that rest on a narrow basis may
differ very widely among themselves.   For the group
of persons supporting the government may stand in
widely different relations to the mass of the community.
One of the commonest of these relations is absolute
undisguised hostility.   A military horde surrounds
the ruler, and enables him to trample the people

under foot. This is in some cases the result of a conquest, but perhaps more often, as is shown in the history of the East, the result of the decay and disruption of military empires, where mercenary armies, breaking loose from the central government, appropriate a portion of territory and make their chief Sultan of it.

The kind of state which comes thus into existence we have considered more than once, and have described it as inorganic. It is so extreme a form that we have held that it ought scarcely to be called a state, but at most only a quasi-state. But we may now observe that there are many other varieties of state which, though much less extreme, have similar characteristics.

In the inorganic state the ruling horde is foreign to the nation over which it tyrannises. Round Haider Ali or Tippu Sultan stood a Mussulman host alien in religion and everything else to the native population of Mysore. But it is easy to imagine a state in which there is no such gulf between the ruling and the subject population, and yet the system of government is closely similar. Without being foreign in blood or religion, the ruling class may still be conscious of a separate interest, and may guide the government not with a view to the welfare of the whole but for its own exclusive objects. Of this kind of partial government, which yet is not in the full sense of the word inorganic, there may be a great many varieties.

In ancient Laconia we find a Dorian host settled as conquerors in an Achæan population. But such a state is much less inorganic than those Oriental states to which I have just referred, since conquerors and conquered were of the same nationality, language, and religion.

The same may be said of the government of Rome established by conquest in the Italian populations, among the Latins and Samnites. It rested on conquest, but there was a tie of kindred and religion between the conquerors and the conquered.

Another variety arises where there has been no foreign intrusion at all, but internal movements have given to some class or section of the community a great superiority in power over all the rest, and the class or section, taking advantage of this superiority, has usurped or appropriated to itself the government.

The commonest case of such usurpation occurs when the government which I call imperialism is set up. A standing army in a state has almost always the power, if it had the will, to usurp the government. By its discipline and organisation it is superior in force to the nation. Circumstances occur not very unfrequently in which it resolves to employ this superior force in taking possession of the government. The result is a government not alien or inorganic, but

resembling inorganic governments to this extent, that
it is at the service of one part of the community, and
likely to consider the interest of that part either
exclusively or at least excessively. Such was the
government of Rome under the emperors, of England
under Cromwell, of France under Napoleon.

What the army is in these states the priesthood
is in another variety. I have insisted upon the
immense influence of religion in the formation and
growth of states. During the period when religion
is the leading influence the ministers of religion have
an opportunity of becoming the dominant class. In
these circumstances it will happen in some degree,
and may happen in a very great degree, that the
whole government of the state is warped to suit the
special interests of the priestly class.

In both these cases the predominating class is very
clearly defined; it is a class that wears a uniform.
We come next to a variety of state in which there is
a similar class predominance, but it is less visible and
obvious to the eye. The government may have fallen
into the hands, not of a profession or class formed
into a corporation, but simply of an interest, that is, of
a number of people who, having a similar occupation
and similar objects, desire the same measures and
instinctively combine to promote them. It may be
the landed interest or the monied interest, or the
manufacturers.

It may happen, you will observe—though historically perhaps it does not often happen—that this predominant class may obtain its predominance by no kind of merit or public service, but only by some accidental advantage. Mere wealth may confer it upon some class of industrialists, the possession of weapons and discipline may give it to an army, superstition and deceit may in some cases give it to a priesthood. This is possible. It is not only possible, but history shows that it often happens that a class which has risen to predominance by great public services remains predominant long after it has lost the qualities which entitled it to be so. Thus the religious faith which enabled the Spaniards to drive out the Moors had been nursed by the priesthood, and as a reward the priesthood obtained an unbounded influence. But two centuries later, when the Bourbon dynasty began to govern Spain, they found the country sacrificed to the Church, and it could no longer be perceived that the Church in any way deserved its predominance.

We must recognise therefore that there exists a large class of states in which the good of the whole is sacrificed to the interest of some one part.

It is the modern practice to call this system *aristocracy,* and the predominant class, which in this manner preys upon the community, we also call an aristocracy. Thus the monopolists of land in

Australia have been called the squatter aristocracy,
and we hear in America of a shoddy aristocracy, a
petroleum aristocracy, and so on. The opposite, the
healthy system in which government is honestly
directed to the welfare of the whole community, we
call *democracy*. The perversion of words from their
original sense is here quite bewildering. In Aristotle
democracy is precisely the contrary of this. It is a
system under which government does not aim at the
welfare of the whole, but is warped to suit the interest
of a part, viz. the common people. And *aristocracy*
in Aristotle *is* a healthy system. It is the government of good people.

We are not bound of course to adopt all the
definitions of Aristotle, but I do not see what we
gain by saying "aristocracy" where he would have
said "oligarchy." A squatter oligarchy, a shoddy
oligarchy, would have been quite satisfactory and
unobjectionable phrases. But when a bad sense is
given to "aristocracy" we lose the word which used
to convey the notion of government by good people
as good people, and in losing the word we are in some
danger of losing the notion itself. How the perversion
has come about it is easy enough to see. An oligarchy
always, as a matter of course, calls itself an aristocracy.
It tries to justify its monopoly of government by
saying that it alone deserves by its virtue to govern,
and it tries to conceal its selfish objects under the

mask of the public good. And it demands, and obtains, as a matter of courtesy, the right of choosing the name by which it will be known.

Nor is it difficult to see why we have forgotten Aristotle's definition of democracy. We readily understand that the good of the whole is liable to be sacrificed to the interest of a part, but in our modern experience the usurping part is always the few, never the many. That the poor should be trampled on by the rich, and little people by great, we recognise as only too possible. But when Aristotle tells us that there is an opposite perversion, by which the rich are sacrificed to the poor, and the few to the many, we are perhaps inclined to smile at such a conceit. It seems to us theoretical and pedantic; and we are not disposed to allow such a good word as democracy to retire altogether from active service by being appointed to the sinecure of representing a system which does not actually exist. The truth is that little Greece had a richer political experience than great modern Europe. The whole popular side of politics was better known there than it is among us, who after a thousand years of landed oligarchy are but beginning to make the acquaintance of democracy. The next generation may perhaps learn to understand Aristotle's use of the word.

We have now, however, distinguished a new kind of states. It is one which seems to stand between the organic and the inorganic. Between the healthy political organism and the quasi-state which only imitates political vitality, we find a kind which seems shaped by vital processes, but in an unhealthy way. One limb here is overgrown and draws all nutriment to itself. But we at the same time discover that this kind does not properly deserve the name that we are seeking to define. Aristocracy is not this, but something different. Such states at present are without a generic name. Oligarchy denotes that variety of them which in the modern world have been commonest. But we see that the predominant class, which is their characteristic feature, is not necessarily small; it may be the majority. For the present, therefore, we can only call them class-states.

But now what is aristocracy? The word ought to mean the government of the good. Of course if " good " is only a euphemistic name meaning simply wealthy or well-born, then aristocracy is only a euphemistic name for oligarchy. But can we distinguish a pure aristocracy by the side of the sham aristocracy? In other words, can we lay it down that there are states in which government and the control of government are in the hands only of the qualified, and others in which no qualification is required?

In the modern discussion this question is scarcely ever considered. Aristocracy is loudly condemned, but when you examine the argument you find it consists in showing that existing systems which call themselves by the name of aristocracy have no right to the name. But if so, their defects can prove nothing against aristocracy. The question, Ought there to be, and may there be, a test by which the fitness of men to take a share in government can be determined, is not answered by showing that wealth is not such a test or that birth is not such a test, still less by showing that in a government of wealth the poor are oppressed and in a government of birth the low-born. Granted that a number of so-called aristocracies are mere oligarchies in disguise, granted that the tests of goodness hitherto applied have been exceedingly rude and almost useless, these may be very good practical arguments against such and such a system professing to be aristocratic, but they prove nothing against the theory of aristocracy. In fact almost the whole popular polemic of the day is not really directed against aristocracy at all, but against oligarchy. Aristocracy is not attacked, but drops out of sight, while people say incredulously, As to a real aristocracy, if such a thing there can be, we will tell you what we think of it when we see it. Practically the question is argued as if the choice lay between democracy and some form of oligarchy.

I use democracy here, in its modern sense, to mean "a government in which every one has a share." That every one should have a share in government is

represented as following from the fact that every one
has an interest in good government; and if it is argued
that some people are not wise enough to understand
even their own interest, much less that of the whole
state, the answer is, The other plan has been tried
long enough, and it has been found that each man
practically understands his own interest well enough,
and that those who profess to be better than others
and to be ready to undertake the tutelage of others
invariably in the long run betray the trust. An
aristocracy, like Bolingbroke's patriot king, is an
empty imagination; in practice it is merely an
oligarchy.

"One man then," we are told, "is just as fit as
another to take part in government, and in arguing
for the admission of a class to the franchise it is only
necessary to show that so long as it is excluded its
interests are certain to be disregarded. The agri-
cultural labourer is treated only with a kind of
patronising benevolence so long as he is excluded;
give him a vote, and his interests will begin to be
considered with quite another kind of earnestness."
Well! if we may abandon ourselves to this view, we
shall perhaps at last arrive at the principle that a
person's right to a share in government is strictly
proportionate to his interest in good government, or
to the risk he runs of being injured if government
neglects him, that is, to his weakness and insignificance.

For instance, a grown man can always do something to protect himself, but a child! How much exposed is a child to ill-treatment, to neglect, to injury from bad education or no education! The child therefore ought certainly to have the franchise, even if the grown man should go without it. And, having once dismissed the notion of qualification, there is no reason why we should stop at the child. If there is any class which is liable to ill-treatment, whose interests therefore require the solicitous attention of government, it is the class of lunatics. But perhaps, on the principle we are considering, the class which would have the most undeniable right to the franchise, which ought to have the largest share in government, would be the criminal class. For how much more intimate, how much more practical and living, is their connection with law and government than ours! Compared to them, we are all mere theorists, mere amateurs in politics! To how many of us after all, if we will confess the truth, it makes little difference what laws are in force! Personally. we never come in contact with these laws. But to the criminal class the question is evidently all-important, in the strictest sense a matter of life and death.

You cannot resist these absurd conclusions except by admitting that after all there must be a standard of qualification, that the lunatic has not judgment enough, the child has not experience enough, the criminal has not virtue enough, to take part in government. And to admit this is to admit the principle of aristocracy. We constantly speak as if the democratic and aristocratic parties were at issue on a principle. But here again, as so often in party conflict, we find that the grand word "principle" is taken in vain. No rational creature disputes either the principle that all interests should be considered, or the other principle that there must be a standard of qualification. But some people think more of the interests to be represented, that is, of the democratic principle; others more of the standard of qualification, that is, of the aristocratic principle.

Again, if we consider aristocratic and democratic states as they appear in history we do not find them founded on principles sharply opposed. I do not know in what part of history you could find a state founded upon the principle that one man is as good as another. Certainly those states which stand out as eminently democratical have in practice applied standards of fitness, though sometimes they have applied them indirectly, and in a manner unconsciously.

Look at Athens. There to be sure it might seem that you had much more even than universal suffrage. Every Athenian was not only what we call a voter— he was actually a member of Parliament. But we see that this appearance of unbounded comprehensiveness is an illusion, when we remark that the Athenians had slaves. What may be thought to incapacitate men for taking a share in government is that unceasing mechanical drudgery which precludes much mental development, and that total want of leisure which makes the study of public affairs impossible. At Athens the whole class which the aristocratic party would disfranchise on the ground of want of education, leisure, and intelligence, was disfranchised without hope of a Reform Bill by the status of slavery. Those poor Athenians, who sat in the Ecclesia by the side of the rich and well-born, were of the class of which Socrates came. They are described to us as having much leisure; and at that period of the world, when there were no universities and no libraries, wealth conferred little intellectual advantage. Such education as there was, was almost absolutely common to all. If there was at Athens no gulf between the rich and the poor, it was because there was a gulf, wider than can now be conceived in the most exclusive society, between the free man and the slave.

And now let us look at the modern form of democracy. Universal suffrage has been introduced in several great modern states; and we ourselves have travelled rapidly on the road that leads to it. But is universal suffrage the negation of aristocracy?

Does it rest on the principle that one man is as good as another?

Not at all. First note that when we say universal we do not mean universal, and that there are some very large exclusions which we do not mention because they are understood without being mentioned. Such are those that I referred to before. Not only children, but the most gifted youths up to a certain age, and all women, are excluded. But secondly, we must bear in mind here the distinction upon which I have laid so much stress. Under the vague word government I have insisted that we confuse together two very different things. It is true that at Athens almost every citizen was called on in rotation to perform actual functions of government, as we remember that Socrates himself, the poor sculptor, found himself on a memorable occasion presiding in the Ecclesia. But this does not happen in modern democracy. Modern democracy gives every man a vote, but it does not make every man in turn Speaker of the House of Commons or Lord Chancellor or Prime Minister. The truth is, it is not a share in government that is conferred with the franchise, but at the utmost a share in the power of making government. And when we grant merely this to all men, we by no means lay it down that all men are equal. How far we are from doing this even in the most democratic

state appears from the astonishment with which we
regard those elections by lot which took place at
Athens. Government, in fact, is understood in this
so-called democratic age, more than at former periods,
to require so much special skill that the whole
number of persons whom we can even conceive as
qualified for high office is exceedingly small. But
now, thirdly, observe that the franchise does not
usually confer even a share in the power of directly
making government. It is not the constituent body
that directly makes the Ministry; it does but make the
Parliament, and the Parliament makes the Ministry.
It is commonly overlooked when we speak of the
steady progress of democracy in these latter times
that modern democracies have the representative
system, and that the representative system is essentially aristocratic. As there may be an elective
monarchy, so there may be elective aristocracy,
and such is every representative Parliament. It
is an elective aristocracy. It is a body of men
who have been selected by the community as more
fit than the average to attend to public affairs, to
make and unmake the government. These men have
stood out in some way above the rest; that is, they
are an aristocracy. And where, as in England and
as in Germany, the members do not receive payment,
they constitute not merely an aristocracy, but even an
aristocracy of wealth, or at least of leisure, since no

one can become a member of Parliament who is not in a condition without a salary to devote a large portion of his time to public affairs.

It appears then that the principle of aristocracy is not and cannot be seriously questioned. Aristocracy therefore stands on quite a different footing from oligarchy. History presents a great number of states founded on the principle of oligarchy, but it does not seem allowable to admit such states as healthy political organisms. Oligarchy is a disease, and where it absolutely prevails a mortal disease. We cannot therefore, I think, put down the oligarchical state in our classification simply as a species, but, as we were disposed to deny to the inorganic state the very name of a state, so we ought to regard the oligarchic state as a state deranged and diseased. The case of the aristocratic state is quite different. It is simply a state in which a sound and necessary principle, admitted in all states, has assumed an unusual prominence. It has all the appearance therefore of being a healthy and legitimate variety. Variation in states is caused by variation in the pressure of their environment. Thus we remarked that when the pressure is light there is liberty; when the pressure is heavy liberty is diminished. Now it is easily conceivable that in certain cases the pressure may be of such a kind as to make great demands upon the capacity, whether intellectual or moral, of govern-

ment. As in some states government, to do its
work, must have great authority, so in others it may
need to have great skill. Where this is the case,
the standard of qualification, which must always
exist, both in the government and the government-
making organ, will need to be raised. High qualification will need to be insisted upon. The aristocratic principle, which before was latent, must henceforward acquire more emphasis. It was always a
matter of course that only the good ought to govern,
but by the good was meant persons of ordinary intelligence, ordinary respectability. Henceforward the
good must be taken to mean persons of more than
ordinary intelligence, of exceptional virtue. And so
arises the aristocratic state.

But this healthy state is pursued by the corrupt
oligarchical state as by its shadow. So much so that,
as I pointed out, the very word aristocracy is now
scarcely understood except as a synonym for oligarchy.
Such a persistent, inveterate confusion could not
arise accidentally. I have pointed out how natural it
is that oligarchy should try to screen its corruptions
under the fair pretext of aristocracy. I have hinted
also at another cause which has been at work. It is
a cause for which, in studying forms of government,
great allowance must constantly be made. A large
proportion of the forms of government which in party
controversy are necessarily denounced as if they

were intrinsically bad are only bad because they have
lasted too long; they are the survivals of good things.
Thus, when I discussed despotism, and showed that
if it were the purely monstrous thing it is imagined
to be it could never have come into existence, I
admitted that many historical despotisms are monstrous enough, because they are survivals, and have
ceased to do the good they once did without ceasing
to do the harm.   Now the same remark may be
made of the aristocratic state.   Strictly it is quite
different from the oligarchical state.   But the survival
of an aristocracy is often an oligarchy; and many
of the states which history presents as aristocracies
are in reality survivals.   Indeed it may be remarked
in general—and the remark shows how difficult it is
not to misunderstand the lessons of history—that the
best and most glorious states have the toughest
survivals, just as the healthiest man may be expected to have the longest old age, and therefore the
best states are most in danger of being discredited by
their survivals.   The oligarchy that Sallust describes,
which displayed its venality in the war with Jugurtha,
and its daring wickedness in the conspiracy of Catiline,
was a survival of the heroic aristocracy that had
conquered Hannibal.   The noblesse that the French
Revolution devoted to exile or the guillotine was a
survival of the aristocracy which had made the staff
of Condé and Turenne.   Public opinion can scarcely

distinguish in these cases the healthy period, on which it looks back through such a vista of gradual corruption, from the survival with which it is familiar.

The confusion is the more inevitable, because aristocracies, like other healthy political forms, spring up, not by well-considered contrivance, but spontaneously, unconsciously. Nothing needs more thought and contrivance than the devising of a test of political capacity. And the tests which have been actually resorted to, even in the most successful aristocracies, have not commonly been the result of thought or contrivance at all, but have been the rudest, most accidental tests imaginable. And in applying these rude tests only the immediate need has been considered; the question how they lent themselves to corruption, what abuses they were likely to give rise to, has been disregarded.

Now the most obvious tests for discovering political capacity lend themselves just as readily to oligarchical exclusiveness.

Birth is a real test of capacity, though a test of a rough kind. The man who is the son of a statesman, who has grown up in the house of a statesman, may be presumed to have learnt something, if only some familiarity with public questions, some knowledge of forms of routine, which other men are likely to want; and there is a fair probability that he may have acquired more, and a certain possibility that, as the younger Pitt, he may have acquired very much and also inherited very much.

But if birth works for true aristocracy, it is still more certain that it works for the false aristocracy, that is, for oligarchy. Aptitudes and maxims may descend in families; but the family has quite another character at the same time. The family is the most intense of cliques; it is nature's clique. And if the government of a state becomes a monopoly in the hands of a few families, we may easily understand that at the outset a healthy aristocratical impulse was at work—the pressure found out the best families, in which the most virtue and the most capacity were stored up;—we may understand, too, that for a certain time the arrangement would really favour true aristocracy—the monopoly would secure for two or three generations a skilful and capable government; but we shall hold also that for true aristocracy the arrangement will not be long adequate, that its effectiveness will steadily diminish,—for a good family tradition is corrupted by power and wealth,—and that after a while it will change its tendency and begin to work steadily and intensely for oligarchy. Insensibly in the course of a few generations an oligarchy will reign where an aristocracy was established.

Precisely the same remark may be applied to wealth. Wealth too is a rough test of the goodness which is wanted in political life. For that is not an abstract ethical goodness, but a goodness relative to the object aimed at. In public life two qualifications are highly important, of which wealth is a guarantee. The wealthy man will have, first, leisure and freedom of action; secondly, he will presumably not be open to corruption.

But then wealth also is oligarchical. The rich are in the main similar in their occupations and objects; they soon discover that they have common interests which make it worth their while to combine and co-operate. In a state which is under the management of the rich, the interests of property will be too much considered, and the government will be regarded as a grand machine for favouring and furthering the enterprises of capital.

Still more, where the two tests are applied together, where birth counts for something and wealth for something, the tendency will be oligarchical as well as aristocratical, and perhaps in the long run oligarchical rather than aristocratical.

You see, then, how many causes are at work leading us to identify aristocracy with oligarchy. First, oligarchy always calls itself aristocracy; secondly, the survival of aristocracy is oligarchy, to which I may add that in the age of the French Revolution such a corrupt survival was found at the same time in almost every country of Europe; thirdly, the tests

employed to maintain aristocracy make equally or
even more for oligarchy.

I must be content to-day if I have succeeded in
clearly distinguishing the aristocratic and democratic
principles. I leave for the next lecture the inquiry
how institutions are practically modified by these
principles; in other words, how the aristocratic state
practically differs from the democratic.

LECTURE VII

My last lecture may have helped us to understand how the name "aristocracy," originally one of the most respectable of all political names, has come in recent times to have disagreeable, almost disreputable associations. Democracy, a word which now excites enthusiasm, had in old times just such disagreeable associations, and even as late as the seventeenth century Corneille writes peremptorily, *Le pire des états c'est l'état populaire.* But the very name "aristocracy" in the ear of Plato or Aristotle seems to have carried an impressive sound. Almost without waiting to argue the question they assume that it must be the best form of government, for indeed to a Greek ear the word aristocracy conveys either "government of the best" or "best government."

But superficially this form of government resembles two other forms, of which the one is wholly illegitimate and immoral, and the other cannot be called either legitimate or moral. The good people who in the aristocracy have a monopoly of the government and of the government-making power seem to answer

to that ruling horde which in the inorganic quasi-
state trample the people under foot, and also to that
ruling class which in the class-state have an unjust
and mischievous predominance. Both these tyrannous
minorities claim the title of an aristocracy. They pro-
claim a doctrine that their ascendency is in itself a
proof of their superiority, that in the main and in
the long-run might is identical with right. Accordingly in practice there is always a strong probability
that what professes to be an aristocracy is really
only a tyrannising class or a tyrannising race, and
the result of a long and wide experience of this im-
posture has been that in our modern political philosophy the sham aristocracy has superseded the true
one, that a true aristocracy is not now believed to
be possible.

But we must not allow this phase of practical
opinion, even though as a practical opinion it may be
reasonable, to enter into theory. We are not to
assume, because we see or fancy we see no real
aristocracy in the actual world, that in other ages
and other states of society there has been none.
Nor again, when we detect a tinge of oligarchy in
some ruling class, are we to assume too readily that
that ruling class is a mere oligarchy, for we are to
bear in mind that it may be an aristocracy in the act
of passing, as we have seen that aristocracies so
readily pass, into an oligarchy. Let us for the

moment at least forget the sham aristocracy and fix our thoughts exclusively upon the true one.

We have regarded the state as an organism, and the development of its institutions as the result of the effort which organisms make to adapt themselves to their environment. But, as this organism is composed of human beings, the struggles of it are indicated not merely by spasms or modifications in the tissue, but by speeches and actions from which we can in the clearest manner infer thoughts, reasonings, wishes, emotions. When we say that in the body politic modifications and developments take. place, we mean that thoughts and feelings pass through the minds of certain individuals belonging to the body politic.

Do we mean that they pass through the mind of every individual and of every individual equally? Surely not. In every community there is a part which has ordinarily no share in those movements which constitute political vitality. In many communities this part is infinitely larger than the part which is disturbed by them. Imagine the condition of the Russian population for many centuries. Serfs scattered through the villages of an enormous territory, they had not only no part in, but no conception of, that which to foreign statesmen constituted Russia. A few nobles, a few soldiers, a few ecclesiastics, and the Czar, these together made up the politically active part of Russia; all the rest had its place in the organisation of the family and of the Church, but politically it was, at ordinary times, altogether inert.

In such a state aristocracy is not only real, but is, as it were, the chief reality. It arises not by contrivance, not out of a theory that some qualifications are necessary, not out of any design on the part of the rich to exclude the poor in order that they may have more freedom to oppress them; it arises inevitably and naturally. The population falls of itself into two parts. On the one side are seen those who have thoughts and feelings about the public welfare; on the other are those who have no such thoughts and feelings. In one sense all are included in the state, for the state protects all and imposes duties upon all. But one of these two classes is normally passive; nothing, therefore, can prevent the other from monopolising public affairs. For purposes of action, or in the eyes of foreign statesmen, these active citizens are the state, and the passive class, often the great mass of the population, do not count.

I have cited the extreme case of Russia. Let me cite another case in order to show that aristocracy of this natural, necessary kind is by no means uncommon. England at the beginning of the eighteenth century stood out as the most political country in Europe—the country in which an interest in public affairs was most widely diffused. Yet at that time

not only the whole lower class, but a very large proportion of the middle class, were excluded from the
franchise, and therefore had no share whatever in
the government of the country or in making the
government. Now, there was at that time nothing
artificial in this exclusion; it caused no discontent;
no cry was then raised for an extension of the franchise. It would seem that the vast excluded class
acquiesced contentedly in its exclusion, and that it
was conscious of having no serious political opinions;
and, indeed, on those rare occasions when it was
roused to express an opinion, as at Sacheverell's trial,
or when Walpole proposed his excise, it proved very
plainly that it was still *minor*, that it had not yet
come to political discretion.

The genesis of aristocracy then is this, that political consciousness or the idea of the state comes to
some minds before it comes to others. Those mono-
polise all the powers of the state who alone enter
into its nature and understand it. These are the
good people. Such a development is perfectly
healthy in itself, and yet we can see that an aristocracy must from the very moment of its birth be exposed to the oligarchical corruption. These good
people are by no means saints. They have virtue
enough to sacrifice something for the commonwealth,
but they have acquired a monopoly, and they will
use it not quite solely for the public good, but also

for their own good and for that of their families. Moreover, these more advanced spirits are likely to be of one class. They will be of those to whom wealth has given leisure, freedom of mind, and the habit of dealing with large affairs. Thus aristocracy and plutocracy come into existence together. They are different aspects of the same thing, and if the spirit of life passes away from an aristocracy, the body which it animated does not dissolve ; it simply becomes a plutocracy.

This view of the origin of aristocracy explains a fact which strikes every one who studies history by the comparative method. In general we find aristocracy prevailing in the earlier period of a state.[1] Where democracy has prevailed in the end, as in Athens and Florence, or the United States, aristocracy has preceded it ; where in the end a moderately liberal system has reigned, it has usually been the result of a long struggle in which a more exclusive system has been overthrown. So in ancient Rome, where first the patricians and then the *nobiles* monopolised power ; so in modern England. This is the natural course of things if we suppose that the state was created, as it were, by a minority in whom political consciousness was first awakened, but that the political life thus put in course of

---

[1] A pencil note suggests that the writer intended to qualify this statement, so far as regards primitive tribal conditions.—ED.

development afterwards diffused itself through a larger number.

When we compare one of these primitive states with Athens under Cleon, or the United States under Jefferson, we see that the difference between aristocracy and democracy is real, and that some states may be called aristocratic and others democratic. At the same time the distinctions I have drawn, the qualifications I have made, very much reduce the importance of the contrast. To the popular view it presents itself everywhere in history, and the struggle between the two systems seems to make a principal part of the development of humanity. And true it is that the oppression of tyrannous minorities has been among the greatest plagues of humanity, but these are not aristocracies, they are corrupt oligarchies or conquering hordes. A struggle which can be strictly described as between aristocracy and democracy is indeed very difficult to find in history, for it is the almost invariable characteristic of the struggles which are commonly so described that the democratic party declare their opponents to be no true aristocracy but a mere oligarchy, to have no real superiority, and if they ever had one to have lost it. And in most cases they have been evidently justified in saying that at least circumstances have changed, that the rulers can no longer urge their former claim of superior capacity, and that the

excluded class have outgrown their original incapacity.
To take the most obvious example from English
history. The aristocracy which in the seventeenth
century hardly encountered opposition consisted of
the landed gentry of the country. But about the
time of William III. there grew up a new class which
in wealth and intelligence, in everything which constitutes political *goodness*, rivalled the landed-gentry;
this was the monied and merchant class of the city,
the magnates of the Bank, the India House, and the
South-Sea House. From this time the old aristocracy is shaken, not because the principle of aristocracy is called in question, but because the right of
the existing aristocracy to call itself an aristocracy is
denied.

And as it is not really aristocracy but oligarchy
that is attacked, so the attacking party does not seem
really democratical. Their argument is not that
there are no degrees of merit among men, that one
man is as good as another. Not only do they not
use this argument; they use the opposite, they use
the aristocratical argument. They attack oligarchy
expressly because it is not aristocracy, not because it
is not democracy. They attack the false tests which
oligarchy applies to men, not because they think no
tests should be applied, but because they think that
the false tests prevent the application of the true
one. This will readily appear from an example.

About thirty years ago the system of patronage was abolished in our Civil Service and in our Indian Service. This was spoken of as another step in the destruction of aristocratic monopoly and in the establishment of democratic freedom. Connection then ceased to constitute a claim to office. In the place of it was substituted the test of examination. Now democracy—if it means the principle that one man is as good as another—did not really gain by this change; that would require that men should be chosen by lot or in some sort of rotation. The change was based on the principle that some men are better than others, and that it is all-important to choose the good and exclude the less good. It introduced a new test on the ground that it was more searching than the old. It rejected the old test on the ground that it was ineffective, that it did not find out the good nor sift out the bad, but introduced an artificial invidious distinction. By this change then aristocracy not democracy gained, oligarchy not aristocracy suffered.

Objections have since been urged to the competitive test which was then introduced. And everywhere in history we see that it has been found infinitely difficult to contrive a test of political goodness which shall be at all satisfactory. But let us make the supposition that this difficulty has been surmounted. Let us suppose that some test better

than birth and wealth has been invented, by adopting
which the danger should be avoided of introducing
oligarchy under the name of aristocracy; and that
this test is also safe against the objections which are
urged against competitive examination. The result
would be that we should see for the first time pure
and true aristocracy; and I think you will see that
every one would hail it with delight, and that it
would appear at once that all the invective against
aristocracy to which we have grown accustomed in
recent times is like a letter which has been mis-
directed; it ought to have been addressed to
oligarchy.

It results from all this that we can hardly expect
to find aristocratic and democratic states in history
sharply distinguished, or marked by palpable differences of organisation, such as those which may be
discovered in city- and country-states or in despotic
and constitutional states. Oligarchic states, such as
Venice, may have their golden book, their *serrata del
gran consiglio*. But aristocracy proper is a principle
which all states admit and in some degree practise,
and democracy is no negation of aristocracy, but only
of oligarchy. We can scarcely say then that there
are any characteristically aristocratic institutions.
At the utmost there is in some states a tinge or
complexion which is aristocratic, and in others a
tinge or complexion which is democratic. I will

illustrate this by an example from ancient and another from modern history.

In antiquity Athens represents democracy and Rome aristocracy. The difference between them is not to be mistaken, yet it is scarcely palpable at any one point. In both states a great part of the labouring class was relentlessly excluded from political rights by the operation of slavery, in both also citizenship was strictly guarded. In both territories therefore the number of persons absolutely excluded was great. So far both states were aristocratic. On the other hand, in both states the ultimate authority lay with vast popular assemblies, in which every citizen had a place. In both states the magistrates were frequently changed, and no citizen was disqualified by station from holding a magistracy. So far both states were democratic. Where then lay the difference? In Athens, as Grote has pointed out, the people inclined towards high station, family, and wealth in filling the most responsible posts. But in Rome they went much further. After the primitive monopoly of the patricians had been broken through by the plebeians a new monopoly gradually grew up. The magistracies were confined in practice to certain families, members of which had already held magistracies. As a rule a new man had no chance with the voters. Here no doubt was aristocracy, corrupted with a strong taint

of oligarchy. But observe that it was a mere usage
and no law, that nothing could prevent the *novus homo*
from becoming a candidate, if he chose, nor the
people, if they chose, from electing him, and that
occasionally they exercised this right.

Again, the Senate was in the best sense an aristocratic assembly. It consisted of those who had held
public office and therefore had experience of public
affairs. There was no assembly answering to this at
Athens, for the "Boulê" had no aristocratic character. Here, then, is something like a characteristic
aristocratic institution. The great authority, however,
which the Senate possessed was rather a matter of
usage than of positive law. The aristocratic feeling
of the community inclined them to leave to this
assembly much of the power which perhaps belonged
more strictly to the popular assemblies.

Lastly, we seem to see in the arrangement of
one of the great popular assemblies an expedient
adopted for the purpose of favouring birth and
wealth. In the *comitia centuriata* the people appear
as an army, and vote not individually but by centuries, that is, military companies. As in the primitive army the citizen provided his own armour, the
richer men, being alone in a condition to arm themselves completely, would occupy the front ranks.
The richer men therefore, the cavalry and the fully
armed infantry, were called up to vote before the

poorer men. And now observe what contrivance was introduced. A century properly consisted of a hundred men, but it was arranged that the poor centuries should be so much fewer and larger than the rich, that the rich centuries should be a majority of the whole number. The consequence was that in this assembly the poor were powerless against the rich. It is to be observed, however, that the poor could take their revenge in the other assembly, the *comitia tributa*, where there was no such restraint upon the numerical majority; and in the declining period of the Roman aristocracy this more demo-cratic assembly grows in power.

Now let us turn to modern times. Here we may discover how an aristocratic state practically differs from a democratic state by comparing the United States with England as England was in the eighteenth century, or by observing what changes have recently been made in England itself, as England has become more democratic.

Modern democracy differs from ancient mainly in this, that it admits the labouring class. In the United States you have not only universal suffrage, not only inclusion of those who at Athens would have been disqualified as slaves, but something still more extreme—inclusion of the emancipated negroes, that is, of an alien race which has not been prepared for political life by the training and experience of centuries, but has known only barbarism and slavery. Compared to such comprehensiveness as this the Athenian system hardly deserves to be called democracy. But the aristocratic principle has made progress not less than the democratic. The inequality of men with respect to abilities is as much clearer to us than it was to the ancients as their equality in respect to certain primary rights. We see with astonishment that both at Athens and Rome one man was thought just as fit as another to be a judge and even to command an army. .To become Prætor Urbanus, the Roman Lord Chancellor, a man needed no special qualifications, and the appointment went by popular election. Cleon, apparently a mere civilian, noted only for his unsparing tongue and rancorous popular eloquence, is put in command of an important expedition against Brasidas. And if this strikes us as an example of extreme democratic recklessness, look at what was done in grave aristocratic Rome. In the last extremity of the state, when Hannibal himself was in the heart of Italy, and Rome was to send against him what seemed her last army, she put it under the command of a successful lawyer in rather a low kind of practice, Terentius Varro, and forth it went to be exterminated by the "dire African" on the field of Cannæ! And to us it seems the height of ludicrous satire to say of a civilian statesman that he would take the command of the Channel Fleet at a moment's notice !

You see, a new aristocratic principle has sprung up which was unknown to those ancient states. Special skill is now recognised. The superiority of one man to another in this respect has become so glaringly obvious, so utterly beyond dispute, that we can scarcely now imagine a state in which it is not acknowledged. Yet the principle is aristocratic. And so as the United States is in one aspect far more democratic than Athens, in another it is far more aristocratic than Rome. For the country is governed in the main by specialists. The President, indeed, may be a man of no very special qualifications, but he will select a Cabinet of specialists. The Secretary of the Treasury will be a financier, the Attorney-General will be a lawyer, and the army will be under the command of a skilled military officer. Elections by lot, armies commanded by lawyers,— these are notions which have become inconceivable, for however democratic we may be, we know at least that men differ infinitely in special skill.

Thus in the executive government of the United States the aristocratic principle prevails. It is recognised that the government should be in the hands of the best, and if in the list of Presidents some unworthy names are found, it is because universal suffrage made a mistake, not because it was held that

for the office of President one man was as good as
another.

Again, in the United States the assemblies are
more aristocratic than at Athens or Rome, for they
are representative both in the Federation and in the
States. As I have said, a representative Parliament
is a kind of elective aristocracy. Where there is
payment of members, as in the United States, it is
true that the members need not be drawn from the
wealthy or cultivated class, but at the lowest representatives are men who give up most of their time
to public affairs. Now at Athens and Rome the
assemblies consisted of men who hurried from their
business to the Assembly, and went back immediately
to their business again. That system assumed that
for deliberative purposes one man was as good as
another; but modern democracy, you will observe,
lays it down that the man who devotes himself to
public affairs is better for these purposes than the
man who does not; and this is an aristocratical
principle.

Lastly, the United States has borrowed from Rome
and England an institution which is avowedly aristocratic, the Senate. The members of it have a longer
term, six years instead of two; they must reach a
certain standard of age, thirty years; and they are
chosen not by the people but by the State Legisla-
tures. All these restrictions are founded on the

aristocratical principle, that men are not equal, but that some men are superior to others.

Our own system, as it has now become, is still in several points more aristocratic than this. We have not universal suffrage, but only household suffrage. That is, a large number, in fact a great majority, of English people have not yet any share in the government of the country. Secondly, our members are not paid. As the expense of elections has been much reduced, this no longer means that only men positively rich can, as a rule, have seats, but it does mean that only men can sit who can command a great deal of leisure for unprofitable work. It creates an aristocracy of leisure. And thirdly, the persons best qualified to fill the highest post, that of Prime Minister, are found out by a most powerful and singular process of natural selection extending over a long time.

But in the last century we had a system which might fairly be selected as the typical aristocracy of the modern world, that is, as the type of that form of government in which the aristocratic principle overpowers the democratic. In the United States we have seen the democratic principle asserted in a manner so daring and impressive by the admission of the negroes that in spite of all aristocratic checks and exclusions which I was able to point out, we cannot help calling the system on the whole a democ-

racy. The old English system was just as decidedly
an aristocracy. Like Rome, England has always had
one institution specially aristocratic, the House of
Lords. But it is less purely aristocratic and more
oligarchic than the Roman Senate. In the Senate all
the great magistrates sat as a matter of course; in
the House of Lords this is as may happen, and
several of the most important Ministers are usually
not members of it. In the House of Lords, birth is
for the most part the absolute and only title to
membership, and this is rather oligarchy than aristocracy : in the Senate there was no such rigid rule,
and birth did not by itself constitute a title, though
the Assembly as a whole consisted of noblemen.

But if England was an aristocracy in the eighteenth
century this was not chiefly on account of the House
of Lords. In the main it was the House of Commons,
not the House of Lords, that was the bulwark of
aristocracy. Here, again, aristocracy rather tinges
institutions than creates institutions peculiar to
itself. By the expense of elections, by the vast
influence of great land-owning families, by the
dependence of the smaller boroughs upon these
families, and by the exclusion of many of the largest
and richest towns, the House of Commons became a
House in no degree representing the lower classes,
but controlled mainly by the landed interest, which,
however, had to struggle against a certain infusion of

the higher commerce. This was in the beginning a moderately pure aristocracy, that is, the landed class and higher commerce really contained at the outset most of the political life of the community, but throughout the eighteenth century it was always growing less aristocratic and more oligarchic. It preserved, however, to the last one highly honourable feature of a true aristocracy, viz. that the owners of rotten boroughs often made an honest search for rising ability, and introduced of set purpose into the House most of those men who in the latter half of the eighteenth century made it renowned for oratory. From this circumstance comes almost all the lustre which surrounds that period in history.

Thus it is that now aristocracy, and now again democracy, tinges the institutions of a state. But though the rival watchwords "equality" and "qualification" prevail more than almost any other watchwords in party conflict, it can hardly be said that. they are of much use to us in classification. For there is no real opposition of principle; the question is only "how much"? If by some happy invention that unlucky connection between aristocracy and oligarchy could be broken once for all, if some test of merit could be devised which should be acknowledged as satisfactory and should not be so terribly liable to perversion as the tests of birth and wealth, the opposition would almost come to an end, and democracy and aristocracy would meet together.

In classifying states we can only say that some are aristocratic and others democratic, but that the difference shows itself on the whole rather in colour than in form. If there were any institution characteristic of aristocracy, we should say it was the Second Chamber. A senate, that is, an assembly of old men; a witenagemot, that is, a meeting of the wise—both are in principle strictly aristocratic, equally opposed to democracy on the one side and to oligarchy on the other. But so little does this institution practically mark aristocratic states that at the present day the most powerful and efficient Second Chamber is to be found in the great typical democracy; it is the Senate of the United States.

Perhaps the most accurate statement would be that there are three kinds of state, one in which the democratic and aristocratic principles are reconciled and balanced, and two in which one or other of them preponderates. For, as I have insisted, there is no opposition between the principles: there is only a practical opposition of tendencies. And the distinction we have drawn between government and government-making power points out how this practical opposition may be prevented by assigning to either principle its proper province. All the democratical arguments, those powerful pleas for comprehensiveness, for the equal representation of all rights and of all interests, do not really refer to government but to the government-making power. Every one would be glad that the poor and the weak should, if possible, have some share in making the government; nobody wishes that the poor or the weak should themselves govern. On the other hand, the aristocratical arguments refer mainly to government. That government is a difficult art, that it requires experience, special knowledge, high education, firm character, and active intelligence,—all this is indisputable; it is less open to dispute now, though democracy prevails, than it was in the aristocratic ages—but it does not refer to the government-making power. Without great skill, without high education or enlightenment, men may either directly or through representatives more skilled than themselves, take part in making and unmaking the government.

But such a reconciliation of the two principles is of course only feasible in states where the government-making power has been developed, and has acquired an organ, and in history such states are rarely met with. In history, therefore, the principles commonly shock against each other, and one excludes the other. In primitive states, as we have seen, aristocracy commonly prevails because the people have not yet acquired political consciousness. But political life is itself an education, and in certain circumstances, if

the people are not brought into misery by chronic
war, a time comes when intelligence is widely diffused
and a certain degree of political consciousness becomes general. The same lapse of time which brings
this about usually suffices to corrupt the ruling
aristocracy, and to turn it into a selfish and indolent
oligarchy. Then begins a democratic period. In the
former age the very notion of democracy seemed
absurd ; the very conception of government in the
hands of the people seemed ludicrous, as it does to
Homer when he pours contempt on Thersites, to
Shakespeare when he paints for us Jack Cade, to
Corneille when he writes *Le pire des états c'est l'état
populaire.* Now, in this period, aristocracy becomes
just as inconceivable. Men's minds refuse to admit
the notion. When you mention aristocracy they
think you mean oligarchy. When you talk of fitness,
of high qualification, of high character, they think
they recognise the world-old sophistries by which in
all ages poor people have been sacrificed to the rich,
and simple people have been hoodwinked by the
clever ; to them it is only the old story of *l'exploitation
de l'homme par l'homme.*

Nevertheless, in these very advanced periods, when
society has grown complex, the absolute necessity of
special skill in rulers forces itself more than ever upon
all eyes. The principle of aristocracy shows itself not
less great and momentous than the principle of

democracy.   We know already that Ministers must be specialists.   The question is whether they ought not to be much more.

But where a popular distinction is drawn between the government and the government-making power, these blind oscillations are no longer unavoidable. We may allow to democracy an almost unbounded province in the government-making power, and yet need not be precluded from maintaining that government itself ought to be not less, but far more aristocratical than in other ages ; that the vastness of modern states and the complexity of modern life calls for more intelligence, severer method, exacter knowledge, and firmer character in government itself than was required in any former period.

LECTURE VIII

A COURSE of lectures can hardly have the complete-
ness of a treatise. I have undertaken to expound to
you political science, but I am compelled to stop
when more than half of it is still untouched, and
when all I can hope is that I may have sketched the
outline sufficiently, and given you sufficient exemplifications of the method to enable you to carry further
the exposition for yourselves.

We have been occupied throughout with a single
task, that of classifying states. We have examined,
as it were, a number of specimens, marked the most
important differences, arranged them in classes accord
ing to these differences, and given to each class a
name. We have done nothing more. Now this
seems to me a most important and necessary part
of any science of politics, but assuredly it is only
a part. At the opening of the course I laid it
down that such a science must necessarily have
two large divisions, of which the second would deal
with the mutual relations of states. This second
division we have left wholly untouched, and the

first we are far enough from having treated completely.

I took pains at the outset to explain that in thus treating political science I did not consider myself to quit the subject of history. According to me the historian when he investigates the great occurrences of the past, verifying every particular, and arranging them in the due relation of cause and effect, is only preparing the materials from which a political science may be formed; and I also hold that the historian ought not to confine himself to preparing materials and leave it to the political philosopher to form the science out of them, but that it is important that he should undertake both functions equally, and that there should be no division of labour between the historian and the political philosopher.

I promised in these lectures to keep close to history, and I think I have kept my word. I have built 'up no imaginary state, I have used no *à priori* method. I have not made the theory first and afterwards applied it to the facts. My method has been to look abroad among the states which history puts before us, to compare one with another, and take a note of the largest resemblances and the most striking differences. We have not indeed confined ourselves to the registration of obvious facts. We have found on the contrary much occasion for thought and reasoning. But the reasoning has not been speculative. It has

been employed mainly in removing the misunder-
standings and illusions which in this subject more
than in any other are caused by laxity and popular
recklessness in the use of words.

I have, in short, regarded states as science regards
plants and animals, but I have treated them, not
exactly as plants and animals are treated by the
physiologist, but rather as plants are treated by the
botanist and animals by the zoologist. If I have
been successful, I have enabled you when, as it
were, a new state is put before you, at once to name
it by a precise name, just as the botanist can name a
flower at sight, and can give it not merely its popular
name, but the descriptive name which it has in the
botanical system.

All names are of the nature of an abridged notation.
The words "dog" or "horse," every time that we use
them, save us the trouble of a long description. In
dealing scientifically with states the first important
step is taken when we furnish ourselves with a stock
of such general names for the varieties of states. As
yet only a few such names have come into general
use, such as monarchy, republic, federation, etc. I
have made it my business both to subject these to
criticism in order to remove any vagueness that may
hang about them, and also to add new names. The
result ought to be that we should find ourselves able
to describe the states and to narrate the developments

and revolution of states in history at once with far greater brevity and with far greater precision.

Perhaps, then, I cannot close this series of lectures more usefully than by showing in such a rapid sketch as I have time for how these names may be used in narrating history. I will take the large outline of history as it is known to us all, not attempting here to criticise or alter or supplement it—not dealing with the new matter introduced by Egyptologists or Assyriologists or Vedists—but simply telling the old tale in the new language which we have now provided ourselves with. You will understand that I must not waste a word.

We find then, first, several small communities on the shores of the Mediterranean, some speaking Greek, others Latin or kindred languages, and one farther east speaking a Semitic language. By comparing the half-effaced primitive history of some of these with the Hebrew history, which in outline is considerably clearer for the early period, we find all alike in the condition of tribes and all alike powerfully shaped by religious beliefs. The religious or theocratic influence emanating from temples modifies the tribes, frequently uniting them into leagues. A number of societies spring up, in which as yet there are few political institutions, but strong clans and highly organised ecclesiastical institutions. The tribe passes, everywhere in a certain degree, and in some

cases decidedly, into the theocracy. These small
societies press upon each other by continual war,
and the pressure calls into existence kingship and
organised government, but this organisation long
continues rudimentary.

Thus the theocracy develops into the state. But
these states are here for the most part city-states,
which are found in cognate groups, the sense of
kindred and the common religion holding a number
of them together in a union at once moral and lin-
guistic but not political. Meanwhile outside the area,
for the most part mountainous, of these communities,
there have grown up to the eastward of Iran in the
table-land and in the Mesopotamian river-valley states
of a different type and on a larger scale. The pressure of these begins at last to be felt: the Hebrew
states are dissolved, and the Hebrew communities
conquered, but after their ruin as states they remain
as a theocracy. The. Greek city-states succeed with
great difficulty in repelling the first attack from a
country-state. The Persian is repelled, but somewhat
later they succumb to another attack of the same
kind made from the north by the country-state of
Macedonia.

Westward, however, the city-state has a different
fortune. Italy is not tried by such formidable
invasions as Greece or Syria. North of the Alps the
populations remain chiefly in the tribal stage, capable

only of barbaric inroads, not of organised attack.
Accordingly the Italian cities are not subjugated by
the foreigner. But their mutual pressure continues.
As in Greece we see sometimes one city, sometimes
another, Athens or Sparta or Thebes, taking precedence of the rest, so in Italy. But here the powerful city-state of Rome advances steadily in power and
overcomes all rivalry. All the other Italian cities
and tribes are either conquered or forced into dependent allowance by her. The result is a kind of
federation which, though widely different in organisation, is equal in military power to the great country-
states. This quasi-federal union when tried by invasion, invaded first by Pyrrhus, then by the mighty
military power of Hannibal, practically king of Spain
and almost king of Carthage, issued triumphant from
the probation.

The one word city-state explains the catastrophe
which overtook the whole eastern side of the antique
world. The city-state is necessarily no match in war
for the organised country-state. That the western
side escaped this fate is due to the union of Italy
under the strong leadership of Rome.

The strong and victorious West now stands side
by side with the subjugated East.

Our principle was that conquest calls into existence the inorganic state. This being generally large
in size and at the same time extremely low in vitality,

is almost always weak. All military empires, after a little time has passed, begin to wear a corpse-like appearance. This weakness showed itself first in the great Persian Empire. When the Macedonian country-state was consolidated by Philip, it saw feeble city-states southward, and this decrepit inorganic Empire to the east. It struck down one after the other; Philip subdued Greece, Alexander subdued Persia. But the Macedonian empires which thus arose were inorganic too, and they too in a few generations became decrepit.

Rome had united Italy in like manner by war, but the result here was not in like manner inorganic. The Italian states were cognate, and the word conquest does not fairly describe the process by which Rome united them: Roman Italy was in-comparably stronger than the inorganic East. In a series of campaigns of which the issue could not be doubtful, Scipio, Flamininus, Paullus, Mummius, Lucullus, Pompey, acquire for Rome most of the Empire of Alexander.

The explanation of all these changes lies in the single word "inorganic."

But the great Italian federation was just as much superior in force to its western as to its eastern neighbours. Hitherto the countries now called Spain, France, England, and Germany had produced no political fabric of any solidity. They had neither city-states nor strong country-states. We are to imagine them, I conceive, as in the tribal stage, though in Gaul and Britain a theocratic system, Druidism, was considerably developed. In parts of this region the population was not yet firmly attached to any definite territory. Migration is the great feature of German history in particular from the earliest times for a thousand years. German tribes frequently pass out of Germany westward, as at an earlier time Gallic tribes had left Gaul for the south—and foreign races at intervals penetrate into Germany from the east. In this fluid condition of society the western nations are strong only in short spasmodic efforts. Rome in its early days was once submerged in a Gallic inundation, and in its greatness was more than once endangered by movements in the tribes beyond the Alps; but in their ordinary condition those tribes were no more capable of resisting Roman power than the inorganic states of the East. Spain, Gaul, and ultimately the chief part of Britain, shared the fate of Alexander's empire. Here the word "tribal" furnishes the explanation, as there the word "inorganic."

Within Italy Rome could conquer without producing an inorganic state. She could not quite do this when her conquests extended over the whole coast of the Mediterranean sea. The government of the provinces was for a long time terribly inorganic.

In the last century and a half of the republic proconsuls and propraetors resembled the satraps of
Persia or the pashas of Turkey. The Roman Empire
showed at once the two characteristic features of the
inorganic state, large extent and low vitality. The
task of defending so vast a frontier was felt to be
overwhelming. It became necessary to differentiate
a special organ for the purpose, and a vast standing
army began to form itself. But this standing army
reflected the low vitality of the Empire ; it was poly-
glot, half barbarous. Moreover, to direct institutions that were on so vast a scale the old constitution
of Rome, the minature system of a city-state, became
wholly insufficient. Hence a great change ripened in
the Roman Empire. A new officer commanding the
vast army and responsible for the frontier had to be
introduced. His power necessarily effaced the old
magistrates of the city-state, nor was it found possible
to subject it to the government-making organ which
had been developed for those magistracies. The
government-making power became latent. Despotism
set in, and along with it a peculiar form of oligarchy.
The army had now gained an ascendency in the state ;
the despotism was at the same time imperialism ; and
though the best emperors studied to balance the
military influence by the influence of the Senate, yet
in the end, from the beginning of the third century
after Christ, militarism tinged everything. In the

2 B

inorganic state military despotism is the favourite
form of government : the vast Roman Empire was, as
it were, half organic, and therefore found this form
suitable.

For the first time Rome had introduced a firm
political organisation into the regions beyond the
Alps.　In Gaul and Britain the germ of native
civilisation was crushed; Druidism disappeared, the
Celtic language died out in the greater part of
Gaul.　Gaul was Latinised in language, religion,
everything.　But in Germany Rome received a
serious check, and was compelled to make the Rhine
the limit of her conquests.　The German tribes,
though unconquered, found themselves thus on this
side subjected henceforth at once to a firm pressure
and to a stimulating influence.　In the second
century after Christ they begin to show signs of
political development caused by this pressure.　The
old German tribes disappear, larger and more
solid political unions, Alemanns, Saxons, Franks,
Goths, take their place.　But there is not only no
city-state, but not even any considerable city, in
Germany.　Hence the Germans are peculiarly liable
to invasion, having no fortified posts, and though the
Romans no longer try to subdue them, they continue
to be attacked from the East.　For they are still in
the main tribal, and the tribe is weak.

This want of fortified posts in Germany led now to

the great revolutions which we call the migration of
nations. Pressed from the East by the invasion of
the Asiatic Huns, and also by the advance of the
Slavonic tribes, Germany threw itself upon the Roman
Empire. First, the more Eastern Germanic tribes,
the Goths and Vandals, spread like a wave over the
West, and set up kingdoms in Spain, Southern Gaul,
Africa, and Italy. The Empire was much transformed
by this immigration, which, however, produced no
durable states. The Germanic kingdoms of Italy and
Africa were destroyed again after a century by the
imperial armies under Belisarius and Narses, nor did
the Gothic kingdom of Spain last much longer. But
a second wave of migration took place in the second
half of the fifth century, which had more durable
results. The Alemanns occupied Switzerland, Alsace,
and Baden, the Franks entered Gaul from the North,
and the Saxons occupied the greater part of Britain.

The Empire submitted to so much invasion because
it laboured under the feebleness of a half-organic
state. But it partly roused itself by two successive
efforts. Large empires fall naturally under the head
of weak federations, that is, the central power in
them is so weak compared to the local power that
they are almost paralysed. Such was the Roman
Empire in the middle of the third century—the time
of the so-called Thirty Tyrants. Two reformers,
Diocletian and Constantine, by a great achievement

of centralisation, changed it from a weak federation into a strong one;—though it did not become vigorous enough to resist finally the Germanic invaders.

This was, as it were, a mechanical remedy, but the disease was moral. The Empire being founded on force was essentially inorganic—it was morally dead. Nevertheless, it contained within it a vast fund of spiritual life, the whole treasure of ancient civilisation. We have analysed the vitality of a state, and found that the principal element in it is religion. Living states must first be theocracies. Now at this moment the Roman Empire found a religion. It became Christian and Catholic. Henceforward it can no longer be called inorganic. The theocratic or hierarchic period of Europe begins. In this great regeneration the Empire begins to fall into two halves, the Western becomes distinct from the Eastern Empire, and gradually this distinctness extends to the religion of the Empire ; the Latin Church separates itself from the Greek.

The new vitality which the Empire derived from religion made it aggressive in the moral order at the very time that it suffered military invasion. The conquering Franks and Saxons became Christians and in the religious sense Roman, and the Saxons of England in their first zeal carried the moral triumphs of Rome into Germany itself.

But the appearance of a world-religion and its

prodigious political effect provoked imitation. A new world-religion, composed partly out of the same materials, appeared in Arabia, and founded a vast number of states hanging together in a loose federation. Soon the world was divided between two rival communities, half political, half religious, Christendom and Islam, the wars of which,—first aggressive on the Mohammedan side, when Syria, Egypt, Africa, and Spain were lost to Christianity, then on the Christian side in the Crusades, then again on the Mohammedan side in the conquest of Greece, Bulgaria, and Constantinople by the Turks, then again on the Christian side in the victorious campaigns of Prince Eugene and the Russians,—fill a thousand years.

The key to all this is in the view we have taken of religion as a principal element in political life, of the theocracy as an early phase of the state.

The great Christian theocracy might, according to this rule, have been expected to develop into a great Christian state, or rather, since schism had taken place between the Latin and Greek Churches, into two Christian states. And this seemed for a long time not unlikely. The Western Empire was revived in the name of the Christian Church. First, Charles the Great at the head of the Franks, and later Otto at the head of the Saxons, give form and shape to the theocratic Empire, the Holy Roman Empire. The Frankish House repels the Saracen in France, the

Saxon House saves Europe from the Magyar. But
beyond these rudiments the Christian state will not
advance. This was owing to the great size of the
territory and the barbaric feebleness of the age in
political construction. This feebleness is expressed
in the system of feudalism, which gives to all government the form of an extremely loose federation. The
Emperor himself, and the kings who reigned in
particular parts of Europe, have at this time little
practical power; the only real government existing
is the rude despotism of the fief. At the moment
when development was thus arrested, when the
universal Christian state was still feeble, there broke
out a fatal discord between the representative of this
state, the Emperor, and the representative of the
theocracy underlying it, viz. the Pope. This discord,
begun by Hildebrand in the eleventh century, raged
for more than two centuries, and was fatal to the
unity of Christendom.

Political development thus arrested turns aside
into another channel. Since Christendom as a whole
cannot develop, the separate parts begin to do so.
The tribal feeling or sense of kindred, which lies at
the root of all politics, but had been repressed in the
Roman Empire, begins to revive. But it takes now a
peculiar shape. The modern nation, of which the
peculiar badge is language, springs up. Europe,
which has hitherto regarded itself as a single theocratic

Empire, begins in the Crusades to appear as a brother-
hood of nations, and among the Christian princes the
Emperor has now at the utmost the precedence of an
Agamemnon.

The growth of the nation-state within the framework of the theocratic Empire was an affair of ·
centuries. Nation-states had been perhaps known to
antiquity, but when they were prosperous they
commonly soon lost their character by undertaking
conquest, and were merged in inorganic empires.
Now, nation-states grew side by side, checking each
other, as city-states had done in ancient Greece.
France and Germany had begun to fall asunder as early
as the ninth century. The growth of France was now
favoured by the Popes, who leaned on her in their
contest with the Emperor, and who destroyed by the
crusade against the Albigenses the germ of an
independent state in the south of her territory. England, first united in her struggle with the Danes, now
owed much to her insular, and Spain much to her
peninsular, position. In the thirteenth century
national legislators appear, Frederick II., Alphonso, .
St. Louis, and Edward I. Soon after national litera-
tures begin to show vigour. But when the nucleus
of each nationality is formed two great problems
remain to be solved. One is to fix the frontier of
each nation ; this cannot be done without an infinity
of wars ; the other is to develop out of the machinery

of the theocratic Empire in its feudal period an organisation which shall be suitable to the nation-state.

The Crusades in the twelfth century show us the European Commonwealth of nations in its Homeric phase, still chaotic ; at the end of the fifteenth century, in the reign of Ferdinand and Isabella, Henry VII., Louis XII., and Maximilian, the outlines and forms of the leading European nation-states have become distinct. England and France have settled their long quarrel, Spain is united and has expelled the Moor, the Burgundian middle-state has fallen, the independence of the Swiss cantons is secure.

In the sixteenth century follows the final dissolution of the old imperial and theocratic framework. Charles V. makes a last attempt to revive the universal Christian Empire. In doing so he revives the irreconcilable enmity of the Popes. The old Guelf and Ghibelline discord, which two centuries earlier had arrested the development of united Europe, now breaks in two the Universal Church. Pope and Emperor are so suspicious of each other that they cannot unite to put down heresy, which accordingly establishes itself in several states. Nation-churches spring up. Rome, the centre of theocratic unity, is treated with complete disregard by England—with respect, but still with independence, by France. Spain and the Empire remain in close connection with her, but the Guelf-Ghibelline discord still secretly smoulders, and Spain, professing to obey Rome, in reality rather dictates to her.

The nation-states are now fairly founded, their distinctness and independence established, but their form of government is still a survival from the theocratic time. It. is borrowed from the fief. Rulers have the character of landowners ; they consider the state they govern as a landed estate which they possess. Kingdoms accordingly descend to heirs like so much property, and as in many countries female succession is admitted, states find themselves united together in the most arbitrary way as the effect of a marriage. Early in the sixteenth century this strange cause threatened once more to destroy the brotherhood of nation-states, and to revive the universal empire under Charles V. It had also, however, accidentally good effects ; as it had created Spain by the marriage of Ferdinand and Isabella, so now by uniting England and Scotland it gradually created Great Britain. After the beginning of the seventeenth century the problem for the nation-state is to develop a national out of a feudal organisation. The old system necessarily tended to become despotic, as soon as it ceased to be feeble. There could not be a government-making organ where government was regarded as landownership, subject to a fixed rule of succession. In the religious wars of the sixteenth century this system was first broken through. A state came into

existence which had a government-making organ. In
the United Provinces the government was sometimes
in the hand of a Stadtholder, who resembled a king
in this, that he was always taken from one family;
sometimes it was in several hands, but in either case
there was a government-making organ—rude, but
effective. In the first half of the seventeenth century
the attempt was made to introduce a similar system in
England and France. In England there was apparent
success. The Parliament destroyed the government
of Charles I., but did not succeed in establishing a
satisfactory system. In the heat of the struggle the
power passed to the army; a class-state, an imperialism,
was set up; and the nation in the end became profoundly dissatisfied. About the same time the
Stadtholderate, or more monarchical form, was
abolished in Holland. But here, and still more in
France, the experiment failed. The attempt made in
the Fronde to set up the Parliament of Paris against
the King proved the absolute impossibility of adapting
the old institutions of France to the purpose now contemplated, and in Holland it was found that nothing
short of the Stadtholderate was adequate in time of
war. Accordingly the second half of the seventeenth
century is a time of Restoration, not in England only,
but in Holland also, and in France where Louis XIV.
appears as the impersonation of hereditary despotism.
So much for reaction; but development, too, has a

memorable triumph at this time in the English
Revolution of 1688, by which the government-making
organ is solidly established, and which serves as a
model soon after for the less successful constitutional
experiments of Sweden and Poland.

Hereditary monarchy is demoralised by its great
successes in the age of Louis XIV. It degenerates
into Sultanism, and leads to chronic wars of ambition
and prodigious financial waste. A fund of revolutionary discontent is gradually stored up, and now for
the first time Europe looks on at the spectacle of the
creation of a new state from the beginning. In
America the government-making organ is seen openly
at work, and a successful government is called into
existence. This ripens at once the development, so
long delayed, of Europe. The process is begun in
France, which leads indeed to unparalleled confusions
and calamities, but does at least develop in France
the government-making organ. Meanwhile by a
circuitous process, England, without disturbance, has
completed the work she began at the Revolution,
reconciling by the contrivance of a responsible Minister
the effective working of the government-making organ
with hereditary monarchy. The two models, the
American and the English, have since been imitated
in most other states of Europe.

Finally, the last trace of the ancient theocratic
system has been removed. The nation-state, estab-

lished everywhere else, had not yet entered Germany
or Italy, that is, the countries of the Emperor and the
Pope. By the revolutions of 1860 and 1866 Italy
and Germany have been set up by the side of the
other nation-states of Europe.

I hope you see why I have made this long recapitulation. I have tried to tell almost the whole
history of the world in half an hour, simply that you
may see what is the practical use of those general
names which I have collected and distinguished with
so much care in these lectures. History is commonly
regarded as a sort of ocean, an immense magazine of
miscellaneous facts which no memory can retain, a
labyrinth in which the mind loses itself. It is my
fixed belief that the study of it can never be profitable
so long as it keeps this unlimited, miscellaneous,
labyrinthine character. My object has been to furnish you with something which may serve as a clue
to the labyrinth.

. I began by laying it down that though the number
and variety of occurrences which in some sense may
be called historical is well-nigh infinite, yet history
proper is only concerned with one class of phenomena,
viz. those political groups which human beings seem
almost everywhere to form. Within these groups,
and under the shelter of their organisation or in the
conflict between them, no doubt almost everything
memorable that human beings have done has been

done. But history proper is concerned not primarily with the individuals composing the groups or their memorable achievements, but with the groups themselves, their development and organisation, their unions and collisions, and with individuals only so far as they have affected that development, that organisation, those unions, and those collisions.

This principle, if it were admitted, would at once alter the appearance of history. It would remove from the mass of facts all its unmanageable infiniteness and miscellaneousness.

But I advance another step. These political groups themselves seem at first sight bewildering by their variety and by the variety of their combinations. I say then, this is an illusion. No doubt there are infinite individual differences, as they say a shepherd can distinguish every sheep in his flock from the others. But these differences are insignificant compared to the resemblances. The number of kinds of state, the number of phases in the development of a state is limited, more limited perhaps than we might suppose. We have tried to distinguish these kinds, using the method of observation and comparison, and avoiding all à *priori* construction. I have not had time for a classification by any means complete. Doubtless you can add to the list we have made other, perhaps many other, kinds. My object has been rather to suggest to you how classification ought to be done, and to give you samples of the process, than to do the necessary work of classification completely for you. Still we have made out a list sufficiently long, attending, moreover, principally to those kinds which occur most frequently in history. If my method is really useful, I ought to be able to show, even with the general names we have collected, that history begins to look really less confused, that we have acquired some sort of clue to the labyrinth. This is why I have taken you to-day with such breathless speed through almost the whole length and through the most crowded part of the history of the world, from the primitive tribal period of antiquity to the revolutions which have happened in our own time.

If I had had more time at my disposal I should have devoted two or three lectures at least to this review of history. But I hope that my hasty recapitulation may serve the purpose I had in view. It strikes me that the current, the generally accepted classification, throws light only upon one or two detached pieces of history. Monarchy and republic, aristocracy and democracy, are words which no doubt are very useful in the history of Greece and Rome, and again in the last century or two of modern history. In the long intervening period they are useful perhaps when we are dealing with the Italian Republics. But in the rest of history, and it is much the larger part, they are of little use. For, first, primitive or barbarous politics cannot be described by these words; the traveller in Asia or Africa or Polynesia gets little help from them; English observers of Hindoo society and Hindoo history seldom want them. Secondly, the student who brings to history no categories but these is disconcerted by finding himself constantly confronted with religion. Religion itself, the promulgation of new religions, the struggle of rival religions, fills a large part of history, and in another very large part what we call politics have a strongly religious tinge. We are driven to evade this difficulty by distinguishing two kinds of history, secular and ecclesiastical. But nothing can be more nugatory than this distinction. Nothing can be more false than the notion that you can give a complete account of the state without mentioning religion, that the state is a secular institution, and only the Church a religious one. Once more, this accepted classification leaves out of account all empires in which a number of nations are brought together by conquest. Yet the Roman Empire in old time, and the Turkish Empire more recently, are examples sufficient to show how important in history these phenomena of conquest are.

We should see more clearly the miserable inadequacy of this classification if we did not confuse ourselves by mixing up what is or has been with

what we think ought to be. Primitive states are
neglected; true; but then they are barbarous. The
phenomena of conquest are neglected; true; but
let us hope that the progress of humanity will more
and more make war and conquest obsolete. Religious
phenomena are neglected; true; it is sadly true that
in past ages the beauty of tolerance was little understood, that it was not then recognised that "religion
is an affair between man and his Maker"; but why
revive now the memory of these wretched disputes?

So long as we reason in this way it is evident that
we can have no political science that will serve as a
clue to history. The principal object of my rapid
review of history has been to show you that by
taking pains to supply these defects instead of
apologising for them we can obtain such a clue. For
this purpose, of all the categories we have collected
the most important are these three—tribal, theocratic,
and inorganic. Mainly by the help of these we can
fill up the gaps which the popular classification leaves,
and bring the whole of history, and not merely a few
detached parts of it, under the light of method.

I hope that some of those who have listened to me
will weigh these suggestions of mine, and so far as
they deserve it, develop them. Upon this generation
of students evidently is laid the task of finding for
history its proper place both in science and in education. The study has reached a critical point. Never

was it regarded with so much interest and curiosity. Never was it prosecuted with so much zeal, or by so large an army of investigators. But there is a hindrance, a hitch, which is caused mainly just by the interesting and popular character of the study. Abstract and abstruse studies, as they want the stimulus of popularity, so are exempt from this hindrance. They are left in the hands of the few people who have a taste for them, and who, being left to themselves, have no temptation to leave the right path. But of the vast number of those who take a strong interest in history more than half have no scientific object at all. Some are antiquarians and collectors of curiosities, some are romancers, some are professional men, lawyers or ecclesiastics ; the vast majority have a literary rather than a scientific habit of mind. All these are tempted, and tempt others away from the straight path of science. They have other objects. This one looks in history for food for the poetic sense, that one for patriotism, another for art, another wants useful information. Even of those who have a scientific object some find in history the materials for one science, others for another. And the best intellects that devote themselves to history end in becoming rather great scholars than great scientists.

Just at this moment it seems to me all-important that the student of history should bethink himself,

should make up his mind what he wants and what
he means to do. The questions to be answered are
such as these: Is there a science at the bottom of
history? Are there several sciences? If several,
does one stand out as more properly historical than
the rest?

Next, in what relation does history stand to these
sciences? If history purveys the facts which the
science is to generalise, is it right that one class of
students should be devoted exclusively to collecting
the facts and another to generalising them? Or
should the historical student be, as a rule, at the
same time an investigator of facts and a theoretic
reasoner.

You see how we answer these questions. We find
at the bottom of history a Political Science, and we
would place all historical investigation, as it were,
under the guidance and government of this science.

But the science is still in the making; we cannot
yet refer to satisfactory text-books. In these circumstances some will doubt whether such a science exists
or can be formed, and many will prefer the old path
of mere erudition, of investigation for investigation's
sake, of collecting facts by endless research and
housing them in scholarly books without asking for
any principle which might bring the confused heap
into order.

The moment, therefore, I say, is critical, and in

these lectures on political science which I now bring to a close I have cast my seed upon the waters, hoping that in the work which will be done in the next few years by the rising teachers of history in this University I shall find it after many days.

INDEX

THE END

Printed by R. & R. CLARK, LIMITED, Edinburgh.

The Eversley Series.

341

Globe 8vo. Cloth. 5s. per volume.

The Works of Matthew Arnold. 6 vols.
ESSAYS IN CRITICISM. First Series.
ESSAYS IN CRITICISM. Second Series.
EARLY AND NARRATIVE POEMS.
LYRIC AND ELEGIAC POEMS.
DRAMATIC AND LATER POEMS.
AMERICAN DISCOURSES.

Essays by George Brimley. Third Edition.

Chaucer's Canterbury Tales. Edited by A. W. POLLARD. 2 Vols.

Dean Church's Miscellaneous Writings. 9 Vols.
MISCELLANEOUS ESSAYS. | DANTE : and other Essays.
ST. ANSELM. | SPENSER. | BACON.
THE OXFORD MOVEMENT. Twelve Years, 1833-1845.
THE BEGINNING OF THE MIDDLE AGES. (Included in this Series
by permission of Messrs. LONGMANS and Co.)
LITERARY REVIEWS AND ESSAYS. 2 Vols. [*In the Press.*

Emerson's Collected Works. 6 Vols. With Introduction by JOHN
MORLEY.
MISCELLANIES. | ESSAYS. | POEMS.
ENGLISH TRAITS AND REPRESENTATIVE MEN.
THE CONDUCT OF LIFE, AND SOCIETY AND SOLITUDE.
LETTERS AND SOCIAL AIMS.

Letters of Edward Fitzgerald. Edited by W. A. WRIGHT. 2 Vols.

Goethe's Prose Maxims. Translated, with Introductions, by T.
BAILEY SAUNDERS.

Thomas Gray's Collected Works in Prose and Verse. Edited
by EDMUND GOSSE. 4 Vols. Poems, Journals, and Essays.—
Letters, 2 Vols.—Notes on Aristophanes and Plato.

Works by John Richard Green.
STRAY STUDIES FROM ENGLAND AND ITALY.
HISTORY OF THE ENGLISH PEOPLE. 8 Vols.

The Choice of Books, and other Literary Pieces. By FREDERIC
HARRISON.

Poems of Thomas Hood. In 2 Vols. Vol. I. SERIOUS POEMS.
Vol. II. HUMOROUS POEMS. Edited, with Prefatory Memoir, by
Canon AINGER.

R. H. Hutton's Collected Essays.
LITERARY ESSAYS.
ESSAYS ON SOME OF THE MODERN GUIDES OF ENGLISH
THOUGHT IN MATTERS OF FAITH.
THEOLOGICAL ESSAYS.
CRITICISMS ON CONTEMPORARY THOUGHT AND THINKERS.
2 Vols.

Thomas Henry Huxley's Collected Works.
METHOD AND RESULTS. | DARWINIANA.
SCIENCE AND EDUCATION.
SCIENCE AND HEBREW TRADITION.
SCIENCE AND CHRISTIAN TRADITION.
HUME. With helps to the Study of Berkeley.
MAN'S PLACE IN NATURE : and other Anthropological Essays.
DISCOURSES, BIOLOGICAL AND GEOLOGICAL.
EVOLUTION AND ETHICS, AND OTHER ESSAYS.

Works by Henry James.
PARTIAL PORTRAITS.
FRENCH POETS AND NOVELISTS.

MACMILLAN AND CO., LTD., LONDON.

The Eversley Series.

Globe 8vo.   Cloth.   5s. per volume.

Letters of John Keats to his Family and Friends. Edited by
SIDNEY COLVIN.

Charles Kingsley's Novels and Poems.

WESTWARD HO! 2 Vols.	TWO YEARS AGO. 2 Vols.
HYPATIA. 2 Vols.	HEREWARD THE WAKE.
YEAST. 1 Vol.	2 Vols.
ALTON LOCKE. 2 Vols.	POEMS. 2 Vols.

Charles Lamb's Collected Works. Edited, with Introduction and
Notes, by Canon AINGER.   6 Vols.
THE ESSAYS OF ELIA.
POEMS, PLAYS, AND MISCELLANEOUS ESSAYS.
MRS. LEICESTER'S SCHOOL, and other Writings.
TALES FROM SHAKESPEARE. By CHARLES and MARY LAMB.
THE LETTERS OF CHARLES LAMB. 2 Vols.

Life of Charles Lamb. By Canon AINGER.

Historical Essays. By J. B. LIGHTFOOT, D.D.

The Poetical Works of John Milton.   Edited, with Memoir,
Introduction, and Notes, by DAVID MASSON, M.A.   3 Vols.
   I. THE MINOR POEMS.
   II. PARADISE LOST.
   III. PARADISE REGAINED, AND SAMSON AGONISTES.

John Morley's Collected Works.   In 11 Vols.

VOLTAIRE. 1 Vol.	ROUSSEAU. 2 Vols.
DIDEROT AND THE ENCYCLOPÆDISTS. 2 Vols.	
ON COMPROMISE. 1 Vol.	MISCELLANIES. 3 Vols.
BURKE. 1 Vol.	STUDIES IN LITERATURE. 1 Vol.

Science and a Future Life, and other Essays.   By F. W. H.
MYERS, M.A.

Records of Tennyson, Ruskin, and Browning.   By ANNE
THACKERAY RITCHIE.

Works by Sir John R. Seeley, K.C.M.G., Litt.D.
THE EXPANSION OF ENGLAND. Two Courses of Lectures.
LECTURES AND ESSAYS.
ECCE HOMO. A Survey of the Life and Work of Jesus Christ.
NATURAL RELIGION.
LECTURES ON POLITICAL SCIENCE.

Sheridan's Plays.   In 2 Vols.   With an Introduction by MOWBRAY
MORRIS.   *[In the Press.*

Works by James Smetham.
LETTERS. With an Introductory Memoir. Edited by SARAH SMETHAM
   and WILLIAM DAVIES. With a Portrait.
LITERARY WORKS. Edited by WILLIAM DAVIES.

Life of Swift. By HENRY CRAIK, C.B. 2 Vols. New Edition.

Selections from the Writings of Thoreau. Edited by H. S. SALT.

Essays in the History of Religious Thought in the West. By
B. F. WESTCOTT, D.D., D.C.L., Lord Bishop of Durham.

The Works of William Wordsworth.   Edited by Professor
KNIGHT.
   POETICAL WORKS. 8 Vols. | PROSE WORKS. 2 Vols.

MACMILLAN AND CO., Ltd., LONDON.